Help Us Keep This Guide Up to Date

Every effort has been made by the author and editors to make this guide as accurate and useful as possible. However, many changes can occur after a guide is published—establishments close, phone numbers change, hiking trails are rerouted, facilities come under new management, etc.

We would love to hear from you concerning your experiences with this guide and how you feel it could be improved and be kept up to date. While we may not be able to respond to all comments and suggestions, we'll take them to heart, and we'll make certain to share them with the author. Please send your comments and suggestions to the following address:

The Globe Pequot Press
Reader Response/Editorial Department
P.O. Box 480
Guilford, CT 06437

Or you may e-mail us at: editorial@GlobePequot.com

Thanks for your input, and happy travels!

INSIDERS'GUIDE®

OFF THE BEATEN PATH® SERIES

Off the Beaten Path®

THIRD EDITION

washington, d.c.

A GUIDE TO UNIQUE PLACES

WILLIAM B. WHITMAN

INSIDERS'GUIDE®

GUILFORD, CONNECTICUT
AN IMPRINT OF THE GLOBE PEQUOT PRESS

The prices, rates, and hours listed in this guidebook
were confirmed at press time. We recommend,
however, that you call establishments to obtain
current information before traveling.

To buy books in quantity for corporate use
or incentives, call **(800) 962–0973, ext. 4551,**
or e-mail **premiums@GlobePequot.com.**

INSIDERS' GUIDE®

Copyright © 2001, 2003, 2005 by The Globe Pequot Press

Text design by Linda Loiewski
Maps created by Equator Graphics © The Globe Pequot Press
Illustrations by Carole Drong
Spot photography throughout © Gail Mooney/Masterfile

ISSN 1541-5201
ISBN 0-7627-3476-0

Manufactured in the United States of America
Third Edition/First Printing

To Cameron, my patient wife, editorial assistant,

and boon companion from the District

to Dubrovnik and lots of places in-between.

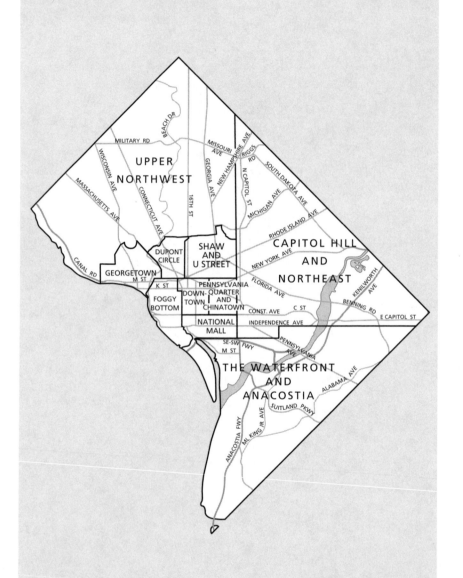

Contents

Acknowledgments

I'd like to thank my editors at The Globe Pequot Press, Laura Strom, Shelley Wolf, and Hrissi Haldezos for their skillful help, sympathetic support, and occasional forbearance in making this guide a reality. Thanks also to friends who told me about their favorite off-the-beaten-path places and to the Washington, D.C. Convention and Visitors Association, which provided valuable advice and information. And last but by no means least, let's not forget the D.C. Heritage Tourism Coalition, which, through its activities and its fascinating book, *Capital Assets*, is helping the District rediscover and rebuild the hidden places that contribute so much to its rich cultural fabric.

Introduction

As world capitals go, Washington is small and compact, but the settlement on the Potomac that became America's capital through—what else?—a political deal, has traditionally packed a planetary political punch as the capital of the world's sole superpower. But, closer to home, Washington is also experiencing an urban renaissance. The benefits of better government, including a plunging crime rate, have restored the city's sense of pride and powered investments downtown, where the construction crane has seemingly replaced the Washington Monument as the city's symbol.

And it's more than just real estate. The excitement also extends to the District's lively cultural and arts scene where internationally renowned institutions like the Kennedy Center, the Shakespeare Theater, and the National Gallery of Art are being joined by small experimental theaters and flocks of new and imaginative art galleries. And, as you're about to find out, Washington's renaissance also includes seemingly nonstop openings of exciting new restaurants and hotels. Although President Kennedy once quipped that Washington is a town of "southern efficiency and northern charm," it's certain that today he'd want to, as they say on Capitol Hill, "amend his remarks."

All of this is very good news for travelers, who have an extraordinary and expanding variety of visit choices. Most tourists often follow well-worn paths to wander through Official Washington, which lines Pennsylvania Avenue from the White House to Capitol Hill, and, of course, Monumental Washington, the marble palaces of government and megamuseums that line the Mall from the Capitol to the Lincoln Memorial. And it's only right that tourists and first-time visitors see the great symbols of our nation's heritage and democracy. But, as the D.C. Heritage Tourism Coalition, which promotes visitor travel to Washington's vibrant neighborhoods, points out, "these sites are overcrowded; tourists are seeing only a fraction of what there is to see."

Tourists become travelers when they move off the Mall to explore Washington's historic neighborhoods to see great history, art, and culture without the crowds and packaging. This guide is aimed at taking you and other urban adventurers to Washington's secret places, where you'll visit often overlooked spots (some even in downtown Washington) that most visitors miss and most other guidebooks don't even mention. That's why you won't find the Capitol, the great Mall Museums, including the Holocaust Museum and the National Gallery and other much-visited attractions in this guide. What you will find are the city's hidden corners where you can explore art galleries, great architecture, world-class house museums, cultural landmarks, restaurants, and even shops that are indeed "Off the Beaten Path."

History

As you might have guessed, Washington became our capital as part of a political deal, in this case a 1790 trade-off of Southern congressional support for funding Northern state debts in exchange for moving the capital from Philadelphia to a southern location. George Washington determined that the new capital should be at the confluence of the Potomac and Anacostia Rivers, between the thriving ports of Georgetown, Maryland, and Alexandria, Virginia. Washington hired a young Frenchman, Pierre-Charles L'Enfant, who had been one of his staff officers at Valley Forge, to design the new capital. Peering down from the hill that now holds Arlington Cemetery and Lee House at a rural valley of woods and marshlands, L'Enfant saw instead a monumental city—the "Territory of Columbia"—a dream capital with parks, canals, fountains, grand public buildings, and an orderly grid of north-south and east-west streets overlaid by broad diagonal boulevards.

The Grid

Although some of L'Enfant's original plans may have faded away, that combination of a street grid and diagonal avenues, which now bear the names of all fifty states, remains today, sometimes to the confusion of visiting motorists trying to navigate the traffic circles at many of the places where grid and diagonal intersect.

The grid itself is pretty simple: North-south streets are numbered; east-west streets are lettered, starting with A, but there is no J, X, Y, or Z Street. When the east-west grid runs out of single letters, it continues in alphabetical order with two-syllable streets (Adams, Belmont, Channing, and so on), until it reaches Windom or Yuma, after which it resumes in alphabetical order with three-syllable names (Appleton, Brandywine, and so on).

Washington is divided into four quadrants—Northeast (NE), Northwest (NW), Southeast (SE), and Southwest (SW)—which converge at the dome of the U.S. Capitol, the geographic center of Washington. The dividing lines of those quadrants—North Capitol Street, East Capitol Street, South Capitol Street, and the National Mall—radiate out from the Capitol. For example, an address with NW in its street name means the street is north of the Mall and west of North Capitol Street. Pay careful attention to the quadrant abbreviation that follows the street name; seemingly identical addresses can occur in all four quadrants, and you don't want to learn the hard way that the corner of 17th Street and Pennsylvania Avenue NW is a long, long way from that of 17th Street and Pennsylvania Avenue SE.

Getting In from the Airport

A taxi from Dulles Airport costs around $50.00 and the 26-mile ride takes about forty-five minutes. Dulles to downtown bus service is available only via the West Falls Church Metro stop; the bus-Metro connection takes about an hour and costs $8.00 one-way. A cab from Reagan National Airport to your hotel should run around $15.00 and take twenty minutes. You can also take a blue or yellow line Metrorail from National Airport to downtown Washington for $1.10.

Both Dulles and National are served by the "Super Shuttle," which will take you and other passengers to and from your hotels. Call 296–6662 to book a seat, or look for the blue van in the taxi area; rates to downtown Washington are around $22.00 from Dulles and $10.00 from National.

Although Dulles has no direct rail or Metrorail connections with downtown Washington, here's a tip about a bus service known only to District Denizens. You can avoid an expensive 26-mile cab ride to and from Dulles by taking Metrobus line 5A, which connects Dulles with the Metro station at L'Enfant Plaza, conveniently located on the yellow, green, orange, and blue lines. The trip takes fifty-five minutes and will cost you only $1.10. Buses run hourly seven days a week from 5:30 A.M. to 11:30 P.M. For exact times visit www.wmata.com/timetables.

Washington's third airport is Baltimore-Washington International, always referred to as BWI, (www.bwiairport.com) and located much nearer Baltimore than D.C. A taxi from BWI to the center of Washington will run you anywhere from $55.00 to $70.00 and take about an hour. However, for a much cheaper and more satisfactory trip, take the free shuttle bus (marked "BWI Rail") from your arrival area about a mile to the airport's rail station, then take either a MARC commuter train or Amtrak to Union Station, where you can take the Metro to your destination. Another option is to take the BWI Express Metro bus service that connects the airport with the Greenbelt Metro station; buses leave every forty minutes and cost $3.15. For more information about rail connections, call the BWI Rail Station, (410) 672–6167; Amtrak, (800) USA–RAIL; or MARC, (800) 325–RAIL. Super Shuttle vans also service BWI and cost $26.00 to $32.00 each way; reserve by phoning (800) 258–3826.

Getting Around

If you enjoy dense traffic, dueling over nonexistent parking spots, and negotiating diabolically difficult traffic circles, you'll love driving in the District. Otherwise, give your jalopy a rest and take advantage of the fact that Washington is compact and a great walking town. Washington is also blessed with an excellent, modern subway system called Metrorail, which starts service at 5:30 A.M. weekdays and 8:00 A.M. weekends. It closes at midnight, except on Friday and Saturday, when the witching hour is 2:00 A.M. Metrorail stations are marked by tall columns that bear a big "M," along with the colors of the lines that serve that station.

Metro fares range from $1.10 to $3.25 depending on the length of the ride and the time of day (rush hour fares are more expensive). You can also buy one-day passes for unlimited travel for $5.00 and there's also a seven-day pass for $25.00.

Because Metro is fast, reliable, and safe, it is usually the best way to get around the city, and the places in this guide are often, but not always, keyed to Metro travel and the name of the nearest stop. When Metrorail is not feasible, there's a good chance that the city's excellent Metrobus system will get you there, and the appropriate route will be given. Metrobus fares run from $1.10 to $2.00 depending on the route; since drivers don't carry money, you'll need exact change when boarding. For more information about Washington's public transit system, go to www.wmata.com or phone 637–7000.

Although many Washington taxis are vintage items that belong in the Smithsonian and not in front of it, they are plentiful, relatively inexpensive, and handy for getting around in unfamiliar or edgy neighborhoods. Keep in mind that, unlike most U.S. cities, Washington's taxis do not use meters, relying instead on a zone system so arcane that it can be fully fathomed only by experienced readers of the *Congressional Record*. Minimum fare: $4.50.

Fees, Prices, and Rates

The good news is that most of Washington's great attractions, both on and off the beaten path, are free. In fact, sightseeing in the nation's capital is a freeloader's dream. Unless this guide mentions an admission fee, you can assume that there isn't one.

Restaurants and lodgings are another matter. Washington consistently ranks as one of America's most expensive cities. This guide will give you an indication of what you can expect to pay for meals: under $15 is considered inexpensive, $15 to $35 is moderate, and $35 and up is expensive.

When it comes to lodgings (a standard double, excluding the District's 13 percent room tax), $125 and under is considered inexpensive, $125 to $225 is moderate, and $225 and up is expensive.

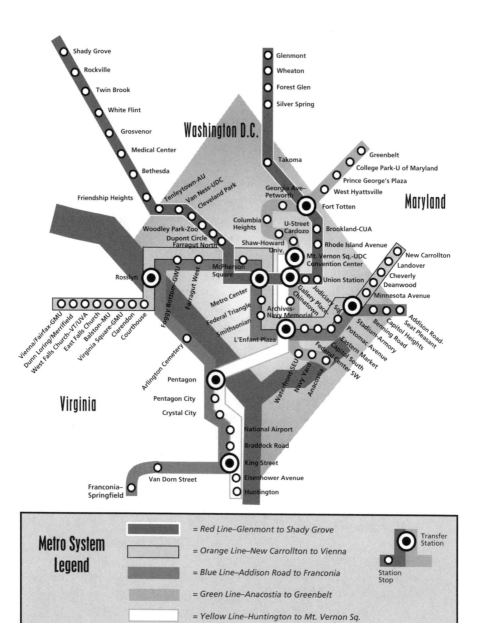

Washington D.C.

Shady Grove
Rockville
Twin Brook
White Flint
Grosvenor
Medical Center
Bethesda
Friendship Heights
Tenleytown-AU
Van Ness-UDC
Cleveland Park
Woodley Park-Zoo
Dupont Circle
Farragut North

Glenmont
Wheaton
Forest Glen
Silver Spring
Takoma
Greenbelt
College Park-U of Maryland
Prince George's Plaza
West Hyattsville
Georgia Ave-Petworth
Fort Totten

Maryland

Columbia Heights
U-Street Cardozo
Shaw-Howard Univ.
Brookland-CUA
Rhode Island Avenue
Mt. Vernon Sq.-UDC Convention Center
New Carrollton
Landover
Cheverly
Deanwood
Minnesota Avenue
Union Station
Judiciary Sq.
Gallery Place-Chinatown
Archives-Navy Memorial?
Stadium-Armory
Benning Road
Capitol Heights
Addison Road-Seat Pleasant
Federal Triangle
Smithsonian
L'Enfant Plaza
Eastern Market
Potomac Avenue
Capitol South
Federal Center SW

Rosslyn
Foggy Bottom-GWU
Farragut West
McPherson Square
Metro Center

Vienna/Fairfax-GMU
Dunn Loring/Merrifield
West Falls Church-VT/UVA
East Falls Church
Balston-MU
Virginia Square-GMU
Clarendon
Courthouse

Arlington Cemetery
Pentagon
Pentagon City
Crystal City
National Airport
Braddock Road
King Street
Eisenhower Avenue
Huntington
Van Dorn Street
Franconia–Springfield
Waterfront-SEU
Navy Yard
Anacostia

Virginia

Metro System Legend

= Red Line–Glenmont to Shady Grove
= Orange Line–New Carrollton to Vienna
= Blue Line–Addison Road to Franconia
= Green Line–Anacostia to Greenbelt
= Yellow Line–Huntington to Mt. Vernon Sq.

Transfer Station
Station Stop

Area Code

Washington's one and only area code is 202. When calling from outside the District, all of the phone numbers in this book (unless otherwise noted) can be reached by using the 202 prefix.

Sources of Info

After you arrive, you'll have several excellent sources for news of what's happening while you're in Washington:

The *Washington Post* (www.washingtonpost.com) is a great national newspaper, but it also pays close attention to its home town. The daily Metro and Style sections are prime sources of news about what's going on, while the Friday Weekend magazine always carries an extensive listing of cultural and other events of the moment.

Washington City Paper (www.washingtoncitypaper.com), widely distributed everywhere (and free!), carries an exhaustive compilation of tours, concerts, and museum happenings, along with highly professional exposés about what's really going on in D.C. Even if you're just hanging out and not thinking much about culture, City Paper is for you.

The *Washingtonian* (www.washingtonian.com), the city's local magazine, is very strong on gallery schedules, details about what's happening at local museums, and superb restaurant coverage. Pick one up for both operational information and a good feel for what Washington is all about.

If you've arrived by air, you've surely seen *Washington Flyer* (www.fly 2dc.com), which is widely circulated at Dulles and National airports. Unlike the usual airport freebie publications, *Flyer* is a magazine with heft and content that will help you get around very nicely, from its front-of-the-book articles on local attractions to its listings of Washington sights, museum happenings, and restaurants. Best of all, *Washington Flyer* regularly covers off-the-beaten-path places like the ones you're going to see.

capitalquote

"Wherever else an American citizen may be a stranger, he should be at home in his nation's capital."

—Frederick Douglass, 1877

Washington contains some of the most distinctive and historic residential architecture found in any American city, from the rarified Federal precincts of Georgetown and the opulent Beaux Arts mansions of Embassy Row to the brownstones and bay fronts of many less exalted neighborhoods. If you'd like to know more about the architects and designs you're seeing, be sure to arm yourself with the *American Institute of Architects (AIA) Guide to the Architecture of Washington, D.C.*

Visitor information is available from the Washington Convention and Visitors Association, 1212 New York Avenue NW (789–7000, www.washington .org) and the D.C. Chamber of Commerce Visitor Information Center, Ronald Reagan Building, 1300 Pennsylvania Avenue NW (first floor, east side); 328–4748; www.dcvisit.com. Open daily 8:00 A.M. to 6:00 P.M.

Tour Groups and Organizers

Although there's no shortage of trolley and bus tours to take you to the usual sites, off-the-beaten-path exploration requires more specific and close-up help, ideally a walking or bus tour with a knowledgeable guide. Here are a few to consider, along with a specialized possibility or two:

Beyond the Monuments is operated by the D.C. Heritage Tourism Coalition, which is dedicated to promoting the tourist potential of Washington's historic neighborhoods. This useful service provides one-stop shopping for clear, detailed information about how to hook up with professionally led walking tours of each area covered in this book. Just call 828–WALK and select the part of the city you're interested in. Many tours are of the walk-up variety and leave from Metro stations. Others are bus tours operated in cooperation with the D.C. Chamber of Commerce. The D.C. Heritage Web site, www.dcheritage.com, has more information.

Anecdotal History Tours. Every Sunday from 11:00 A.M. to 1:00 P.M., tour guide Anthony Pitch takes a group to some of D.C.'s hidden corners. The rotating list includes Georgetown, Around the White House, White House to the Capitol, and Adams Morgan. For a schedule, call (301) 294–9514 or go to www.dcsightseeing.com. Cost is $15 per person. Groups by appointment.

Bike the Sites. Daily three-hour guided bike tours follow paths and trails to visit a number of sites in the District, including Capitol Hill and Georgetown. The $35 price includes bike rental, entrance fees, and snack. Tours can be arranged for small groups, so think about family touring. Visit www.bikethe sites.com online or call 842–2453.

City Scooter Tours. If you'd like to explore some of the city's main monuments and either prefer not to hoof it or need mobility assistance, think about an electric scooter tour. Guided tours of the National Mall and Tidal Basin cost $75, last three hours, and cover 6 miles of historic real estate. Walk-up rentals are also available on an hourly and daily basis, starting at $30 for the first two hours. Tours leave from the Bike the Sites kiosk in the Old Post Office Pavilion at 1100 Pennsylvania Avenue, NW, Wednesday and Sunday from 10:00 A.M. to 1:00 P.M. and on Friday 7:00 to 10:00 P.M. Call (888) 441–7575 or visit www.cityscootertours.com.

D.C. Ducks will take you on a ninety-minute tour of Washington's streets aboard a World War II amphibious troop carrier, after which you'll splash into the Potomac for a short cruise. The charge is $24 for adults and $12 for kids four to twelve. Call 832–9800 or peek at www.dcducks.com.

Spy Drive. Since Washington is said to be the world's spy capital, it's only natural that someone has organized a tour of the city's espionage attractions. In this case "someone" means a group of former (they say) CIA, KGB, and FBI operatives, who will show you all the top secret sites. No security clearance necessary, just call (866) 779–3748 or check out www.spytrek.com. The cost is $35.

Washington Photo Safari. Instead of depending on trite and corny postcards as reminders of your Washington visit, think about making some personal travel statements with your own photographs. On Wednesdays and Saturdays veteran photographer E. David Luria offers tours of the city's neighborhoods, monuments, and memorials. Along the way you'll receive professional advice about finding just the right perspective, lens, or exposure to capture your own D.C. memories. Walking safaris take three hours. Bring your own camera. Half-day tours, $59; full day, $99. Call (877) 512–5969 or 537–0937; the Web site is www.washingtonphotosafari.com.

Tour D.C. offers highly knowledgeable ninety-minute walking tours of Georgetown every Saturday. Also tours of Dupont Circle and other neighborhoods. Call (301) 588–8999 or visit www.tourdc.com for details.

Washington Walks has a selection of about ten possibilities for walks through a number of places in this book, plus a "Capital Hauntings" tour to some of the city's ghostly places. Each walk starts at a Metro station, lasts two hours, and costs $10.00 per person; $5.00 for kids under twelve. For details, call 484–1565 or check out www.washingtonwalks.com.

Annual Events

Washington has literally hundreds of special events every year, but listed here are a few of the city's leading festivals, shows, and special tours. Because the dates for many of these occasions vary from year to year, for most events, you'll also find a phone number or Web site where you can find exact dates and more information. The *Washington Post* and *City Paper* are also excellent sources for the latest about these and other major events.

JANUARY

Martin Luther King Jr. Birthday Celebration. Performances, exhibits, and readings commemorate the life and legacy of the human rights leader. 727–6306.

FEBRUARY

Black History Month at the Smithsonian. Monthlong exhibitions and activities reflecting African-American history and culture. 357–2700.

Chinese Lunar New Year Parade. Chinatown parade plus fireworks, dragon dancers, and lion dancers.

Washington Boat Show. Hundreds of boats ranging from dinghies to motor yachts. (703) 823–7960; www.washingtonboatshow.com.

Abraham Lincoln Birthday Celebration. Reading of the Gettysburg Address at the Lincoln Memorial. 619–7222.

Frederick Douglass Birthday. Frederick Douglass National Historic Site. 426–5961.

MARCH

St. Patrick's Day Parade. Thousands cheer along Constitution Avenue as the Irish march, the dancers dance, and the bagpipes play. 637–2474; www.dcstpatsparade.com.

Smithsonian's Annual Kite Festival. Held the last Saturday in March at the Washington Monument. 357–3030.

LATE MARCH OR EARLY APRIL

Cherry Blossom Parade and Festival. Thousands of cherry blossoms, a parade, and a Festival Queen to boot. For tickets, call 432–SEAT. For details, call the Festival Committee at 547–1500.

Washington Flower and Garden Show. Display gardens with thousands of flowers and trees that are all in full bloom. (703) 569–7141.

APRIL

White House Spring Garden Tour. See the great White House gardens while military bands serenade. 456–2200.

Annual White House Easter Egg Roll. Children ages three to six gather on the White House South Lawn; older children roll their eggs on the Ellipse. Eggs and live entertainment are provided and, just maybe, an appearance by the president. 208–1631 or 456–2121; www.whitehouse.gov/history/tours/easter.

Smithsonian Craft Show. More than 100 leading American artisans display and sell their textiles, ceramics, wood, metal, and glass. 357–2700; www.smith soniancraftshow.org.

Georgetown House Tour. One weekend each spring private homes are open to the public. 338–2287; www.georgetownhousetour.com.

MAY

Georgetown Garden Day. A self-guided walking tour of dozens of beautiful gardens. 965–1950; www.gtowngarden.org.

The National Cathedral Flower Mart. Flower booths, crafts, and demonstrations, held the first weekend in May. 537–6200; www.cathedral.org.

Annual Goodwill Embassy Tour. On the second Saturday in May, embassies open their doors to the public. 636–4225.

Annual Candlelight Vigil Ceremony. National Law Enforcement Officers Memorial. 737–3400.

Memorial Day Weekend Concerts. The National Symphony Orchestra performs on the West Lawn of the Capitol. 619–7222.

Memorial Day Ceremonies. Arlington National Cemetery. (703–607–8585), Vietnam Veterans Memorial (619–7222), and the U.S. Navy Memorial (737–2300).

MAY–AUGUST

Twilight Tattoo. At 7:00 P.M. every Wednesday from mid-April until early August the U.S. Army Military District of Washington stages a stirring sunset parade on the Ellipse, south of the White House. The U.S. Army Band plays and the army's precision drill team performs. Seating in the bleachers or on the lawn is first come, first served. 685–2888; www.mdw.army.mil/tlt/tlt.html.

JUNE

Dupont-Kalorama Museum Walk Weekend. Visits to six neighborhood museums and historic houses. 387–4062, ext. 12.

Shakespeare Theatre Free for All. Carter Barron Amphitheatre. An annual festival put on by the Shakespeare Theatre in Rock Creek Park's Carter Barron Amphitheatre. 334–4790; www.shakespearetheatre.org.

Smithsonian Folklife Festival. This annual festival of food, crafts, music, and dance is held on the National Mall and runs until July 4. 275–1150; www.folk life.si.edu.

JUNE–AUGUST

Marine Band Summer Concert Series. Wednesday at 8:00 P.M. at the U.S. Capitol and Sunday at 8:00 P.M. on the Mall. 433–4011.

U.S. Army Band Summer Concert Series. Tuesday and Friday at 8:00 P.M. on the steps of the U.S. Capitol. (703) 696–3399; www.army.mil/armyband.

JULY

National Independence Day Celebration. Daylong concerts, a morning parade, and the famed National Symphony Orchestra Concert on the National Mall. 619–7222.

Soap Box Derby. Independence day race on Constitution Avenue. (216) 733–8723.

Bastille Day. Always ready for a party, Washington celebrates French Independence Day on July 14 with live entertainment and a race to the U.S. Capitol and back by tray-bearing waiters and waitresses. 296–7200.

SEPTEMBER

National Symphony Orchestra's Labor Day Concert. West Lawn of the U.S. Capitol. 619–7222.

Black Family Reunion Celebration. The annual celebration of the African-American family features live entertainment, food, and pavilions. 737–0120; www.ncnw.org/blackfamily.htm.

Kennedy Center Open House. Free concerts and performances. 467–4600.

National Cathedral Open House. Cathedral-related music, tours, tower climbs, and entertainment. 537–6200; www.cathedral.org.

SEPTEMBER–OCTOBER

Hispanic Heritage Month. The Smithsonian hosts a month of arts, entertainment, and educational activities celebrating Hispanic culture and traditions. 357–2700; www.si.edu.

OCTOBER

Taste of D.C. Festival. Pennsylvania Avenue is lined with stands offering foods from forty of D.C.'s hottest restaurants. Live entertainment too. 789–7002; www.washington.org/taste.

Outdoor Sculpture

Washington is supercharged with grandiose outdoor sculpture, much of it decorating federal buildings or paying official tribute to American leaders. But there's a parallel world of unconventional work in D.C. that's sure to revive your interest just when you're sated with the usual tourist fare. Local art maven and sculptor Vlad Lehovich shares his offbeat favorites.

PENNSYLVANIA QUARTER AND CHINATOWN

Viewed from the north, **Guns into Plowshares** (1997) looks just like a giant, 14-foot-high plow, but view it from the south and you'll see exciting metal texture. And close up you'll find that it's made from innumerable confiscated handguns, welded together. This virtuoso piece by Esther and Michael Augsberger is in an area filled with sculpture related to law enforcement. The title is from Isaiah, 2:4. *Judiciary Square, Fourth Street between D and E.*

DOWNTOWN

In perhaps the most bizarre work in town, the **Boy Scout Memorial** (1964), an 8-foot tall scout in full uniform strides doggedly toward the Mall, which was the site of the first national Boy Scout jamboree in Washington in 1937. But why is he accompanied by his enormous, naked parents? Good grief! Sculptor Donald DeLue maintained that they represent American manhood and womanhood—you judge! *The Ellipse, near 15th and E Streets NW.*

Two blocks west of the White House, **Don Quixote** (1981) cuts an extraordinary figure in Miles Rolph's tour de force of welded steel. Note how the Don's horse, Rosinante, snarls in anger as her master prepares for another hopeless foray. *1776 G Street NW, in courtyard between F and G and 17th and 18th Streets.*

GEORGETOWN

Four imposing bronze **Dumbarton Buffaloes** (1914) guard the bridge across Rock Creek to eastern Georgetown, splendid despite the ravages of weathering. Locals love these evocative tributes by sculptor Alex Phimester Proctor and call the bridge "Buffalo Bridge." *Dumbarton Bridge at Q Street NW.*

UPPER NORTHWEST

One of D.C.'s noblest pieces of stainless steel, the giant **Behrend Menorah** (1984) by Saunders Schultz and William Severson is a spiritual statement and a gleaming work of art. See it on a sunny day to catch reflections of nearby trees and bushes. Washington Hebrew Congregation, *3935 Macomb Street NW, off Massachusetts Avenue.*

Nudes on the central doorway arch of the National Cathedral? They've been controversial ever since designs were chosen for the central section of **Ex Nihilo** (Out of Nothing), Frederick Hart's interpretation of the Creation. Some find his vision edifying; others recall *Playboy*'s legendary Marilyn Monroe centerfold and other air-brushed females. Hart's smaller lucite and bronze figures are a staple at upscale malls. Completed 1990. *Massachusetts and Wisconsin Avenues NW.*

Methodist leader John Wesley, who said, "I look on the world as my parish," bows wearily over his equally tired horse as he rides westward into the New World. Instead of a sword, he brandishes an open Bible; instead of being heroic, he is slightly smaller than life. Arthur Walker's sensitive 1961 sculpture is at *Wesley Theological Seminary, 4500 Massachusetts Avenue at Tilden Street NW.*

DUPONT CIRCLE

Shirtless, with steel-rimmed glasses and staff, **Mohandas Gandhi** (2000) is a forceful presence on Massachusetts Avenue as he strides forward, seemingly leading a protest march. Calcutta sculptor Gautam Pal's tall bronze blends well with elegant surroundings on a picturesque traffic island opposite the Indian Embassy. *Massachusetts Avenue between Q and 21st Streets NW.*

Saint Jerome the Priest (1954) sits on the curb off bustling Massachusetts Avenue in front of the Croatian Embassy. Oblivious to nearby traffic, the surreal curvature and power of his body obscure the upturned Bible he reads. Croat sculptor Ivan Mestrovic's lugubrious interpretation of the fourth-century hermit and scholar is one of D.C.'s finest grotesques. *2343 Massachusetts Avenue NW.*

THE WATERFRONT AND ANACOSTIA

The **Big Chair** has long become part of the neighborhood in Anacostia. Visitors gape while locals hardly notice. Built in 1959 as a furniture store display, this 19-foot mahogany Duncan Phyfe-style chair has weathered well and packs one of the biggest visual wallops in town. Unpretentious, it is an interesting challenge to culturally correct pop art like Oldenbourg's giant eraser off Constitution Avenue. *Martin Luther King Jr. Avenue and V Street SE.*

White House Fall Garden and House Tours. Visit the White House gardens and public rooms while military bands entertain. 208–1631 or 456–2322.

Marine Corps Marathon. Thousands run in this annual marathon from the Iwo Jima Memorial in Arlington to the Capitol and back. Applications available February 1. (800) RUN–USMC; www.marinemarathon.com.

Washington International Horse Show. One of the East's premier shows, where hunting and jumping horses compete for prizes at the D.C. Armory. 432–SEAT; www.wihs.org.

NOVEMBER

American Indian Heritage Month. The Smithsonian celebrates with special programs and exhibitions. 357–2700.

Veterans Day Ceremonies. Arlington National Cemetery (703–607–8585), the Vietnam Veterans Memorial (619–7222), and Navy Memorial (737–2300).

DECEMBER

Kennedy Center Holiday Festival. Free performances and holiday concerts all month. 467–4600.

National Cathedral Christmas Services. A month of pageants, carols, and choruses. 537–2700.

National Christmas Tree Lighting and Pageant of Peace. The president lights the nation's Christmas tree on the Ellipse behind the White House, to begin a month-long Pageant of Peace. Events include nightly choral performances, a Nativity scene, and the Pathway of Peace. A collection of smaller, decoratively lit Christmas trees represents each of the nation's fifty-six states and territories. 208–1631; www.pageantofpeace.org.

The Washington Ballet's The Nutcracker. A Washington holiday tradition. 432–SEAT.

White House Christmas Candlelight Tours. Evening tours of the White House, its Christmas decorations, and holiday candlelight. 208–1631 or 456–2322.

Downtown

Like the rings of a great tree, Washington's buildings and public spaces trace the American past, from the outer layers of Watergate and the Vietnam Memorial down to the innermost bands of pre-Revolutionary Georgetown and the Marine Barracks. But the city's core has always been the White House, more modest by far than the mansions occupied by heads of state in many less affluent or powerful countries, but for more than 200 years the symbol of America all over the planet. Thousands of tourists pour through the Executive Mansion every year before following well-worn paths to the next attraction. More inquisitive travelers with historic perspectives think of the White House in its original role as the center of an old Washington neighborhood. Start exploring the president's neighborhood in *Lafayette Square,* which was the Pierce family farm, orchard, and burial ground when L'Enfant's plan projected it as the President's Park, where the chief executive could relax and seek relief from the capital's sizzling summers.

It may have been named for the Revolutionary War hero the Marquis de Lafayette, but the Square really belongs to Andrew Jackson, starting with the Spanish cannon captured by Old Hickory at Pensacola to the statue of Jackson on a capering horse, as Henry James put it, "as archaic as a Ninevite king,

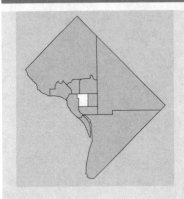

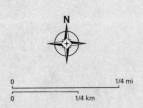

N

0 | 1/4 mi
0 | 1/4 km

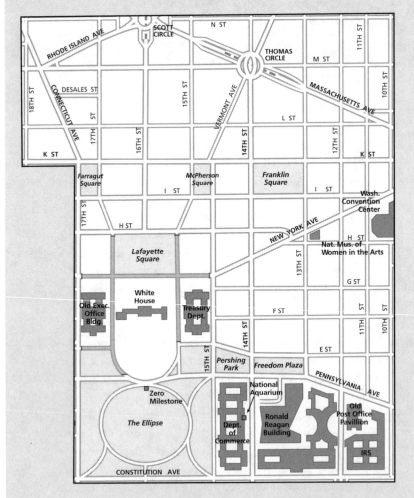

RHODE ISLAND AVE

SCOTT CIRCLE

N ST

11TH ST

THOMAS CIRCLE

M ST

10TH ST

18TH ST

CONNECTICUT AVE

DESALES ST

15TH ST

VERMONT AVE

MASSACHUSETTS AVE

17TH

16TH ST

14TH ST

L ST

12TH ST

K ST

K ST

Farragut Square

I ST

McPherson Square

Franklin Square

I ST

Wash. Convention Center

17TH ST

H ST

NEW YORK AVE

Nat. Mus. of Women in the Arts

H ST

13TH ST

Lafayette Square

G ST

White House

ST

ST

Old Exec. Office Bldg.

Treasury Dept.

F ST

14TH ST

11TH

10TH

E ST

15TH ST

Pershing Park

Freedom Plaza

PENNSYLVANIA AVE

Zero Milestone

National Aquarium

Old Post Office Pavillion

The Ellipse

Dept. of Commerce

Ronald Reagan Building

IRS

CONSTITUTION AVE

prancing and rocking through the ages." Jackson's statue looks down on the scene of his notorious 1829 inaugural, when tubs of whiskey and high-octane orange punch were rolled into the square to lure the drunken, coonskin-capped crowds out of the White House, touching off a wild melee that prompted the Chief Justice to sniff that "the reign of King Mob seemed triumphant."

The Square has also seen military service, when soldiers bivouacked there, first during the War of 1812 and again during the Civil War, turning it both times into a muddy swamp. President Grant later used it as his private zoo until the aroma of the presidential prairie dogs became intolerable.

But the Square's most distinctive and enduring role was as the social headquarters of antebellum Washington, a time when, as Square-dweller Henry Adams recalled, "beyond the square the country began." President and Mrs. Kennedy rescued many of the Square's elegant town houses from demolition in the 1960s, when the so-called planners saw this as the place for a government office complex.

On your stroll along the east side of the Square you'll pass the **_Tayloe House_** at number 721 Madison Place, a Federal beauty with an ironwork balcony that was known as "The Little White House" when it was the home of Mark Hanna, President McKinley's éminence grise. The widowed Dolley Madison lived in the Madison-Cutts House, where the Square meets H Street, until her death in 1849. During the Civil War the house belonged to General George McClellan, who, one night in November 1862, deliberately snubbed Abraham Lincoln. After waiting an hour in the parlor to see the absent general, the president was told that McClellan had in the meantime returned but had gone to bed.

At the top of the square stands St. John's Episcopal Church, "the church of the presidents," where every president since Madison has worshiped in pew 54. The parish house next door is Ashburton House, which was the British legation in the 1840s.

TOP ATTRACTIONS DOWNTOWN

Treasury Building	National Museum of Women in the Arts
National Geographic Society	
Old Executive Office Building	National Theater
Renwick Gallery	B'nai B'rith National Jewish Museum
Decatur House	Old Post Office Pavilion Observation Deck

At the corner of H Street and Jackson Place visitors get a crash course on the history of Washington social life. Capital insiders have gathered for almost two centuries at **Decatur House,** built in 1819 by Commodore Stephen Decatur, the swashbuckling hero of the War of 1812, with prize money earned from his naval victories. Decatur's architect was the equally distinguished Benjamin Henry Latrobe, known as the "father of American architecture." Decatur's exquisite Federal townhouse soon became one of the young capital's social and power centers, but not for long; a year later Decatur was mortally wounded in a duel. His house later became the residence of three secretaries of state— Martin Van Buren, Edward Livingston, and Henry Clay, who bragged (correctly) that he was "living in the best home of the city."

In the house's downstairs rooms you'd swear that the Decaturs had just stepped out, perhaps to pay a call on President Monroe just across the park. In the front parlor a gleaming eighteenth-century writing desk and secretary await the commodore's return while a vintage sewing kit reminds us that his wife Susan took an interest in what guys back in 1819 used to call "women's pastimes." On the wall you'll see a painting on glass of the 1812 naval battle where Decatur seized the British warship *Macedonian,* and in doing so made the money to pay for this glorious house. In the stately dining room a table set with Chinese export porcelain awaits the Decaturs' return. On the ground floor you'll also see the kitchen, which is being painstakingly restored with the help of a combination of original drawings and historical sleuthing.

As of mid-2004 visitors to the second floor enter a time warp and fast-forward to the end of the nineteenth-century and the grand Victorian living room of the socially prominent Beale family, who lived in Decatur House from 1871 to 1957. The Beales entertained here in late nineteenth-century grandeur amid an eclectic collection of furnishings, ranging from delicate Japanese screens to ornate Belter-style American furniture of rosewood and red velvet. In the center of the dining room floor the Beales placed a seal of California inlaid in rare woods to remind them of the source of the family's ranching fortune.

This, however, is slated to change over the next few years. While many reminders of the Beales remain, the National Trust for Historic Preservation, which manages the house, is in the process of phasing out the Beale era and returning these parlors to the Decatur days, when these upstairs rooms were the scene of numerous "crushes" and "squeezes"—the 1820 ancestors of the infamous Washington cocktail party. This ambitious project will also restore the Decaturs' original upstairs bedroom, from which you can look down on an interior courtyard and garden. Here prominent Washingtonians still gather for twenty-first century crushes, a.k.a. fundraisers.

The house also has a permanent exhibit space where you can trace Decatur's home, life, and times; there's also more about his naval victories. In addition, don't miss the museum's nifty gift shop, where first ladies Nancy Reagan and Laura Bush have shopped for books and Christmas ornaments.

Decatur House, at 748 Jackson Place NW (entrance at 1610 H Street); 842–0920; www.decaturhouse.org. Both the museum and its shop are open 10:00 A.M. to 5:00 P.M. Tuesday through Saturday and noon to 4:00 P.M. Sunday. Suggested donation $5.00. This is the only Lafayette Square home open to the public. Metro: Farragut West (orange and blue lines).

Tucked away in one of those wonderful Jackson Place town houses is one of the city's top gift shops, the ***White House Historical Association.*** Here you'll find a marvelous collection of books and other items that commemorate "The President's House," including splendid photographic studies of the White House and its public rooms, along with histories and official portraits of the presidents. For the kids, the shop offers educational games, coloring books, and guides to the White House. If you visit in November and December, you'll be able to take away distinctive tree ornaments from many different administrations (check out Teddy Roosevelt's 1902 ornament in Bohemian glass), greeting cards, and notepaper. The White House Historical Association, at 740 Jackson Place NW, is open from 9:00 A.M. to 4:00 P.M. Monday through Friday; 737–8292; www.whitehousehistory.org/shop.

Before you leave the Square be sure to visit each corner to inspect the statues of foreign heroes of the Revolution: de Rochambeau, Kosciusko, von Steuben, and Lafayette himself at the southeast corner.

Near the corner where Lafayette Square meets Pennsylvania Avenue, you'll find ***Blair House,*** one of Washington's most historic mansions and now the president's guest house, where visiting heads of state and royalty spend their official days in Washington. The patrician Blair family of Maryland built the original Blair House in 1824, which is the white Federal mansion at 1653 Pennsylvania, while the ***Lee House*** next door belonged to the aristocratic Lees of Virginia. These two elegant homes lived separate and stately lives until World War II, when Eleanor Roosevelt, wearied of having houseguest Winston Churchill padding around the White House in his Doctor Dentons, a brandy glass in hand, looking for FDR (so would you), used the merged

> # capitalquote
>
> "Washington talks about herself, and about almost nothing else. It is about herself as the City of Conversation that she incessantly converses."
>
> —Henry James

houses to put up visiting dignitaries. In 1950, when Harry and Bess Truman were using Blair House as a temporary White House while 1600 was being rebuilt, Puerto Rican nationalists stormed the buildings in an assassination attempt. A plaque on the Blair House fence honors the bravery of Secret Service agent Leslie Coffelt, who was shot and killed defending the president. In 1969 Blair House was again expanded to include two adjoining 1860s row houses around the corner on Jackson Place, facing Lafayette Park. These additions turned the original Blair House into a 70,000-square-foot, four-house complex that's larger by far than the White House itself.

Although Blair House is not open to the public, suffice it to say that as a special and small hotel for America's most important foreign guests, it is a treasure trove of the best in American art, interior design, and furnishings. And, of course, of American history. Just behind the deceptively plain front door are the spacious parlors where Andrew Jackson called his cronies together in the original "kitchen cabinet" and where, in wartime, Abraham Lincoln frequently conferred with his friend and confidant, Postmaster General Montgomery Blair after a short stroll across Pennsylvania Avenue. Metro: Farragut West (orange and blue lines).

Next door to Blair House, the **Renwick Gallery** exhibits the best in American arts, crafts, and design. Its gingerbread building was designed by James Renwick (also the architect of the Smithsonian "castle" on the National Mall) to hold the art collection of local banker William Corcoran. Alas, Mr. Corcoran's new toy was completed in 1861, just in time to be seized by the government and used as a warehouse for Army uniforms; when it reopened in 1869 it became Washington's first art museum. When the Corcoran collection moved

Renwick Gallery

down 17th Street (see the Foggy Bottom chapter) in 1897, this became the U.S. Court of Claims building until 1964, when it was transferred to the Smithsonian.

After ascending the Renwick's imposing staircase, just as President Grant did at the gala ball that reopened Corcoran's collection, you'll find the gallery's permanent exhibits of furniture, glassware, and textiles, a nice combination of the traditional and contemporary.

But prepare to be astonished by the sumptuous "Grand Salon" at the top of the stairs. It's always the Gilded Age in this grand, almost overwhelming room, where dozens of great paintings from every era of American history are beautifully hung, salon-style, on high silk-covered walls. Among the most memorable are the George Catlins, with fabulous scenes of the West in the 1830s and portraits of great warrior chiefs in full war dress. The Salon also has some rare pieces by California artist Hugo Ballin, and two Albert Henderson Thayer portraits of his children and family. The Renwick Gallery, at Pennsylvania Avenue and 17th Street (357–2531; www.americanart.si.edu), is open from 10:00 A.M. to 5:30 P.M. every day. Metro: Farragut West (blue and orange lines) and Farragut North (red line).

Across Pennsylvania Avenue looms the ***Eisenhower Executive Office Building,*** another ornate Victorian that somehow manages to be both highly visible and rarely visited. Tourists and Washingtonians hurrying along Pennsylvania Avenue never fail to gaze in wonderment at this massive granite ziggurat next door to the White House. But few realize that behind that operatic facade bristling with columns, pilasters, and porticoes lies a bygone world where graceful stairways, exquisite architectural details, and elegant rooms exude both refinement and power.

As of mid-2004, tours of this Washington landmark had been suspended for security reasons but would be renewed "as soon as possible." To find out if they're being given during your visit, phone 395–5895 between 8:00 A.M. and 5:00 P.M. Monday through Friday. To get a preview visit www.white house.gov/history/eeobtour/.

If you go, you'll see why a visit to what was formerly called the Old Executive Office Building, and still the OEOB to its friends, is a must for anyone interested in American design, politics, and history. This Victorian dowager has been the ground zero of American strength and decision-making since the day it opened in 1875, when it accommodated three entire government departments—State, War, and Navy. Several presidents, including both Roosevelts, Eisenhower, and Taft, worked here before moving next door to 1600 Pennsylvania, while twenty-five secretaries of state have had their offices in the south wing overlooking the Ellipse. The west wing, which once housed the War Department, has its own memories of George C. Marshall, Douglas MacArthur, and

**Eisenhower Executive
Office Building**

Major Dwight D. Eisenhower. Although the three original agencies left long ago, OEOB is still the home of the powerful, whose list of tenants includes the vice president and the chairmen of the Council of Economic Advisors and the National Security Council, where Ollie North and his sidekick Fawn Hall shredded the Iran-Contra documents.

Members of the regular Saturday morning tour of OEOB follow high-ceilinged hallways to explore hidden treasures like the Indian Treaty Room, a jewel box of brightly tiled floors and wrought-iron balconies where presidents since Harry Truman have held press conferences. Another visitor favorite is room 274, once the office of Franklin Roosevelt and other secretaries of the navy and now the ceremonial office of the vice president, where marble fireplaces, gleaming marquetry floors, and gold-framed mirrors epitomize Victorian elegance. Other stops include the former State Department library, with three stories of lacy white and gold railings, a ceiling of filigreed glass, and a floor of antique Minton tile. You'll be impressed by the wealth of architectural craftsmanship on the tour, from grand staircases that swoop up to coffered domes and stained glass rotundas, down to details such as intricately cast doorknobs and trash chutes.

Although security considerations rule out casual strolls around the OEOB, look for some special places in a building where every office has a history. In room 208, on the morning of December 7, 1941, Secretary of State Cordell Hull received, then ejected, Japan's emissaries. Room 488 was once the top secret "black room," where American cryptographers broke enemy codes. Metro: Farragut West (blue and orange lines) and Farragut North (red line).

Yes Virginia, there were coffee houses and bars in Washington long before Starbucks. Just off 17th Street, across from the OEOB, you'll find a classic coffee house at 1702 G Street NW, that will warp you back into the days of yore when Woodrow Wilson was president and "latte" was Italian for milk. ***M.E. Swing Coffee Roasters*** has been a local institution since 1916, and it shows in the mahogany fixtures, mirrored walls, marble bar, and the vintage burr grinder that will pulverize your espresso beans. If your taste runs to other types, there's a wide assortment of freshly roasted beans from everywhere from Ethiopia to South America. Open: Monday through Friday 7:00 A.M. to 6:00 P.M. 628–7601; www.swingscoffee.com.

You'll find one of D.C.'s best-kept secrets at 1500 Pennsylvania Avenue, a.k.a. the **Treasury Department.** Security considerations since September 11 have caused Treasury to suspend the regular Saturday morning tour. Call 622–0896 or visit www.ustreasury.gov to see if tours have been reinstated when you're in town. If they have, you'll walk directly from a busy twentieth-century street into the Treasury Department of 1842. The austerity of these Tyler administration corridors of power, with their cast-iron columns and graceful stairways, seems to embody the spartan tastes of a young, egalitarian republic, that is, until your guide takes you behind those louvered office doors into the suite used by Treasury Secretary Salmon P. Chase during the Civil War, where the simple gives way to the sumptuous.

Everything in these handsome offices— the decoratively stenciled ceilings with allegorical themes, the fireplace with its mammoth over-mantel mirror, and the glossy leather furniture—has been meticulously restored to reflect the days when Lincoln ambled over from the White House to anguish with Chase about finding ways to finance the war effort. Don't let this spoil your tour, but these splendid rooms are the birthplace of the income tax, first levied in 1862 to raise money for the Union cause.

macarthur's flowerpower

Displaying his hitherto unseen and unsuspected feminine side, General of the Army Douglas MacArthur designed the flower planters that flank the main entrance to the Eisenhower Executive Office Building.

Just after Lincoln's assassination, the Andrew Johnson Suite down the hall was turned into Johnson's Oval Office, where, as vintage prints show, the new president conducted his first cabinet meetings and received foreign funeral delegations. In the office next door, which once belonged to the secretary of the treasury and is now used by a senior department official, computers and

AUTHOR'S FAVORITES IN DOWNTOWN

Eisenhower Executive Office Building	Treasury Department
Lafayette Square and Decatur House	The Palm

printers coexist nicely with the massive conference tables, richly upholstered chairs, and thick drapes of 1875.

Treasury architect Alfred Mullett wanted the building's Cash Room to be "emblematic of the dignity of the nation and the stability of its credit," so he designed it as an Italian palazzo, its two-story walls covered with colored marble and ringed by a balcony with exquisitely wrought bronze railings. Immense gaslight chandeliers look down on the banking floor where tellers once sold bonds, cashed government checks, and redeemed banknotes with silver and gold

mayflowermadam

Dressed in basic black (no pearls), FBI Director J. Edgar Hoover lunched at the same table at the Mayflower Hotel every day for twenty years.

hauled from the currency and bullion vaults just below. Although it was called "the most expensive room in the world" when it opened, the Cash Room started off with a social calamity: At Grant's 1869 inaugural reception, hungry guests stampeded the kitchen, women fainted in the crush, and the search for coats went on all night. Be glad you weren't invited.

Treasury Department tours last ninety minutes and start at the visitor area inside the building's 15th Street entrance on Saturday mornings at 10:00, 10:20, 10:40, and 11:00. Reservations are essential and must be made at least three days in advance by calling 622–0896 or 622–0692. For security reasons you'll also need a picture ID. Children under twelve are not admitted. Metro: Metro Center (red, orange, and blue lines).

If you're looking for a map to chart your hike across New Guinea, a guide for your next safari along Namibia's Skeleton Coast, or a bicycle tour of Des Moines, **ADC Map and Travel Center** is just the place for you. ADC offers a huge collection of guides and maps covering the planet and, if you're planning a really long trip, charts of the solar system. ADC is located at 1636 I Street NW, and is open Monday through Thursday from 9:00 A.M. to 6:30 P.M., Friday

thezeromilestone

All distances within the United States to Washington are measured from that oblong milestone on the Ellipse directly behind the White House.

9:00 A.M. to 5:30 P.M., and Saturday 11:00 A.M. to 5:00 P.M. Closed Sunday. Metro: ADC is atop the Farragut West station (orange and blue lines).

The **National Museum of Women in the Arts** is probably the only museum anywhere dedicated to the achievements of women in every area of the arts. Its large and thoughtfully assembled permanent collection showcases women's achievements over five centuries, beginning with rare portraits by two of the few women painters of the Italian Renaissance, Sofonisba Anguissola and Lavinia Fontana. The exhibit continues chronologically through Mary Cassatt right down to the vibrant oils of contemporary artists; the museum also regularly hosts special traveling exhibits. Oddly enough, the museum is located in what was once one of the ultimate boys' clubs, a handsome Renaissance Revival building erected in 1908 as Washington's Masonic Temple. The knockout entrance hall exhibit area dates from its later days as a 1930s movie palace. Adding to the abundance, the fine museum shop is dedicated to books, images, and posters by women artists and photographers. The museum, at 1250 New York Avenue NW, is open Monday through Saturday 10:00 A.M. to 5:00 P.M. and Sunday from noon to 5:00 P.M. Voluntary contribution. Call 783–5000 or (800) 222–7270, fax 393–3234, or visit www.nmwa.org. Metro: Metro Center (red, blue, and orange lines).

Red Meat Department

Washington opened the twenty-first century with a stampede of New York steak houses. The venerable Palm, always a White House–media clubhouse and hangout for local movers and shakers, was joined by fellow New Yorkers Smith and Wollensky and Bobby Van's Steakhouse. So for a thick steak or mammoth lobster, here's what you need to know; just don't tell your cardiologist:

The Palm,
1225 19th Street NW;
293–9091.
Open Monday through Friday 11:45 A.M. to 10:30 P.M., Saturday and Sunday 5:30 to 10:30 P.M. Expensive. Located downtown.

Smith and Wollensky,
1112 19th Street NW;
466–1100.
Open Monday through Friday 11:30 A.M. to 11:30 P.M., Saturday and Sunday 5:00 to 11:00 P.M. Upstairs grill room open 11:30 A.M. to 2:00 A.M. every day. Expensive. Located downtown.

Bobby Van's Steakhouse,
809 15th Street NW;
589–0060.
Open Monday through Friday 11:30 A.M. to 10:30 P.M., Saturday 5:00 to 10:30 P.M. Closed Sunday. Expensive. Located downtown.

The **National Theatre,** where greats like Helen Hayes, John Barrymore, and Sarah Bernhardt once performed, has been part of America's theatrical tradition since 1835. On a nonperfoming level, Shirley McLaine and her brother, Warren Beatty, worked as usher and stage doorman, respectively, in the 1950s.

The current theater, at 1321 Pennsylvania Avenue NW, is the fifth edition of the National on this site. Like the Paris Opera, the National also has its very own phantom, the occasionally spotted ghost of John McCullough, a prominent actor of the 1880s who was murdered precisely where the present-day stage is located.

The National is still very much a prominent part of Washington's cultural scene and regularly hosts many pre- and post-Broadway performances, but three much less publicized (and free) presentations are also on the National's regular schedule. Every Monday at 6:00 and 7:30 P.M. from September to May, "Monday Night at the National," features mainly local performers in plays, readings, and performances of dance and music. "Saturday Morning at the National," a children's program that often includes storytellers and puppets, is presented each Saturday from September to May at 9:30 and 11:00 A.M. Every Monday at 6:30 P.M. from June through August, the National hosts a "Summer Cinema Program" of classic films.

Although these events are free, you'll still need tickets to get in. To get them, on a first-come first-served basis, turn up at the box office at least thirty minutes prior to the performance. For information about these and any other performances (or if you run into Mr. McCullough), call 628–6161; www.nation altheater.org. Metro: Federal Triangle (orange and blue lines).

Right on the Money

If you want to watch the sun set over some of the nation's most hallowed places, including the Jefferson Memorial and Arlington Cemetery across the Potomac, then head for the **Sky Terrace** on the roof of the Washington Hotel at 515 15th Street NW. While you're up there you'll also have a bird's-eye view of those equally famous buildings that appear on our $5, $10, and $20 bills—the White House, the Treasury, and the Lincoln Memorial. The eleventh-floor Terrace serves cocktails, sandwiches, salads, and cold platters every day from 11:30 A.M. to 1:30 A.M. from the end of April until the end of October. No reservations. While Sky Terrace prices are moderate, the panorama is anything but.

More formal dinners are available atop the Washington in the **Sky Room,** with a memorable view south to the memorials and the Pentagon. The Sky Room, open for dinner only from 6:00 to 10:00 P.M., is also a good choice for dining before performances at the National Theater. Reserve by calling 347–4499 or at www.hotelwashington.com.

Tokyo on the Potomac

If you're in Washington for the National Cherry Blossom Festival, don't forget to visit the Sakura Matsuri Japanese Street Festival, which is held every year in tandem with its better-known cousin. When Sakura Matsuri time rolls around, Pennsylvania Avenue becomes the Ginza, with a Japanese street festival and shopping on 12th Street NW, music and dancing in Freedom Plaza at Pennsylvania and 13th, and exhibits of Japanese woodworking and other arts and crafts. There's even a demonstration of Japanese martial arts and sumo wrestling competitions. The festival is sponsored by the Japan-America Society of Washington. For information about dates and event schedules, phone 833–2210 or visit www.us-japan.org/dc/events/matsuriindex.html.

When it opened in 1997, the **Ronald Reagan Building and International Trade Center,** named for the president who strongly favored a massive rollback in the bureaucracy, became the second largest federal office building in the United States, surpassed in floor space only by the Pentagon. The ultimate paradox? Two of its major tenants are agencies The Gipper had sworn to eliminate. Anyway, just because it's full of feds, don't pass up a chance to peer inside this massive structure at the corner of 13th Street and Pennsylvania Avenue NW. Once beyond that ostentatious facade, visitors gaze out over a stunning atrium used for special occasions and regular art exhibits. Free guided tours of the Ronald Reagan Building and International Trade Center start from the concierge desk at the 14th Street entrance on Monday, Wednesday, and Friday at 11:00 A.M. Self-guided walking tours are also available; see the concierge at each entrance for details.

The Reagan building also contains the well-stocked D.C. Visitor Information Center (328–4748) with interactive tours of the city and tickets for real tours. Open Monday through Friday 8:30 A.M. to 5:30 P.M., Saturday 9:00 A.M. to 4:00 P.M.; www.dcvisit.com. If it's lunchtime, the building also has a major-league food court that is open Monday through Friday from 7:00 A.M. to 7:00 P.M., Saturday 11:00 A.M. to 6:00 P.M. and on Sunday between March 1 and August 31 from noon to 5:00 P.M.

See vicious sharks dining on the lower end of the food chain! Thrill to razor-toothed piranha fighting for their seafood dinner! Are we somewhere along the Amazon or on a Pacific reef? Not at all; we're in the basement of an utterly prosaic government building, where most of the infighting goes on upstairs in offices and not downstairs in fish tanks. The **National Aquarium,** on the lower level of the Commerce Department Building at 14th Street and Constitution Avenue NW, has seventy tanks teeming with every form of aquatic

Stop the Presses!!

Well, they don't really yell that anymore, as you'll see if you take the Monday tour of the *Washington Post*. This is your chance to see how one of America's great newspapers is put together, as the tour winds through an exhibit of the newspaper's history, then moves on to visit the newsroom and the editorial offices. You'll also look in on the paper's graphics and photography departments. Although the folks at the *Post* are very informative, you will not be briefed on the identity of Deep Throat. Tours are given only for organized groups of ten to thirty on Mondays at 10:00 and 11:00 A.M. and 1:00, 2:00, and 3:00 P.M. Tours leave from the Post's main lobby at 1150 15th Street NW. Reservations are essential, and, for security reasons, well before your intended date you'll have to send the name of your group and the names of all participating members, preferred dates, and other information to the *Post* by fax (202–334–4963) or by mail (*The Washington Post,* Tours, 1150 15th Street NW, Washington, DC 20071). For more information call 334–7969. No children under eleven. Metro: McPherson Square (orange and blue lines).

life, including sea turtles, alligators, and tropical fish; the shark and piranha feedings, however, are the biggest draw. To see why, go there Monday, Wednesday, or Saturday at 2:00 P.M. to watch the sharks get a late lunch; the piranha dine at 2:00 P.M. on Tuesday, Thursday, and Sunday. Friday it's the alligators. Keep a close eye on the kids! Fortunately, you won't have to fight for an inexpensive lunch at the Commerce Department cafeteria on the same floor. The aquarium is open from 9:00 A.M. to 5:00 P.M. daily; 482–2825 (information tape) or 482–2826 (live person), fax 482–4946; www.nationalaquarium.com. Admission is charged. Metro: Federal Triangle (orange and blue lines).

For the full D.C. experience think about dining at the **Fourth Estate,** where you might find yourself seated next to one of the pundits or talking heads you've seen on TV shows and C-Span. Located on the twelfth floor of the National Press Building at 529 14th Street NW, the Fourth Estate was for decades open only to Press Club members, but is now open to all for lunch and dinner. The Fourth Estate gets good marks from local restaurant critics for its seafood entrees and desserts, which are made by Patisserie Poupon and imported from exotic Georgetown. Open Monday through Friday for lunch from 11:30 A.M. to 3:00 P.M. and dinner from 5:30 to 8:30 P.M. 662–7638. Expensive, but prices for members are discounted. For reservations and information about joining, visit www.press.org/abouttheclub/fourthestate.cfm.

There's no way you're going to overlook the **Old Post Office Pavilion** on Pennsylvania Avenue between 11th and 12th Streets, another grand old building that narrowly escaped the wrecker's ball. When it was built in 1899 as headquarters for the Postmaster General and the Post Office Department, this twelve-story fortress of steel and granite was Washington's first "skyscraper," but the Post Office, known to its detractors as "The Old Tooth," fell into disfavor in later years because its massive design overwhelmed that of other buildings in the Federal Triangle area. This Victorian veteran was saved and rebuilt in 1977 and lives on as a combination of government offices and tourist attraction.

Although the building's multistory atrium draws many visitors for its architecture, busy food court, and tourist-oriented shops, the main attraction is the ride up the 315-foot clock tower to the observation deck, where National Park Service rangers will show you around and explain the building's history. If you go, expect a terrific view out over the capital and its suburbs and, on a clear day, even as far as Virginia's Blue Ridge Mountains. While up there you'll also see the Congress Bells, a bicentennial gift from Britain, which replicate the bells in London's Westminster Abbey. The Pavilion (289–4224) is open from 8:00 A.M. to 10:45 P.M. from mid-April to Labor Day; the rest of the year it's 10:00 A.M. to 6:15 P.M. Individual shops may keep different hours. The Web site for the pavilion is www.oldpostofficedc.com and for the tower, www.nps.gov/opot/index.htm. Metro: Federal Triangle (orange and blue lines).

Political junkies visiting our nation's capital will find their special bliss at **Capitol Coin and Stamp,** where they can browse and buy from one of America's greatest collections of political memorabilia. At Capitol, owner Nelson Whitman (no relation to the author) has a huge supply of campaign buttons and stickers, tickets for the Clinton impeachment trials, and presidential Christmas cards from every president since Kennedy. Whitman also has an unparalleled stock of White House gift items reserved for special friends or contributors such as cufflinks and tie clips, plus glassware from Air Force One and a selection of china from Camp David. Lots of posters too, plus videotapes of presidential speeches. Capitol Coin and Stamp, at 1100 17th Street NW, Suite 503, is

Book Lover's Delight

There's not a dot-com in sight at **Chapters Literary Bookstore,** 445 11th Street NW, (347–5495), one of my favorite Washington bookstores, on or off the beaten path. As its name implies, this is a place for book lovers, with a large selection of fiction and literary biography, along with a good selection of poetry and travel literature. Check with the friendly, well-informed staff about Chapters' extensive program of readings and signings. Open Monday through Friday 10:00 A.M. to 7:00 P.M., Saturday 11:00 A.M. to 5:00 P.M., Sunday 1:00 to 5:00 P.M. Metro stop: Metro Center (all lines).

open from 10:00 A.M. to 6:00 P.M. Monday through Friday. 296–0400; www.cap itol coin.com. Metro: Farragut North (red line).

If the words ***National Geographic Society*** conjure up images of grandma's attic and stacks of dusty magazines with yellow borders, a visit to Society headquarters at 1145 17th Street NW, will help bring you up to date fast. In Explorer's Hall, on the first floor, you'll find special exhibits of great explorations or destinations and live music presentations from all over the world. Explorer's Hall is open for self-guided tours from 9:00 A.M. to 5:00 P.M. Monday through Saturday and from 10:00 A.M. to 5:00 P.M. Sunday. No charge.

Nothing demonstrates the "new" National Geographic as much as its bright, colorful store, which sells the Society's excellent travel guides and videos, plus the great photos and maps everyone expects from the National Geographic. If you want to become an intrepid National Geographic Explorer, even if you're just hiking to school, buy yourself an official knapsack or tote. Open Monday through Saturday 9:00 A.M. to 5:00 P.M., Sunday 10:00 A.M. to 5:00 P.M., holidays 9:00 A.M. to 5:00 P.M. Call 857–7588.

The Society also sponsors a little-publicized lecture and film series, often about adventure travel, in the ***Grosvenor Auditorium*** around the corner at 1600 M Street NW. Tickets, which range from $4.00 to $15.00 per event, can get scarce, so check the schedule and buy in advance by calling 857–7700 (fax 857–7747). The Grosvenor's box office is open 9:00 A.M. to 5:00 P.M. Monday through Friday. Every Tuesday at noon from October to May the Society sponsors a free film program in Grosvenor Auditorium. Call 857–7700 for details. Metro: Farragut North (red line) and Farragut West (orange line). Tickets, along with other information about the National Geographic, are also available at www. nationalgeographic.com.

Across M Street from the National Geographic is the Sumner School, named after Senator Charles Sumner, who was caned on the floor of the Senate after giving a speech against slavery. The school played a historic and crucial role in the education of black students in the District ever since it opened in 1873 as the city's first high school for blacks. In 1979 this classic redbrick schoolhouse became the ***Sumner School Museum and Archives,*** dedicated

Homeopathic Heaven

Didn't I tell you that Washington has a statue for everything? Dr. Samuel Hahnemann, who of course you always knew as the father of modern homeopathy, is commemorated with one on the east side of Scott Circle at 16th Street and Massachusetts Avenue NW. A colorful mosaic rounds out the tribute. Metro: Farragut North (red line).

to fostering African-American culture, history, and accomplishment. Exhibits of art and history predominate, but you also might find displays of textiles from Nigeria, paintings by black artists, or historic photographs of African-American life in bygone times. Charles Sumner School Museum, 1201 17th Street NW (442–6060, fax 727–6812), is open Monday through Saturday from 10:00 A.M. to 5:00 P.M. Metro: Farragut North (red line) and Farragut West (orange line).

Chess buffs should make a series of lightning moves to the **_U.S. Chess Center_** at 1501 M Street NW, where they'll find one of America's few chess museums. The center's exhibits contain scorebooks of great matches, chess trophies, and art, along with a vast assortment of chess memorabilia. On the walls, photographs and other mementos make up the Chess Hall of Fame, a series of displays honoring American chess champions, and in the center's gift shop, enthusiasts can pick up chess books, boards and sets, and even chess-themed T-shirts. The center emphasizes its instructional programs for children, in which about 2,000 local schoolkids are enrolled. The center also sponsors tournaments and evening games, but I'm told that walk-ins are only rarely able to find a pickup game. The center is open Monday through Thursday nights, starting at 6:00 P.M. and on weekends from noon to 6:00 P.M. Closed Friday. Call 857–4922 or visit www.chessctr.org. Metro: McPherson Square (orange and blue lines).

Places to Stay in Downtown

The Governor's House,
1615 Rhode Island
Avenue NW;
296–2100 or
(800) 784–1180.
A distinctive, recently renovated boutique hotel with spacious, well-furnished rooms. Located downtown near the National Geographic, but only 4 blocks from Dupont Circle. There's also a fitness center and large outdoor pool for escaping those Washington summers. Moderate. Metro: Dupont Circle or Farragut North (both on red line).

Hotel Harrington,
436 11th Street NW;
628–8140 or
(800) 424–8532;
www.hotelharrington.com
This family-owned, frill-free hostelry is a Washington institution and a perennial favorite of budget travelers and tour groups. The main reasons are its value and great location, where downtown Washington meets Pennsylvania Avenue and only a short walk from the National Mall. A cafeteria, coin laundry, and pub round out the package. Inexpensive. Metro: Metro Center (red, orange, and blue lines).

Hotel Mayflower,
1127 Connecticut
Avenue NW;
347–3000;
This National Historic Landmark opened in 1925 with

Calvin Coolidge's inaugural ball, and it's been attracting the important and powerful ever since. FDR and Eleanor stayed here while waiting for the Hoovers to move out of 1600 Pennsylvania; Charles De Gaulle and Nikita Khrushchev also signed the register. With its majestic main promenade, top restaurants, and luxurious rooms, it's easy to see why. Molto expensive. Metro: Farragut North (red line).

Hotel Washington,
15th Street and Pennsylvania Avenue NW;
638–5900;
www.hotelwashington.com
Talk about a great location! This first-rate Italian Renaissance hotel built in 1918 overlooks the Washington Monument and the Treasury; many rooms have great views

down Pennsylvania Avenue to the Capitol dome. Expensive. Metro: Metro Center (red, orange, and blue lines).

J. W. Marriott,
1331 Pennsylvania
Avenue NW;
393–2000.
Large (773 rooms) and a major meeting/convention place, this is the flagship of the Marriott chain. The J. W. Marriott is located at the crosshairs of downtown Washington, convenient to everything in the city center, including the White House, National Theater, and Lafayette Square. The hotel sits on top of National Place, a large shopping center with an assortment of stores and restaurants. Expensive. Metro: Metro Center (red, orange, and blue lines).

The Sofitel Lafayette Square,
806 15th Street NW;
737–8800.
This is the downtown Washington outpost of France's top luxury hotel chain, and it is très magnifique. Located in a 1920s Art Moderne office building, the elegance starts in the original marble lobby, with its 17-foot ceilings, and continues on upstairs in the Sofitel's 237 sleek and

understated guest rooms. Because it's French, the Sofitel has loads of élan, not to mention panache, along with a certain je ne sais quoi. A first-class restaurant, Cafe 15, and impeccable service make this a great, if expensive, experience. Metro: McPherson Square (orange and blue lines).

Places to Eat in Downtown

Bobby Van's Steakhouse,
809 15th Street NW;
589–0060.
See page 11 for full description.

Cosi Sandwich Bar,
1700 Pennsylvania
Avenue NW;
638–7101.
If you haven't been invited to lunch at 1600 Pennsylvania, don't despair. At Cosi you'll see oodles of White House staff dining decisively on tailor-made sandwiches of tandoori chicken or tuna salad and brie, or you can watch the president's men and women lining up boldly to

carry out grilled vegetables and tasty salads. This branch of a successful New York chain has caught on in a big way in D.C., mainly because of its encyclopedic range of sandwich ingredients and its patented focaccia-style bread. Great for lunch after touring the Lafayette Square/White House neighborhood. No reservations. Inexpensive. Open Monday through Friday 7:00 A.M. to 7:00 P.M., Saturday and Sunday 9:00 A.M. to 5:00 P.M. Metro: Farragut West (blue and orange lines).

Fourth Estate,
529 14th Street;
662–7638.
See page 11 for full description.

Loeb's,
832 15th Street;
371–1150.
If Kosher food had a mecca, this would be it. This storefront deli is for homesick New Yorkers or anyone else who likes thick sandwiches of corned beef, pastrami, or tongue. Cream soda and bagels too—so what's not to like? Just around the corner from Lafayette Square. Open 6:00 A.M. to 4:30 P.M. Monday through Friday. No reservations. Inexpensive.

AUTHOR'S FAVORITE PLACES TO EAT IN DOWNTOWN

The Old Ebbitt Grill	Loeb's
The Palm	Cafe 15 (in Sofitel Hotel)
Red Sage	Smith and Wollensky

Metro: McPherson Square (orange and blue lines).

M&S Grill,

600 13th Street NW; 347–1500; www.mccormickand schimck.com

The atmosphere is late Victorian mansion, with Tiffany glass ceilings, chandeliers, and polished walnut paneled walls. J. P. Morgan would feel right at home. M&S's American bistro menu includes steaks, chops, and well-prepared fish and scampi, which is understandable in a restaurant owned by Seattle's McCormick and Schmick (M&S—get it?). Inventive salads and sides too. The wine list is good and well priced, but could be a tad longer. All this plus friendly, professional service. Open Monday through Friday 11:30 A.M. to 11:00 P.M., Saturday 4:00 to 11:00 P.M., Sunday 4:00 to 10:00 P.M. Moderate. Metro: Metro Center (red, orange, and blue lines).

The Old Ebbitt Grill,

675 15th Street NW; 347–4801; www.clydes.com

Located across from Treasury this is a big local favorite with a long history, where the decor is early McKinley and the food is refined American bistro. Favorites include steaks, grilled fish of all kinds, great crab cakes, and fresh oysters from all over. The liver and onions will make you forget mom's forced feeding; the burgers are classics. The Ebbitt's two immense bars are always crowded. First-rate Sunday brunch. Very popular with politicos, real Washingtonians

and visitors, making reservations a must. Moderate. Open Monday through Friday 7:30 A.M. to 1:00 A.M., Saturday and Sunday 8:30 A.M. to 1:00 A.M. Metro: Metro Center (red, orange, and blue lines).

The Palm,

1225 19th Street NW; 293–9091.

See page 11 for full description.

Red Sage,

605 14th Street NW; 638–4444.

This dazzling Southwestern favorite is actually two restaurants in one. The always busy street-level bar and dining area is lively and informal, with a chili bar, lighter fare, and moderate prices; in the grill room downstairs the action is more serious (and expensive) with dishes such as chorizos and black bean terrine or chipotle shrimp on a buttermilk corncake. No reservations upstairs, but essential for downstairs dining. Upstairs hours: Monday through Saturday 11:45 A.M. to 11:45 P.M., Sunday 4:30 to 11:00 P.M. Grill hours: Monday through Friday 11:30 A.M. to 2:00 P.M., Saturday and Sunday 5:00 to 10:30 P.M. Moderate upstairs; expensive downstairs. If you liked Red Sage and want to take it home with you, go next door to the Red Sage Bakery and Store, practically incandescent with all those spices, hot sauces, and dried peppers. Open Monday through Friday 8:00 A.M. to 3:00 P.M. Metro: Metro Center (red, orange, and blue lines).

17th Street Bar and Grill,

1615 Rhode Island Avenue NW (in the Governor's House Hotel); 872–1126.

This attractive bistro with friendly service is well located for downtown lunches and dinners. American bistro also describes the food, which ranges from sandwiches, large salads, and pizza to grilled fish and steaks. Outside patio is open in good weather. Reserve, especially for lunch, when the National Geographic folks get out their maps and head this way. Moderate. Open Monday through Friday 7:00 A.M. to 10:00 P.M., Saturday 6:30 to 11:00 P.M., and Sunday 5:00 to 10:00 P.M. Metro: Farragut North (red line) and Farragut West (orange line).

Smith and Wollensky,

1112 19th Street NW; 446–1100.

See page 11 for full description.

Tuscana West,

1350 I Street NW; 289–7300.

This downtown Italian is a favorite of the lawyers, lobbyists, and other denizens of nearby K Street's "glitter gulch." Despite its name, Tuscana West offers dishes from all over Italy, including hearty northern risottos and southern pastas with heavy-duty red sauce, along with Tuscany's famed veal chops and seafood. Reservations advised. Moderate. Open Monday through Friday 11:30 A.M. to 10:00 P.M., Saturday 5:30 to 10:00 P.M.; closed Sunday. Metro: McPherson Square (blue and orange lines).

Pennsylvania Quarter and Chinatown

L'Enfant's original plan for Washington envisioned the area around Seventh Street and Pennsylvania Avenue as the hub of the capital's civic life, where the courts, main government buildings, and city hall would be located. And they were. Washington's courthouse and judicial complex, along with great neoclassic public buildings, like the Patent Office and the now abandoned Old Post Office at Seventh and E Streets, were built in this neighborhood and are still there. In later years, the Seventh Street area also became the place to shop for produce at the mammoth Center Market on Pennsylvania Avenue, which operated from 1801 to 1931 on the site of today's National Archives. Seventh Street also became the heart of the city's dry goods district, where Mr. Saks built his first store before moving on to New York's Fifth Avenue. Local department stores like Hecht's, Kann's, and Woodward and Lothrop dominated the area until the 1960s, when the Seventh Street neighborhood fell into disrepair.

The late 1980s saw the Seventh Street corridor, now known as the "New Downtown" or "Pennsylvania Quarter," stage a rebound that's still in progress, thanks in part to the construction of the MCI sports complex and the arrival of trendy art galleries and restaurants. Today the revitalized Seventh Street

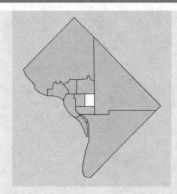

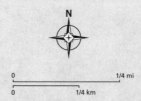

N

| 0 | | 1/4 mi |
| 0 | | 1/4 km |

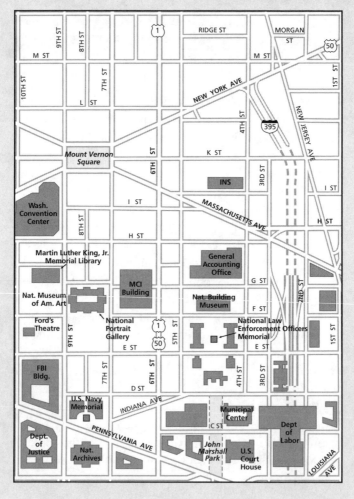

9TH ST
8TH ST
M ST
10TH ST
7TH ST
L ST
RIDGE ST
MORGAN ST
M ST
1ST ST
50
NEW YORK AVE
4TH ST
395
K ST
NEW JERSEY AVE
Mount Vernon Square
6TH ST
Wash. Convention Center
8TH ST
I ST
INS
3RD ST
I ST
MASSACHUSETTS AVE
H ST
H ST
Martin Luther King, Jr. Memorial Library
General Accounting Office
G ST
MCI Building
Nat. Museum of Am. Art
Nat. Building Museum
F ST
2ND ST
Ford's Theatre
9TH ST
National Portrait Gallery
5TH ST
National Law Enforcement Officers Memorial
1ST ST
E ST
E ST
FBI Bldg.
7TH ST
6TH ST
D ST
4TH ST
3RD ST
U.S. Navy Memorial
INDIANA AVE
Municipal Center
Dept of Labor
Dept. of Justice
Nat. Archives
PENNSYLVANIA AVE
C ST
John Marshall Park
U.S. Court House
LOUISIANA AVE

corridor boasts an intense gallery and art scene, some of the city's most inno-vative restaurants, a world-class Shakespearean theater, and a pair of unforget-table museums. It is also the gateway to Washington's Chinatown.

Two Metro stops serve the Pennsylvania Quarter: at the Chinatown end through the Gallery Place/Chinatown stop on the yellow, red, and green lines and at the Pennsylvania Avenue end through the Archives/Navy Memorial stop on the blue, yellow, orange, and green lines.

Start your visit to the Pennsylvania Quarter at the ***Navy Memorial,*** which proves that even well-beaten paths like Pennsylvania Avenue can have hidden corners. This impressive but simple memorial—with its fountains, ship's masts with signal flags, and the touching statue of the *Lone Sailor*—commemorates the Navy's battles, heroism, and achievements. Two curved sculpture walls record important Navy accomplishments and scenes from Navy history. With any luck at all, you'll be there for one of the frequent outdoor concerts by the Navy Band or a visiting musical group.

But less well known, even to many Washingtonians, is the privately funded ***Naval Heritage Center.*** The center's entrance hall adjoins the Memorial on street level, but the real action is below deck, on an underground floor where exhibits depict Navy traditions and a "Ship's Store" sells nautical mementos, prints, and books. The center also has a state-of-the-art theater showing *At Sea,* an action-packed film about carrier life. And don't miss "Navy Log," where you can search military records on a 250,000-name computerized database to see if your Navy or Marine pals haven't been exaggerating their war stories.

The Naval Heritage Center, at 701 Pennsylvania Avenue NW (737–2300), is open Tuesday through Saturday 9:30 A.M. to 5:00 P.M.; closed Sunday. From

---

TOP ATTRACTIONS IN THE PENNSYLVANIA QUARTER AND CHINATOWN

National Museum of American Art	National Building Museum
National Portrait Gallery	Cafe Atlantico
Naval Heritage Center	MCI Center
406 Seventh Street	Chinatown
Footnotes Cafe	National Law Enforcement Officers Memorial
Shakespeare Theater	
Old Pension Building	Morrison-Clark Inn

November to February the center is also closed Mondays. E-mail ahoy@lone sailor.org or visit www.lonesailor.org. Metro: Archives/Navy Memorial (green and yellow lines).

Just off Seventh Street on Indiana Avenue stand a trio of well-preserved 1820 houses that knew Lincoln when the president's carriage took him up Seventh Street to his summer White House at the Soldier's Home. Fine residential dwellings in their day, these antebellum homes have long since been converted to commercial use. The house at 641 Indiana is where you'll find **Artifactory,** a large collection of art and handicrafts unearthed by owner Dominick Cardella on his travels in Africa and Asia. Cardella's shop is packed with an eclectic and tasteful selection of artifacts that includes marionettes from Burma and Indonesia, Balinese masks, and traditional African art and statuary. Artifactory is open Monday through Saturday 10:00 A.M. to 6:00 P.M. Call 393–2727. Metro: Archives/Navy Memorial (yellow and green lines).

america'soldest otiselevator

The 1852 vintage rope-powered lift in Litwin's Furniture and Antiques at 637 Indiana Avenue is the oldest known Otis elevator in America, and it's still in use.

The top three floors of 406 Seventh Street are entirely given over to several of Washington's top galleries, where a range of artists, from New York's best painters and photographers to Washington's own up-and-coming talent, exhibit in spare, high-ceilinged rooms perfect for showing off their colorful art and photography. In addition to their regular hours, all of the galleries are open from 6:00 to 8:00 P.M. on the third Thursday of every month.

The third-floor **Numark Gallery** features New York artists such as David Row, David Shapiro, and minimalist Sol Lewitt, along with Washingtonians like Robin Rose and Christopher French. Numark Gallery (628–3810, www.numark gallery.com) is open Tuesday through Saturday 11:00 A.M. to 6:00 P.M. Next door, the **David Adamson Gallery** focuses on digital printmaking and photography, but also offers prints and paintings by New York and local artists. Open Tuesday through Saturday 11:00 A.M. to 5:00 P.M. Call 628–0257.

In the sprawling second-floor **Apex Gallery,** there's enough space for up to five artists to stage their own shows simultaneously. During one of my visits I got a world tour of art and artists from Washington, France, New York, and the Czech Republic, including an inspired and slightly wacky model by Museum Director David Stainback of a windowed Washington Monument converted to a condominium. Apex Gallery is open Wednesday through Sunday 11:00 A.M. to 5:00 P.M. Call 638–7001 or e-mail amuseum@erols.com or visit www.artistsmuseum.com. Visitors to 406 Seventh Street can also browse and buy a variety of media, including abstract paintings, sculpture, and installation art at **Touchstone Gallery,** a cooperative gallery on the second floor. Open Wednesday through Friday 11:00 A.M. to 5:00 P.M., Saturday and Sunday noon to 5:00 P.M. Call 347–2787.

Even the storefront at 406 offers art, but of a slightly different kind. At **Apartment Zero** you'll find one of D.C.'s hippest home furnishings stores, with cutting-edge office and home furniture, standing lamps of sculptured paper, and, in season, unique Christmas tree ornaments. Nick and Nora Charles would really go for Apartment Zero's collection of '30s era martini shakers, glassware, and other cocktail paraphernalia, minus the olives. Shop here and your house will never be the same. Open Wednesday through Saturday 11:00 A.M. to 6:00 P.M., Sunday noon to 5:00 P.M. Call 628–4067 or visit www .apartmentzero.com. Metro: Archives/Navy Memorial (yellow and green lines).

Although there's a Starbucks in the next block, **Footnotes Cafe** seems to be the coffeehouse of choice for Penn Quarter gallery goers and book browsers. Located in the Seventh Street branch of Olsson's, an outstanding local chain of book and record sellers, Footnotes has a wide range of coffees and teas, a good but short wine list, and a selection of erudite sandwiches for literary noshing. Try ordering the Charles Dickens (traditional roast beef), the Herman Melville ("a whale of a tuna sandwich"), or, if the bambini are along, the Dr. Seuss, which (no surprise here) is peanut butter and jelly. Tables with chairs and sofas round out the picture and, should you feel like falling into a literary swoon, there's a cut velvet chaise longue available in the window. Footnotes, located at 418 Seventh Street, is open Monday 8:00 A.M. to 5:00 P.M., Tuesday through Friday 8:00 A.M. to 7:30 P.M., Saturday 10:00 A.M. to 7:00 P.M., Sunday noon to 7:00 P.M.; afternoon tea from 3:00 to 6:00 P.M. Call 638–4882. Metro: Archives/Navy Memorial (yellow and green lines).

Pua, the shop at 444 Seventh Street NW, takes its name from a natural plant fiber produced in the Himalayas, then spun and woven by hand by Nepalese craftswomen. Pua's designs include quilted cotton coats and jackets,

AUTHOR'S FAVORITES IN THE PENNSYLVANIA QUARTER AND CHINATOWN

International Spy Museum	Jaleo
Hotel Monaco	Teaism
Old Pension Building	Temperance Fountain

colorful and attractive dresses, and block printed skirts and pants. While you're deciding, have a cup of Darjeeling in Pua's little tearoom. Open Monday noon to 6:00 P.M., Tuesday through Friday noon to 7:30 P.M., Saturday and Sunday 1:00 to 7:30 P.M. Call 347–4543. Metro: Archives/Navy Memorial (yellow and green lines).

In Spanish *Andale* means "let's go"—not a bad idea if you're in the Pennsylvania Quarter and looking for a delightful place to dine. The cuisine is authentic and professionally prepared Mexican, with familiar dishes like queso fundido and chorizo balanced against fresh and inventive versions of red snapper seviche and zesty pork carnitas. The *Washingtonian*'s food critic gave high marks to the airy Enchiladas Zapotecas and called the Barbacoa de Borrego Andale's "unchallenged gem." And if you go on Monday night, every bottle of wine on the list is half price. Que alegria!! Andale, 401 Seventh Street NW, is open Monday through Friday for lunch from 11:30 A.M. to 3:00 P.M. and for dinner 5:00 to 10:00 P.M., until 11:00 P.M. on Friday and Saturday. Dinner reservations suggested. Call 783–3133.

The *Zenith Gallery* is a Pennsylvania Quarter pioneer, having arrived at 413 Seventh Street in 1986. It is also one of the neighborhood's more eclectic galleries, where you'll find sculptures in bronze, steel, wood, and ceramic, abstract and realistic paintings, and other media ranging from light sculptures to wearable art, furniture, and comical figures of papier-mâché and resin. If you have a taste for whimsy, the Zenith is for you. The Zenith Gallery is open Tuesday through Saturday 11:00 A.M. to 6:00 P.M., and Sunday noon to 5:00 P.M. Call 783–2963, fax 783–0050, e-mail zenithga@erols.com or visit www.zenith gallery.com. Metro: Archives/Navy Memorial (yellow and green lines).

The Venerable Bead

Whoever said, "when you've seen one bead museum, you've seen 'em all" clearly had never cast a beady eye at 400 Seventh Street NW. The *Washington Bead Museum's* spacious loft hosts a continuous round of exhibits of handmade glass beads, period glass, and jewelry from all over, most recently the United States, the Czech Republic, India, and Africa. Aside from attracting a worldwide audience of bead enthusiasts, the museum also sponsors a series of educational programs to illustrate how beadwork reflects a society's craftsmanship, traditions, and history. Open Wednesday through Saturday 11:00 A.M. to 4:00 P.M., Sunday 1:00 to 4:00 P.M. Closed Monday and Tuesday. Call 624–4500, visit www.beadmuseumdc.org, or e-mail info@beadmuseumdc.org.

Tucked away behind the modest marquee at 450 Seventh Street is the 441-seat **Shakespeare Theater,** which the *Economist* called "one of the world's three great Shakespearean theatres," and the *Wall Street Journal* dubbed "the nation's foremost Shakespeare company." Since the Shakespeare opened in 1986, its performances have racked up dozens of awards, plus acclaim from the *New York Times* as a "critical and popular success." Outstanding guest actors such as Elizabeth Ashley, Hal Holbrook, and Patrick Stewart often join the resident company in staging Shakespearean and other classical plays during the theater's September to July season. Call 547–1122 for information on what's playing, to book seats, or to ask about the Shakespeare's outdoor summer performances in Rock Creek Park or visit www.shakespearetheater.org. The box office is open Monday 10:00 A.M. to 6:00 P.M., Tuesday through Saturday 10:00 A.M. to 6:30 P.M., and Sunday noon to 6:30 P.M. Metro: Archives/Navy Memorial (yellow and green lines).

Those walls covered with colorful plates and a giant mural of a flamenco dancer announce that you've arrived at **Jaleo,** a lively storefront Spanish bistro on the corner of Seventh and E Streets. If you're headed for the Shakespeare Theatre next door or the MCI Center up the street, this bright and bustling restaurant with friendly service is perfect for a pre- or postperformance snack or meal. Choose four or five hot or cold tapas, maybe some garlic shrimp, grilled lamb, or peppers stuffed with goat cheese, and you're off and running. But for a lot of people (like me), that's just the beginning, so they move on to Chef Jose Andres's excellent paellas, grilled fish, or fish stew. Grilled spicy Spanish chorizos (sausages), either as tapas or as a main dish with beans and asparagus, are always a good choice. And, no surprise, the gazpacho and sangria are terrific. As in Madrid, the dinner and bar action goes on until late, when a trendy younger crowd takes over and Jaleo begins to live up to its name—which translates as uproar or revelry—especially on Wednesday nights, when the dancers from Seville perform. Bring castanets. Jaleo, 480 Seventh Street NW (628–7949), is open Sunday and Monday 11:30 A.M. to 10:00 P.M., Tuesday through Thursday 11:30 A.M. to 11:30 P.M., Friday and Saturday 11:30 A.M. to midnight. Although Jaleo accepts a limited number of preshow reservations from 5:00 to 6:30 P.M., seating at other times is walk-in. Moderate. Metro: Archives/Navy Memorial (yellow and green lines).

The neoclassical gem that occupies the block that stretches from Seventh to Eighth Streets between E and F Streets was designed by Robert Mills, who was also the architect of the Treasury Building and the Washington Monument. When it opened in 1842 as Washington's General Post Office, Charles Dickens loved this building, calling it "very compact and very beautiful," making it practically the only thing in Washington that Dickens *did* approve of during his

1842 visit. This is also where the first telegraph message, "what hath God wrought," was transmitted by Samuel F. B. Morse in 1845. During the Civil War the building saw duty as a barracks and hospital. The Post Office ended its official days as the home of the Tariff Commission, after which it stood abandoned for many years until, in 2002, as a prime example of downtown Washington's dramatic renaissance, it was restored, rehabbed, and reopened as the **_Hotel Monaco,_** one of the city's very best hotels. Guests check in at a period reception desk located where clerks sold stamps to 1840s Washingtonians (and maybe even Dickens himself). And the Monaco's Poste-Moderne Brasserie restaurant, overlooks the courtyard where the Pony Express riders and Wells-Fargo wagons once brought in mail for sorting by clerks who worked right about where diners now sit.

That massive Greek Revival building on Seventh between F and G Streets is the **_Old Patent Office,_** which dates from the 1830s, when old photos show its elegant columns beginning to rise above the swamplands and meadows of a distinctly rustic Washington. During the Civil War the Patent Office became a Union Army barracks and hospital where two government clerks, poet Walt Whitman and American Red Cross founder Clara Barton, served as volunteer nurses. Lincoln's second inaugural ball was held in the vast, marble-columned room on the third floor known today as the Lincoln Gallery. The building's Victorian gingerbread Great Hall was once the largest room in America and is still one of the most ornate and beautiful.

Since 1968 this Washington landmark has housed two of the capital's finest museums: the National Portrait Gallery, with stunning portraits of the men and women who shaped American history, from George Washington to Ernest

National Portrait Gallery, Old Patent Office

Clandestine Collection

It wouldn't make much sense in your average American city but, when you're the "World's Spy Capital," (that's Washington) you've just gotta have a spy museum. D.C. has the first and only museum dedicated to espionage, and it's a good one. Even if you left your cloak and dagger in the drawer back home, you'll still enjoy the **International Spy Museum,** which occupies five landmark buildings, with its main entrance at 800 F Street NW. The museum offers a number of lively exhibits of international intelligence artifacts, including the legendary Enigma cipher machine, an orientation into the world of spy tradecraft, and videos of famous and real-life espionage and counterespionage stories, including historic capers involving the Berlin Wall and some current cases involving turncoats like Aldrich Ames and Robert Hanssen. Not only that, the museum has two excellent restaurants, **Zola,** where, under deep cover, you can join James Bond in dining on modern American cooking in a large loft space (open daily 11:30 A.M. to midnight) and, for more casual fare, including salads and sandwiches, try the **Spy City Cafe,** (open daily 8:00 A.M. to 8:00 P.M.). Both the museum and its excellent shop specializing in spook lore are open daily from November to March 10:00 A.M. to 6:00 P.M. and until 8:00 P.M. from April through October; 393–7798; www.spymuseum.org. Admission is $13 for adults and $10 for children and students; secret agents under five are admitted free. Red Alert: Since the museum is a major attraction, long lines are frequent so book ahead. Metro stops: Gallery Place/Chinatown (red, yellow, and green lines) and Archives/Navy Memorial (blue,yellow,orange and green lines).

Hemingway, and the National Museum of American Art, dedicated to the entire span of American artistic creativity. Alas, you won't be able to wander the antebellum corridors to enjoy these two museums until July 4, 2006, when the building reopens after an extensive renovation. But on the Internet you can get a good idea of what you'll see when they reopen. The National Museum of American Art address is www.americanart.si.edu, while many of the National Portrait Gallery's treasures can be found at www.npg.si.edu.

The District's **Recorder of Deeds Building** at 515 D Street NW, may not amount to much aesthetically, but it contains a set of wonderful murals representing important leaders and events throughout African-American history. The series begins in the entrance hall by honoring scientist Benjamin Banneker; six others depict Frederick Douglass in his role as adviser to Abraham Lincoln, Col. Robert Shaw and the 54th Massachusetts at the siege of Confederate Fort Wagner, and explorer Matthew Henson at the South Pole with Admiral Peary. These imposing paintings, like many in post offices and other public buildings throughout the United States, were commissioned by the Public Works Administration, which means that they date from the early 1940s. The building is

Honoring the Men in Blue

The *National Law Enforcement Officers Memorial,* across F Street from the National Building Museum, bears the names of the 14,500 American law enforcement officers killed in the line of duty since 1794. Like the Vietnam Memorial, the wall of inscriptions is frequently visited by relatives or colleagues of the fallen officers, who often leave flowers in remembrance. Although the memorial reminds visitors that violence is always just around the corner for law enforcers, it is also a restful, nicely landscaped place to stroll or take a break from gallery- and museum-hopping.

The *National Law Enforcement Visitor Center,* a short walk away at 605 E Street, is the memorial's companion, a collection of exhibits honoring officers killed in the line of duty. There is also a display of legendary policemen, whose ranks include New York Police Commissioner Teddy Roosevelt, "Untouchable" Eliot Ness, and Wild West lawman Wyatt Earp. The visitor center is open Monday through Friday 9:00 A.M. to 5:00 P.M., Saturday 10:00 A.M. to 5:00 P.M., and Sunday noon to 5:00 P.M. Call 737–3213, visit www.nleomf.com, or e-mail info@ nleomf.com.

open Monday through Friday from 8:30 A.M. to 4:00 P.M. Metro: Archives/Navy Memorial (yellow and green lines).

Tucked away in a tidy little garden at the corner of Third and G Streets NW is the 1876 redbrick synagogue that houses the **Lillian and Albert Small Jewish Museum.** The museum, run by the Jewish Historical Society of Greater Washington, brings together archives and records of Jewish history in Washington over the years. A series of exhibits profile Jewish life in the capital; one of the recent ones, "Kronheim's Washington," was a collection of photographs and other mementos of one of the Jewish community's top movers and shakers. The museum is located at 701 Third Street NW; 789–0900; Sunday through Thursday noon to 4:00 P.M. Suggested donation $2.00. Metro: Judiciary Square (red line).

At **Cafe Atlantico** the accent is on Latin America and its exciting *nueva cocina*. Dining is on three dramatically staged levels, each displaying the work of South American and Caribbean artists. Thirsty gringos can belly up to the bar for potent *bebidas latinas* like silky margaritas and tasty but lethal pisco sours. If a few of these Pan-American powerhouses haven't sent you south of the border, order one of the restaurant's imaginative specialties such as Brazilian feijoada with an Asian spin, duck confit, or a plump grilled salmon wrapped in papaya. There's usually a tasting menu, and at Saturday lunch the main attraction is an inventive and popular Latin American dim sum platter. Reservations recommended; to get them, call 393–0812. Cafe Atlantico, at 405 Eighth Street NW, serves lunch 11:30 A.M. to 2:30 P.M. Monday through Friday and dinner from

5:00 to 10:00 P.M. On Friday and Saturday dinner is served from 5:00 to 11:00 P.M. Sunday it's dinner only, from 5:00 to 10:00 P.M. Expensive.

Across the street at 400 Eighth Street, in the bright, airy ***Teaism*** restaurant, you can dine in utter tranquility on everything from miso soup and soba noodle salad to *ochazuke,* which is Japanese rice and tea soup. Teaism also specializes in "big dishes" of curries and rice, but for a real change of pace, try a "bento" or Japanese meal box based on salmon, beef, or tuna. Teaism's eclectic menu also offers breakfasts of French toast, chicken sausage with naan and raita, and (need we say it?) a vast repertoire of teas and tisanes. Open Monday through Friday 7:30 A.M. to 10:00 P.M., Saturday and Sunday 9:30 A.M. to 9:30 P.M. Call 638–6010.

If you liked Teaism enough to take it home with you, pop into the restaurant's tea shop next door to pick up some Jasmine Pearl or Anxi for your very own, and carry it away in a gorgeous tea box made with colorful washi paper. Here you'll also find all the tea paraphernalia you could ever need, including all of the exotic sweets, jams, and chocolates needed to wow your pals with a great high tea. Open Monday through Friday 7:30 A.M. to 9:00 P.M., Saturday and Sunday 9:30 A.M. to 9:00 P.M. Call 638–7740.

The ***MCI Center,*** with its banners and imposing facade, has been the centerpiece of this neighborhood and of the Washington sports and cultural scene since the day it opened its doors in 1998. The center hosts professional teams like the NBA Wizards, the WNBA Mystics, the NHL Capitals, and the Georgetown University Hoyas, along with a variety of concerts.

The MCI Center, at 601 F Street NW, is open daily 10:00 A.M. to 10:00 P.M. (or one hour after center events conclude), Sunday 10:00 A.M. to 6:00 P.M. For

MCI Center

Hooker's Army

When the Civil War brought hundreds of thousands of soldiers to Washington, something occurred that Pierre L'Enfant, the great planner, could never have foreseen. Pennsylvania Avenue, a.k.a. "America's Main Street," turned into America's leading red-light district, where hundreds of Washington hostesses gathered every evening around Seventh Street. Union General Joseph Hooker, concerned about this, ordered the ladies and their activities confined to a nearby neighborhood known today as Federal Triangle, a command that caused them to refer to themselves sarcastically as "Hooker's Army," and so the term "hooker" was born. Archaeological note: Excavations for major buildings in this area have turned up perfume and liquor bottles, combs, and garter hooks.

information, call 628–3200; for seats it's 432–7328, or go online at www.mci center.com. And on the way out, don't miss the photographic exhibit of neighborhood history just inside the F Street entrance. Metro: Gallery Place/Chinatown (red, yellow, and green lines).

You can't miss the **Old Pension Building,** the spectacular redbrick Victorian pile on F Street that occupies the entire block between Fourth and Fifth Streets. The building, inspired by Rome's Palazzo Farnese, is circled by a terracotta frieze of the Union Army and Navy in action, complete with bayonet charges, sea battles, and gallant generals on rearing chargers, your clue that the building was constructed to process Civil War veterans benefits. But this is far from being a maze of cubicles for civil service paper pushers. You'll be astounded by the grandeur of the Pension Building's Great Hall—a 300-foot-long interior courtyard supported by eight colossal marble columns with a fountain in the center. It's the perfect place for a large and elegant party, which is exactly why presidents since Grover Cleveland have been using the Great Hall for their inaugural balls.

The magnificent setting tends to overshadow the **National Building Museum,** which now occupies part of this grand space. The museum, which celebrates the building arts, nevertheless holds its own with a series of lively exhibits ranging from the American country store to the impact of air-conditioning on everyday life. Don't miss the permanent exhibit *Washington: Symbol and City,* an excellent orientation to the history of the Federal City, the evolution of its architecture, and the impact of European cities on Washington's urban plan. The museum shop is one of the city's best—well stocked with imaginative gifts along with books on buildings and architecture. In High Noon, the museum's cafe, you'll find coffee, salads, and a wide selection of sandwiches. The Building Museum is at 401 F Street NW, 272–2448; www.nbm.org.

Museum hours are Monday through Saturday 10:00 A.M. to 5:00 P.M., Sunday 11:00 A.M. to 5:00 P.M. Building tours, which last forty-five minutes, are given Monday through Wednesday at 12:30 P.M., Thursday through Saturday at 11:30 A.M., 12:30 and 1:30 P.M., and Sunday at 12:30 and 1:30 P.M. Reservations are not needed and there is no charge. Metro: Judiciary Square (red line).

One of Washington's newest and most thoughtful museums is the *Marion Koshland Science Museum,* located at the corner of Sixth and E Streets NW. The Koshland, which is part of the National Academy of Sciences, features a series of exhibits, many of them interactive and based on studies carried out by

Urban Preservation

The *Morrison-Clark Inn* is a prime example of how urban preservation and restoration can enrich the lives of Washington's residents and visitors. This grand Victorian mansion at Massachusetts Avenue and 11th Street actually represents the twentieth-century merger of a pair of handsome homes built in 1864 by wealthy merchants David Morrison and Reuben Clark. A subsequent owner of the Morrison house (obviously a Sinophile) added the grand Chinese Chippendale porch and graceful Shanghai roof visible on the Massachusetts Avenue side of the inn. Through fifty-seven years and two world wars, the house served as an inexpensive residence and club for enlisted men until 1987, when it was extensively renovated and opened as the elegant hotel and restaurant that it is today.

As men of wealth and taste, Messrs. Morrison and Clark would feel right at home in this upscale urban inn. Floor-to-ceiling pier mirrors face each other across a lobby with antebellum furniture and a marble fireplace. The Victorian feel is reflected in the upstairs guest rooms, with their massive armoires, antique furnishings, and imposing mahogany headboards. If you go, ask about room 215, with its private entrance to the porch and a great view up and down Massachusetts Avenue. The inn also offers its guests several French country–style rooms and parlor suites with wicker furniture and pine armoires.

The inn is home to one of Washington's top restaurants, which specializes in imaginative American cuisine. Entrees are seasonal and might include roast quail or Dijon-crusted salmon. All of this culinary delight takes place in an elegant Victorian dining room with tall windows, more full-length gilded mirrors and drapes, and a central banquette of unobtrusive chinoiserie. It is regularly named as one of Washington's most romantic restaurants.

The Morrison-Clark Inn (www.morrisonclark.com) is located at 1015 L Street NW, in the Penn Quarter. Call 898–1200 or (800) 332–7898; fax 289–8576. The dining room is open Monday through Friday 11:30 A.M. to 2:00 P.M. and 6:00 to 9:30 P.M., Saturday 5:30 to 10:00 P.M., Sunday brunch 11:00 A.M. to 2:00 P.M. and dinner 6:00 to 9:30 P.M. The inn and its restaurant are both expensive. Metro: Mt. Vernon. Square (yellow and green lines).

the academy. Some will introduce visitors to the wonders of science in general and dramatize the role of science in our everyday world, while others are targeted on subjects like the uses of DNA sequencing and the implications of global warming for the planet. The museum is open 10:00 A.M. to 6:00 P.M. daily except Tuesday. 334–1201; www.koshland-science-museum.org. Admission is $5.00 for adults and $3.00 for seniors and students. Metro: Judiciary Square (red line).

If you're accustomed to visiting Chinatowns in San Francisco or New York, D.C.'s version is going to seem pretty puny, its main attraction being the ornate and colorful archway at Seventh and H Streets. Chinatown's Metro stop is, logically enough, Gallery Place/Chinatown on the red, yellow, and green lines.

chinese newyear

If you're in town during early February, call 638–1041 to learn the date and other details about Washington's annual Chinese New Year celebration, which is great fun, with plenty of fireworks and a parade led by a giant dragon.

Although it lacks the scale and variety of its counterparts elsewhere, Washington's *Chinatown* does offer a broad array of good and inexpensive Chinese restaurants. My favorite is *Hunan Chinatown* at 624 H Street (783–5858), where the fried dumplings and the smoked duck are memorable. If you want to combine dining with history, head for *Wok n' Roll* at 604 H Street (347–4656), a modest but good restaurant located in the house of Mary Surratt, where the Lincoln assassination conspiracy was hatched. Mary was hanged for her role in the plot, but don't let that spoil your General Tso's chicken or shredded beef. Both restaurants are open daily for lunch and dinner.

Then there's the "only in America" block, the 800 block of Seventh Street. Here, in the heart of Chinatown and surrounded by street and other signs in Chinese, you'll find lined up *(a)* an Irish pub and restaurant, *(b)* a Texas barbeque restaurant, and *(c)* the German Cultural Institute, which presents rich programs of German film, music, and theater.

At 707 H Street, literally in the shadow of Chinatown's signature ceremonial arch, *Capital Q* serves up Texas-style chow. Instead of hunkering down around the campfire, you'll grab a tray and load your paper plate with smoky sausages, pulled pork, and chicken with collards and slaw. The decor is Early Texas Shrine, with license plates and other Lone Star mementos on the walls. Open Monday through Thursday 11:00 A.M. to 7:00 P.M., Friday and Saturday until 8:00 P.M. Call 347–TEXN.

The Irish bar is *Fado,* which specializes in boxty (an Irish potato pancake stuffed with salmon or steak), shepherd's pie, and the inevitable corned beef and cabbage. Fado is located at 808 Seventh Street NW, and is open Sunday through Thursday 11:30 A.M. to 2:00 A.M., Friday and Saturday 11:30 A.M. to 3:00 A.M. Call 789–0066, or visit www.fadoirishpub.com. Inexpensive.

The German Cultural Center, the ***Goethe Institute,*** sponsors a wide selection of art exhibits, lectures, and other cultural programs. And if you've always wanted to learn a little Deutsch, there are courses for that as well. The institute is located at 814 Seventh Street and is open Monday through Thursay 9:00 A.M. to 5:00 P.M., Friday 9:00 A.M. to 3:00 P.M. Call 289–1200 for information about exhibits and cultural programs.

You'll find two of this neighborhood's liveliest spots right next to each other in an out-of-the-way neighborhood on an out-of-the-way street adjacent to the Labor Department. ***The Flying Scotsman,*** at 233 Second Street NW, offers up a menu of American bistro favorites with a smattering of Scottish dishes like Shepherd's Pie, lamb braised in Guinness, and fish and chips. Sorry, no haggis, but you will find a staggering (literally) selection of single malts and other Highland dews at the major-league bar upstairs. The pub atmosphere attracts Hill staffers and other young professionals. Call 783–3848; the Web site is www.flyingscotsman-dc.com. Open from 11:00 A.M. until very late.

My Brother's Place, next door at 237 Second Street NW, describes itself as "old-time Irish pub meets sports bar and grill," but also has an extensive variety of salads and sandwiches. While its Scottish neighbor may be leading the league in whiskies, My Brother's Place seems ahead in the beer department, at least among the lively crowd that clusters around a cozy and well-populated bar, especially during one of the many happy hours. Outdoor seating too. Call 347–1350 or log on to www.mybrothersplace.com. Open Monday to Tuesday 11:00 A.M. to 10:00 P.M.,Wednesday 11:00 A.M. to midnight, Thursday and Friday 11:00 A.M. to 2:00 A.M. and Saturday 8:00 A.M. to 2:00 A.M. Closed Sunday.

Strange Monument to Sobriety

A few steps from the Navy Memorial, on Indiana Plaza at Seventh Street and Pennsylvania, stands the **Temperance Fountain,** one of the weirdest statues in a city where bizarre statuary is as common as fund-raising. Note the intertwined fish under four granite pillars surmounted by a triumphant bronze heron (I am not making this up). This powerful inducement to sobriety was erected in the city's former good-time district by (wait, this gets even more bizarre) a California temperance crusader who made his fortune making false teeth. The fountain once spouted water to give thirsty passersby a big, free drink, but the spigot was turned off long ago and the fountain went dry. The city definitely did not.

That glass building to the right of Mount Vernon Square is the headquarters of **National Public Radio.** If you're an NPR fan you should, all things considered, think about taking the regular weekly tour of this national institution. On the tour you'll see photos of your favorite NPR personalities and the studios where they broadcast. And if there's a show in progress, you'll see that too. No reservations are needed for the tour—just turn up any Thursday at 11:00 A.M. at NPR's main door, which is 635 Massachusetts Avenue NW. If you'd be interested in attending a live broadcast of the classical music series *Live in Studio 4A,* a feature of NPR's *Performance Today* program, call Andrea Danyo at 513–2301 in advance to find out what's going on the dates you're in town. You can also e-mail her at adanyo@npr.org to get on the program's mailing and waiting list. Tickets go to the first forty respondents. Metro: Gallery Place/Chinatown (yellow and green lines).

The **Sixth and I Historic Synagogue,** one of Washington's dazzling "new" buildings, was actually built in 1908, when part of what is now Chinatown was the site of a vibrant Jewish community. In 1951, in an ecumenical leap rarely seen in any city, this 1,000-seat synagogue became the home of the Turner Memorial AME church and its African-American congregation. In 2002, just as it was about to be converted again this time into a nightclub, the synagogue was purchased by a group of Washington's Jewish leaders and, after a $2 million renovation, meticulously restored to its former glory. To see its glorious, stenciled 70-foot dome, the original religious artifacts, some rescued from oblivion, and the gorgeous stained glass windows, take one of the tours given Monday through Thursday at 11:30 A.M., and 12:30 and 1:30 P.M. Reserve by calling 408–3100. The entrance is at 606 I Street NW. Metro: Mt. Vernon Square/Convention Center (yellow and green lines) and Gallery Place/Chinatown (red, yellow, and green lines).

Places to Stay in the Pennsylvania Quarter and Chinatown

Courtyard by Marriott,
Ninth and F Streets NW; 638–4600.
If, like Gordon Gekko in Wall Street, you think that "greed is good," and the idea of spending the night snuggled up with some cash has a certain appeal, then this is just the place for you. The Courtyard is located in an 1891 vintage bank that was clearly designed to impress depositors, with its massive stone facade, coffered ceilings, and marble staircases in the lobby. This classic example of urban conversion features a restaurant, the Courtyard Cafe (located among the safe deposit boxes), and a conference area in the former vault. The rooms are equally imposing. Moderate.

Henley Park Hotel,
926 Massachusetts Avenue NW; 638–5200 or (800) 222–8474.
This Tudor-style building began life in 1918 as an apartment house, but it's now the urban equivalent of an English country inn. Its seventy-nine rooms and seventeen suites are mainly done in Chippendale, with

four-poster beds, antiques, parquet floors, and over-stuffed chairs. Cozy, well-mannered, and chintzy in the nice sense—Edith Wharton will be along any minute. The Henley's restaurant, *Coeur de Lion* is, however, strictly non-British, intimate, and hugely romantic with dim lights and a fireplace. And best of all there's wonderful food from a French-trained chef, including veal and foie gras en croute and a spectacular bouillabaisse. One of the best restaurants in the city. Every Thursday, Friday, and Saturday evening you'll hear live music during the "Jazz Chic" program that takes place in the adjoining Blue Bar. Hotel and restaurant are both expensive.

Hotel Monaco,
700 F Street NW;
682-7177.
See page 28 for full description.

Morrison-Clark Inn,
1015 L Street NW;
898-1200 or (800) 332-7898.
See page 33 for full description.

Places to Eat in the Pennsylvania Quarter and Chinatown

Andale,
401 Seventh Street;
783-3133.
See page 26 for full description.

Austin Grill,
750 E Street NW;
393-3776.
You'll see why this Penn Quarter outpost of a local chain is so popular when you tuck into the quesadillas and fajitas, not to mention all those silky margaritas. Standard Tex-Mex offerings in a relaxed atmosphere, probably because the decor is early Texas roadhouse. Open Tuesday through Thursday 11:30 A.M. to 10:00 P.M., Friday and Saturday until 11:00 P.M., Sunday and Monday 11:00 A.M. to 9:30 P.M. No reservations. Inexpensive.

Cafe Atlantico,
405 Eighth Street NW;
393-0812.
See page 30 for full description.

Capital Grill,
601 Pennsylvania Avenue NW; 737-6200.
The sides of beef hanging in the window say it all. This upscale steak house lures political moguls of both parties from Capitol Hill, probably because of the men's club atmosphere and lively bar scene. All this and terrific steaks and lobsters too. Testosterone levels positively soar in the special cigar areas. Reservations essential. Open Monday through Thursday 11:30 A.M. to 10:00 P.M., Friday until 11:00 P.M., Saturday 11:30 A.M. to 11:00 P.M., Sunday 11:30 A.M. to 10:00 P.M. Expensive.

Capital Q,
707 H Street;
347-TEXN.
See page 34 for full description.

District Chop House,
509 Seventh Street;
347-3434.
Just what its name says, this steak house with billiard tables, oceans of beer, and early twentieth-century kitsch is another good place to know about if you're headed for the MCI Center or the Shakespeare Theater. Contrived but fun. Open Tuesday through Saturday 11:00 A.M.

AUTHOR'S FAVORITE PLACES TO EAT IN PENNSYLVANIA QUARTER AND CHINATOWN

Cafe Atlantico	Zola
Coeur de Lion	Luigino
Poste-Moderne Brasserie	Jaleo

to 11:00 P.M., Sunday and Monday 11:00 A.M. to 10:00 P.M. Inexpensive.

Fado,
808 Seventh Street NW; 789–0066.
See page 34 for full description.

Flying Scotsman,
233 Second Street NW; 783–3848
See page 35 for full description.

Hunan Chinatown,
624 H Street; 738–5858.
See page 34 for full description.

Jaleo,
480 Seventh Street NW; 628–7949.
See page 27 for full description.

Luigino,
1100 New York Avenue; 371–0595,
www.luigino.com
Every meal in this handsome, bustling restaurant brings back memories of my favorite ristorante in Milan. Signor Luigino serves up northern Italian favorites like

risotto, sweetbreads, and game specialties, plus pastas made *in casa,* including my all-time favorite, pappardelle in hare sauce. Open for lunch 11:30 A.M. to 2:30 P.M. weekdays. Dinner is served Monday through Thursday 5:30 to 10:30 P.M., Friday and Saturday 5:30 to 11:00 P.M., Sunday 5:30 to 10:00 P.M. Moderate.

Morrison-Clark Inn,
1015 L Street NW; 898–1200 or
(800) 332–7898.
See page 33 for full description.

My Brother's Place,
237 Second Street NW; 347–1350
See page 35 for a full description.

Poste-Moderne Brasserie,
555 Eighth Street NW (in Hotel Monaco);
783–6060.
See page 28 for full description.

Teaism,
400 Eighth Street NW; 638–6010.
See page 31 for full description.

Tony Cheng's,
619 H Street; 842–8669.
Actually two restaurants in one. Upstairs the specialty is dim sum and seafood, such as stir-fried grouper or shrimp with asparagus in black bean sauce. Downstairs try your hand at Mongolian barbecue or hot pot; the all-you-can-eat barbecue involves selecting the ingredients and giving them to the cooks for grilling, while the hot pot has you cooking your own vegetables and noodles in a pot of boiling stock. Open Sunday through Thursday 11:00 A.M. to 11:00 P.M., Friday and Saturday until midnight. Inexpensive.

Wok n' Roll,
604 H Street; 347–4656.
See page 34 for full description.

Zola,
800 F Street; 393–7798.
See page 29 for full description.

Capitol Hill and Northeast

When Pierre L'Enfant was asked by George Washington to find a site for "the Congress House," he selected Jenkins Hill, an elevation with a commanding view of the future capital, a place he told Washington was "a pedestal waiting for a superstructure." Construction of the Capitol building began in 1793, when President Washington, wearing Masonic regalia, laid the building's cornerstone. The House and Senate wings were completed by 1803 and connected by a wooden bridge erected where the main building and great rotunda now stand. A 1930s guidebook to the District reports that the Hill was so rural in 1809 that, "the British Ambassador put up a covey of partridge" only 300 yards from the Capitol buildings. The unfinished Capitol was torched by the British during the War of 1812. Long story short, the two wings were reconstructed by 1826, but crowned with a low wooden dome; the huge, twin-shelled iron dome that you now see was completed in 1863 by President Lincoln, who saw its completion as symbolic of the survival of the Union.

The area around the Capitol, once you get past the monumental eastern fringe of the Supreme Court and the Library of Congress, is essentially the eighteenth- and nineteenth-century neighborhood that began as a collection of boardinghouses

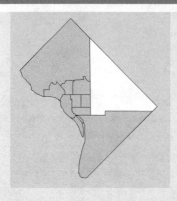

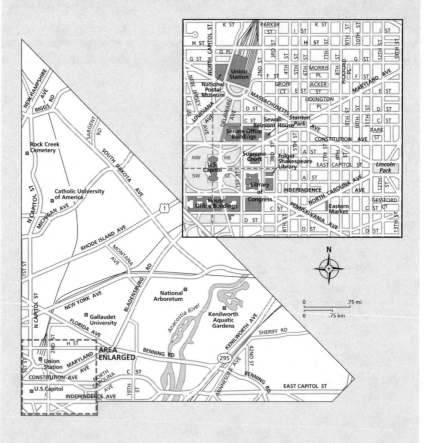

where representatives and senators lodged during congressional sessions. In fact, in 1793 Thomas Jefferson walked from one of those boardinghouses on New Jersey Avenue along the unpaved streets of the new capital to take his oath of office as president. The Hill, as Washingtonians call it, later became one of the city's prime residential areas, which accounts for the neighborhood's wonderful, large, and completely intact collection of fine homes that trace nineteenth-century residential architecture from antebellum Federal houses to Victorian-era Queen Annes.

Although young and youngish Hill staffers make up a large proportion of neighborhood residents, and crowd the streets during the day and on weekends, the area is surprisingly short of night life. The Hill's restaurant scene, aside from Union Station, is pretty much limited to the restaurant clusters along Pennsylvania Avenue SE and Massachusetts Avenue NE.

Although visitor- and constituent-friendly Capitol Hill has been a major beneficiary of the District's steep decline in crime, you should still exercise the usual street smarts after dark.

Start your Capitol Hill visit at the *Sewall-Belmont House,* one of Capitol Hill's oldest and best examples of Federal architecture and one of the top women's history sites in the United States. The small original house on this site, built in 1750, was expanded into the current mansion in 1800 by Robert Sewall and is now its rear wing and kitchen. Because American snipers fired from it on their commanding general, British troops burned the house during the War of 1812, the only private home in Washington to suffer that fate. After rebuilding, the Sewall-Belmont House was home to many distinguished officials, including Albert Gallatin, secretary of the treasury under Jefferson and Monroe, who may have worked out details of the Louisiana Purchase in the house's front rooms, and a slew of U.S. senators. In 1929 the house became the headquarters of the National Women's Party, the militant wing of the feminist movement founded by Alice Paul, the radical strategist who led hunger strikes and

TOP ATTRACTIONS IN
CAPITOL HILL AND NORTHEAST

Supreme Court	Eastern Market
Union Station	Library of Congress
National Postal Museum	Kenilworth Aquatic Gardens
Folger Shakespeare Library	

marches and, in 1923, drafted the Equal Rights Amendment on a desk displayed in this house.

The house's feminist library contains a vast and valuable collection of suffragist archives and exhibits celebrating women's history; its rooms are filled with mementos of the early days of the suffrage movement. Your guide will also show you *We Were Arrested, Of Course,* a film chronicling the days before 1920, when the Nineteenth Amendment passed, when a women's right to vote was not only controversial, but insisting on it could land you in the cooler. At the Sewall-Belmont House you'll also look in on some historic rooms, including an elegant front parlor straight out of 1880, with Victorian gilt mirrors, period furniture, and a square 1875 piano. There is also a small gift shop. The Sewall-Belmont House, 144 Constitution Avenue NE, has guided tours Tuesday through Friday at 11:00 A.M., noon, 1:00, and 2:00 P.M., and Saturday at noon, 1:00, 2:00, and 3:00 P.M., 546–1210, fax 546–3997; www.sewallbelmont.org. Contributions appreciated. Metro: Union Station (red line).

Walk down Maryland Avenue NE to the ***Supreme Court,*** where most visitors troop through the first floor and the tours that go to the building's courtroom, America's ultimate judicial chamber, for a potted lecture. You, however, should head downstairs to the lower level to see lively exhibits that document the fascinating history of the building and its architectural evolution; other displays recount the gypsy nature of the Court, which had no home to call its own for 146 years until this imposing Greek marble temple was opened in 1935. In the theater, also downstairs, every half hour between 9:00 A.M. and 4:00 P.M. you can watch a twenty-four-minute film about the Court's operations and proceedings. Around the corner there's a gift shop selling legal lore, including law books, judicial neckties, and other Court marginalia. Best of all, you'll also find on this level a reasonably priced cafeteria and elaborate snack bar, with good food and (naturally) the most dignified surroundings of any federal government eatery. The Supreme Court building itself is at First Street NE, 479–3000; www.supremecourtus.gov. Open 9:00 A.M. to 4:30 P.M. Monday through Friday; closed Saturday and Sunday. The building's cafeteria is open Monday through Friday from 7:30 A.M. to 10:30 A.M. and from 11:30 A.M. to 2:00 P.M. The snack bar's hours are 10:30 A.M. to 3:30 P.M. Monday through Friday. Gift shop hours: 9:00 A.M. to 4:25 P.M., Monday through Friday. Metro: Union Station (red line).

When the Supreme Court is in session, which starts on the first Monday in October and ends in April, you can sit in on the one-hour oral arguments the Supremes will hear in each case. Oral arguments are conducted on Mondays, Tuesdays, and Wednesdays for two weeks in each month. To see them, join one of the two lines that form in front of the Court steps before sessions begin at 10:00 A.M. One is for legal buffs who want to attend an entire argument,

Flying the Flag

Would you like to have that flag flying over the U.S. Capitol for your very own? Ask your congressman or senator to order one from the Capitol's Flag Office, which will fly one from the building, then send it to you. It'll cost about $15, after which you can start building that shiny white dome for your house.

while the other is a three-minute line for those satisfied with a brief look at the proceedings. Seating for these events is first-come first-served and begins at 9:30 A.M. so you need to get in line well before that. To see what's scheduled when you're in town, consult the Court schedules in the first section of the *Washington Post*.

Inside a classic Art Deco building across from the Supreme Court, is the **Folger Shakespeare Library,** containing possibly the world's greatest collection of works by and about William Shakespeare. The library and its priceless artifacts, the Elizabethan Theater, and the Folger Consort, with its regular programs of early English music, constitute one of the capital's greatest cultural and intellectual treasures. The much-praised facade of this building is worth examining for its carved motifs from Shakespeare's plays

You'll experience a major time shift beyond that 1930s facade when you enter sixteenth-century England in the Folger's majestic Great Hall, inspired by a grand and historic room of Brasenose College, Oxford. The hall's oak-paneled walls and its high, vaulted ceiling display Shakespeare's coat of arms plus motifs from his plays that the docents call "hints and clues." The Great Hall is also the exhibition space for rare artifacts of Shakespeare's work and his period from the Folger's own collections. During my visit the exhibit subject was *Fortune,* a favorite theme of Shakespeare and his contemporaries and the displays

AUTHOR'S FAVORITES IN CAPITOL HILL AND NORTHEAST

Eastern Market	La Colline
St. Mark's Episcopal Church	Dubliner Pub
Market Lunch	Kenilworth Aquatic Gardens
Capitol Hill Books	

Rome the Dome

If you want a special and definitely off the beaten path tour of the Capitol, call 223–9800, ext. 27, to find out when the Italian Cultural Institute is running its next tour of the famed *Brumidi frescoes* that adorn the Capitol. Roman artist Constantino Brumidi came to the United States in 1852 after painting murals in the Vatican, and immediately began work on the still-unfinished building. On the tour you'll see many of his masterpieces, including the famed Brumidi Corridors, ornate hallways inspired by designs uncovered in Pompei and by Raffaello's works in the Vatican. Some of Brumidi's frescoes depict events from American history, such as the 1770 Boston Massacre, while others portray North American wildlife and birds. Brumidi also painted the frieze that circles the Rotunda dome. Thanks to a recent restoration, all of Brumidi's work is in top shape—vibrant with brilliant details. Hint: If you go, take field glasses to see details of the higher frescoes. Be advised that since tour groups are small, reservations are essential. Get them by contacting mgiacalone@italcultusa.

included sixteenth-century playing cards and other ancient gambling devices. Another case contained the only known first folio of *Titus Andronicus.*

The Elizabethan Theater, where the Folger stages educational symposia and an annual cycle of Shakespeare plays, is a timbered replica of an inn-yard theater of Shakespeare's day.

Before leaving check out the Folger's spiffy little museum store, with lots of books and plays by and about the Bard. For information about the Folger's many programs, including the Consort and Theatre schedules, call 544–7077. The Folger, at 201 East Capitol Street SE, is open 10:00 A.M. to 4:00 P.M. Monday through Saturday. Tours of the Folger rooms and architecture are given Monday through Friday at 11:00 A.M.; Saturdays at 11:00 A.M. and 1:00 P.M. Tours of the garden occur every third Saturday from April through October at 10:00 and 11:00 A.M. 544–4600; www.folger .edu. Metro: Capitol South (orange and blue lines) or Union Station (red line).

greatideas fromthefolger

Among the best-selling items at the Folger Library's excellent gift shop are mugs and T-shirts bearing the popular Shakespeare quote "The first thing we do, let's kill all the lawyers." And this just across the street from the Supreme Court?

After leaving the Folger, turn right and get an idea of Capitol Hill as a neighborhood by sauntering along *East Capitol Street.* The Metro stop for this walk is Eastern Market (orange and blue lines).

Heading east toward Lincoln Park you'll pass an eclectic mix of ornate Victorian row houses, Federal beauties from the Hill's earliest days and even a sprinkling of Washington's first apartment houses, most of them dating back to Victorian times. To make this stroll even more pleasant, most houses have deep setbacks, in keeping with L'Enfant's original plan to make East Capitol Street a commercial area; these are now handsome front yards with gardens, trees, and benches for sitting and gazing.

Local shops from another era contribute to East Capitol Street's small-town feel, especially *Grubb's Pharmacy,* at East Capitol and Fourth Streets NE, which, like much of this neighborhood, could have been marooned in a 1900s time warp. Grubb's resembles an old-time general store more than a pharmacy, piled high with medical equipment and supplies of every imaginable kind, plus a huge stock of homeopathic remedies. Grubb's, 543–4400, is open 9:00 A.M. to 7:00 P.M. Monday through Friday and 9:00 A.M. to 3:00 P.M. on Saturday. Closed Sundays.

Nearby at 417 East Capitol Street is the local bookstore, and it's a good one. *Riverby Books* carries an outstanding collection of new, used, and rare books on Washington history. If the Folger has sharpened your appetite for the Bard, you'll also find a trove of Shakespeariana. Open daily 10:00 A.M. to 6:00 P.M.; 543–4342.

And at East Capitol and Fifth Streets SE stands *Jimmy T's,* a frill-free zone where you can sit at the Formica counter and join the neighbors for megabreakfasts and basic diner fare. Open Wednesday, Thursday, and Friday 7:00 A.M. to 3:00 P.M., Saturday and Sunday 8:00 A.M. to 3:00 P.M.; closed Monday and Tuesday. Call 546–3646. Farther along, in the 500 and 600 blocks of East Capitol Street you'll pass some of the area's finest examples of Queen Anne houses.

Mother's Day Tour

A number of those wonderful Federal row houses you'll see on Capitol Hill and their elaborate gardens are open to the public every Mother's Day weekend on the annual "Capitol Hill Restoration Society House and Garden Tour." The tour begins Saturday evening with a Candlelight Tour from 5:00 to 8:00 P.M., then continues on Sunday with open houses from noon to 5:00 P.M. Also on Sunday there's a reception from 3:00 to 6:00 P.M. at the Folger Library, which is a Capitol Hill "must" in itself. Jitneys will take you from house to house. Tickets are $15 in advance and can be purchased at Eastern Market and other Hill locations or by writing to the Restoration Society at P.O. Box 15264, Washington, DC 20003-0264. If you wait until the day of the tour you'll pay $20. Call 543–0425 for more information.

Lincoln Park, a neighborhood hangout for dogs and families, begins at 11th Street. The park contains two great statues—the 1876 Emancipation Monument, a statue of Abraham Lincoln holding the Emancipation Proclamation, and an imposing one of black activist and educator Mary McLeod Bethune. The Lincoln statue was the original Lincoln memorial erected in the District, about fifty years before its far more famous counterpart, the Memorial on the Mall. It was paid for by contributions from freed slaves.

A stroll through the park leads to the charming *Park Cafe,* a bright and attractive restaurant with modern art on the walls and a great view of Lincoln Park. Here the menu carries Chilean specialties such as pescado criollo, grilled sea bass, and pollo asado. The Park also offers terrific paella. The Park Cafe, at 106 13th Street SE, is open Monday through Saturday from 5:30 to 10:00 P.M. and Sunday from 5:30 to 8:30 P.M.

One of the main goals of the D.C. Heritage Coalition is the restoration of the *Old Naval Hospital* at 921 Pennsylvania Avenue SE. This grand old building, which was built to treat wounded Civil War sailors who were carried there from the Navy Yard, is in dire need of restoration. Nevertheless, as you walk by you'll see an urban fly in amber—a virtually intact 1865 building, complete with carriage house and original wrought-iron fence.

If you've been missing those terrific European food halls where glistening fish and artistic cuts of meat vie for attention with geometric displays of fruit, exotic cheeses, and vegetables, you'll enjoy visiting the *Eastern Market,* 225 Seventh Street SE (between C Street and North Carolina Avenue). To see Eastern Market's food pageant at its peak, go early on Saturday morning, when trucks packed with crates of fresh produce, game, fish, and meats roll in from Virginia farms and Chesapeake Bay, followed closely by finicky buyers from some of Washington's top restaurants.

> ## capitalquote
>
> "I believe there's something out there watching over us. Unfortunately, it's the government."
>
> —Woody Allen

Eastern Market (www.easternmarket.net) is open from Tuesday through Friday from 10:00 A.M. to 6:00 P.M., Saturday 8:00 A.M. to 6:00 P.M., Sunday 8:00 A.M. to 4:00 P.M. Metro stop for the market and its neighbors? Why it's Eastern Market on the orange and blue lines.

Folks from this neighborhood usually head for the market's specialty food shops like The Union Meat Co., for its meats and half smokes on a bun or The Fine Sweete Shoppe. But truckers, locals, and tourists alike usually end up at the *Market Lunch,* a stools-and-paper plate cafeteria famous for crab cakes, fried oysters, and shrimp, along with immense breakfasts that would

The Market Lunch

horrify your cardiologist. Market Lunch, Tuesday through Saturday 7:30 A.M. to 3:00 P.M. Expect long lines on Sunday, when the Market Lunch is open from 11:00 A.M. to 4:00 P.M.

But the Eastern Market is more than just food; this redbrick food hall and its surrounding stores and stands is also the epicenter of Capitol Hill social and cultural life, especially in the market's north wing, which is given over to exhibits of crafts, wearable art, and jewelry by neighborhood artists and artisans. Outside, surrounding the market building, you'll find a bustling combination of vegetable market and flea market with vendors selling an eclectic mix of everything from prints, clothing, and jewelry to apple pie and flowers. Across Seventh Street there's an even larger flea market that fills a large playground every Sunday from 10:00 A.M. to 5:00 P.M.

This vibrant neighborhood also boasts a first-class used bookstore. **Capitol Hill Books,** at 657 C Street SE, is stacked high with books of every vintage and description and literally overflows with language books, which are located in the shop's toilet. Cookbooks naturally are filed in the kitchen sink of this former row house, but owner Jim Toole's excellent collection of District of Columbia history and books on American politics are shelved out front next to the counter. Open Monday through Friday 11:30 A.M. to 6:00 P.M. and weekends 9:00 A.M. to 6:00 P.M.; 544–1621.

Leaving the Eastern Market, a right turn will take you to **Woven History,** worth seeing even if your interest in fine rugs and carpets is only minimal. The shop has a wide selection of dazzling vegetable-dyed, hand-spun wool carpets made in camps in Pakistan by refugees from Afghanistan, Tibet, and Nepal, along with other carpets imported from Turkey and Azerbaijan. Its companion shop, **Silk Road,** under the same management, specializes in exquisite woven goods and tribal and village arts and crafts from all along the route of Asia's fabled Silk Road. These shops—two treasures, one gate—are located at 311–315 Seventh Street SE. Open daily 10:00 A.M. to 6:00 P.M.; 543–1705; www .wovenhistory.com.

In this block, at 327 Seventh Street SE, you'll also find one of the Hill's restaurant stars, **Montmartre.** The specialties in this cheerful and intimate French bistro include typical fare such as hanger steak and rabbit served over pasta. This is also the place to come if you like perfectly cooked liver and onions and venison. Open Tuesday through Friday 11:30 A.M. to 2:30 P.M., Tuesday through Thursday 5:30 to 10:00 P.M., Friday and Saturday until 10:30 P.M.; open Sunday 11:00 A.M. to 2:30 P.M. Closed Monday. 544–1244.

Next door, at 325 Seventh Street SE, check out the bright and colorful **Gallery 325,** which hosts a regular series of group exhibitions by regional artists and photographers. Open Tuesday through Thursday noon to 6:00 P.M., Friday and Saturday 11:00 A.M. to 9:00 P.M., Sunday 11:00 A.M. to 5:00 P.M.; 547–7900.

When you proceed down Seventh Street to the corner of Pennsylvania Avenue, you'll be standing in front of **Bread and Chocolate,** the local outpost of a highly successful Washington group that specializes in specialty coffees, great pastry, and sandwiches. Bread and Chocolate is also famous for its Sunday brunch and its daily breakfasts, where you'd be well advised to throw dietary caution to the winds and order the divine French toast. Bread and Chocolate, 666 Pennsylvania Avenue SE; 547–2875. Open Monday through Saturday 7:00 A.M. to 7:00 P.M. and Sunday 8:00 A.M. to 6:00 P.M.

In 1871, Frederick Douglass, already distinguished for his writings, his memoirs about his life as a slave, and his wartime role as close adviser to President Lincoln on African-American matters, moved from Rochester, New York, and bought a home on Capitol Hill. His first home in the District is now a small and highly interesting house museum—the **Frederick Douglass Museum and Hall of Fame for Caring Americans.**

The front parlor, Douglass's former study, is a wonderful re-creation of an upper class Washington parlor of the period. The room contains Douglass's violin, comfortable chairs, and a writing desk with some of his papers, including his "freed man" papers signed by Lincoln, and an invitation to the dedication ceremonies for the Washington Monument. Next door, in the dining room-library, the walls are lined with photographs and mementos of people important to Douglass such as Booker T. Washington, Harriet Tubman, and Sojourner Truth. Next to the original fireplace, which was uncovered during restoration, you'll see the "Paper of Manumission" that gave Douglass his freedom and an 1863 safe conduct pass signed by Lincoln allowing him to pass through Union lines on missions for the president. Douglass moved to Cedar Hill, his Anacostia home, in 1878 (see chapter on Anacostia).

The back half of the ground floor and the upstairs bedrooms are devoted to photographs of and awards to "Caring Americans" who have distinguished themselves through their good works in helping others and in their philanthropic activities.

The Frederick Douglass Museum and Hall of Fame for Caring Americans, 316–320 A Street NE; 547–4273. Open Monday, Wednesday, and Friday from noon to 2:00 P.M.; www.caring-institute.org/html/fdm/fdm.html. Metro: Capitol South (orange and blue lines).

High on my list of candidates for the city's most glorious church is *St. Mark's Episcopal Church,* built in 1888 and located at Third and A Streets SE,

Legislative Lunching

If it's noon and you don't know where your senator or representative is, it's a pretty good bet you'll find him or her schmoozing with other politicos or, heaven forbid, even those satanic lobbyists, at one of two restaurants where more decisions than you'd like to think are made over top-notch food.

The Monocle,
107 D Street NE;
546–4488.
The atmosphere here is strictly old-time Capitol Hill, with signed photos of national luminaries and walls bearing famous political quotes like, "I give special consideration to everybody," and "Washington is the only city where sound travels faster than light." This is where our nation's lawgivers gather for power breakfasts and lunches or dinners of crab cakes, filets, rib eyes, and large salads. Jack Kennedy liked the roast beef so much that, after becoming president, he regularly sent a limo over for sandwiches, making the Monocle, according to one wit, "JFK's favorite pickup place." Open Monday through Friday only from 11:30 A.M. to midnight. Expensive. Metro: Union Station (red line).

La Colline,
400 North Capitol Street NW;
737–0400.
One of the city's top French restaurants, with or without the congressional crowd. This warm and inviting bistro serves up great seafood and vegetable dishes, along with a super duck l'orange. Ravioli stuffed with wild mushrooms is another good choice, as are French standbys like cassoulet and choucroute garni. And if you like foie gras, this one's for you. Desserts are exceptional. Reservations a must. Open Monday through Friday 7:00 to 10:00 P.M. Saturday 6:00 to 10:00 P.M. Expensive. Metro: Union Station (red line).

behind the Library of Congress's Adams Building. The tall, high-ceilinged nave of this Romanesque beauty is lined with exposed red brick that makes a simple background for a dazzling collection of stained glass windows that is capped by a splendid Louis Tiffany masterpiece in the baptistery at the north end. A colorful cross made from children's drawings hangs from the nave's beamed ceiling. If St. Mark's should be locked, ask at Baxter House, the church offices at 118 Third Street SE, and someone will show you around. 543–0053; www.stmarks.net.

Capitol Hill also includes one of Washington's liveliest specialty stores and a must for anyone interested in the performing arts. **Backstage,** at 545 Eighth Street SE; 544–5744; www.backstagebooks.com, is D.C.'s showbiz equipment headquarters, with a large repertoire of ready-made costumes and wigs for sale or rent; theatrical books and scripts; stage makeup and theatrical posters too. Monday through Saturday 11:00 A.M. to 7:00 P.M.

The **Library of Congress,** the world's largest library, is definitely not an off-the-beaten-path destination, although many of its visitors probably don't take full advantage of its many exhibitions, concerts and lectures. Film buffs shouldn't overlook the free showings of classic films from the library's enormous film archive in the Mary Pickford Theater. To get an idea about what's available, including the superb special and permanent exhibits, watch the twelve-minute orientation film, then take one of the four full tours of the Jefferson Building that begin Monday through Friday at 10:30 and 11:30 A.M., and 1:30, 2:30, and 3:30 P.M.; Saturday every hour on the half hour from 10:30 A.M. to 2:30 P.M. Don't forget to look up every so often to see the murals scattered around the library ceiling, especially those depicting "Government" around the doors of the Main Reading Room.

capitalquote

"In your country club, your church, and business, about 15 percent of the people are screwballs, lightweights, and boobs, and you would not want those people unrepresented in Congress."

—Former Senator
Alan Simpson

The facade of the library's main building is inspired by the Paris Opera House, which makes it a bit grandiose for some critics. But the interior, with its grand staircase and the octagonal main reading room, excites the admiration of every visitor, even stodgy Henry James who pronounced it "magnificent."

Although it's the Jefferson Building that gets all the attention, and with good reason, you might, especially around lunchtime, consider crossing Independence Avenue to visit the library's newish **Madison Building**, at the corner of First Street and Independence Avenue SE. On the sixth floor you'll find one of the best government cafeterias in town, with good food, plenty of space, and a fabulous panoramic view out over

Holiday Concerts

If you're in Washington on Memorial Day, July 4, or Labor Day, be sure to attend the National Symphony's gala holiday concert on the West Lawn of the Capitol. Concerts start at 8:00 P.M., but most people arrive well before that with a blanket and a picnic supper. Prepare for a real patriotic surge and an intensely patriotic experience by tucking a few flags into your hamper.

southeast Washington and northern Virginia. The cafeteria is open for lunch Monday through Friday from 12:30 to 3:00 P.M. The Madison Building also has an excellent gift shop, where the emphasis is on American history and literature. Open 9:30 A.M. to 5:00 P.M. Monday through Saturday.

After leaving the Library of Congress, walk down Capitol Hill, following Independence Avenue SW past the three House office buildings. That giant glass birdcage you'll spot at the foot of the Hill is in fact the conservatory of the **U.S. Botanic Garden,** one of the city's greatest treasures. The garden was established by Congress in 1820, closed because of general dilapidation in 1997, and reopened in 2001 after a massive and ongoing reconstruction that will end only in 2006 with the completion of a National Garden to the west of the main building.

After entering the garden you'll follow a path through endless summer to visit a number of different plant ecosystems, including Garden Primeval, a mini-Jurassic Park with primitive ferns and plants that have existed for 150 million years; the Desert House, with cacti and other plants from arid areas; and the popular favorite, the perfumed Orchid House, where up to 150 gorgeous orchids flower at any one time. The Palm House, with a controlled climate similar to that of Washington in August, features a teeming jungle scene of vines, ferns, and palms, along with an example of the tropical pitcher plant, which lures insects with its nectar, then devours them. It's a plant jungle in there. And whatever you do, don't miss the Garden's most famous (and aromatic) resident, the gigantic *titan arum,* dubbed the "corpse flower" for its disgusting aroma. See it anyway—it's one of the world's rarest (certainly ripest) plants. If you're lucky you'll be there when it blooms; trouble is the plant is totally unpredictable and blooms whenever the nutrients are right—usually every few years. The Botanical Garden also has a cafe from which you can gaze up at Washington's other hothouse with rare flowerings, the U.S. Capitol. The U.S. Botanical Garden, at First Street and Maryland Avenue SW, is open daily from 10:00 A.M. to 5:00 P.M.; 225–8333; www.usbg.gov.

From the garden, cross Independence Avenue to see the park named for Frederic Auguste Bartholdi, the sculptor of the Statue of Liberty and creator of the elegant and historic fountain located at the center of **Bartholdi Park.** The park is a glorious showcase of contemporary trends in American horticulture and a series of model gardens. If you're a backyard gardener, you might get some ideas from the innovative plant combinations in a variety of styles and design themes.

Backtracking to the Botanic Garden, stroll down First Street SW along the foot of Capitol Hill past the **Garfield Monument** to the colossal **Ulysses S. Grant Memorial,** with heroic groupings, "Artillery" and "Cavalry," that depict in bronze the heat and anguish of battle. The centerpiece is the statue of Grant, forever astride his horse *Cincinnatus* and coolly contemplating a battle scene. You, however, are more likely to be struck by the general's great and unending view down the Mall past the Washington Monument to the Lincoln Memorial. The Grant Memorial is so grand and complex that it took twenty years to complete and killed its sculptor, Henry Shrady, who died of overwork two weeks before it was dedicated.

capitalquote

"Reader, suppose you were an idiot. And suppose you were a Member of Congress. But I repeat myself."

—Mark Twain

Continuing on around the base of Capitol Hill you'll pass the **Peace Monument,** a memorial full of allegorical figures (America weeps on History's shoulder while Mars, the God of War himself, stands by) that honors sailors killed during the Civil War.

At this point you'll see an azalea-lined path winding up Capitol Hill to the rarely visited *"Summer House,"* hidden among the hedges and shrubs of the Capitol grounds. The Summer House was designed in 1880 by Frederick Law Olmsted, the creator of New York's Central Park, as a Victorian-era oasis from Washington's summer heat. You'll find it refreshing too, as you enter this hexagonal red brick building, then relax on one of the benches and enjoy the sound and sight of the Summer House's ornamental fountain and a stream that bubbles over rocks. For a terrific source of information on the Summer House and other places around the Capitol, visit the Architect of the Capitol Web site, www.aoc.gov.

While you're there you'll hear the bells of the 100-foot-high **Taft Carillon,** just across Constitution Avenue, which forms part of the **Robert A. Taft Memorial,** a tribute to the Ohio statesman and presidential candidate.

When you see the Irish flag flying from the corner of North Capitol and F Streets NW, it's not the Irish Embassy, but a corner of the old sod that's a lot more fun. Under the Hibernian tricolor is the **Phoenix Park Hotel,** which

Statuary Symbolism

That statue atop the Capitol dome is **Freedom,** cast from a plaster model that sculptor Thomas Crawford made in Rome, but not after considerable political flak. Crawford had originally designed a simple cloth covering for Freedom's head called a Phrygian cap, which was an ancient symbol of freed slaves, who used them to cover their shaved heads. This did not sit well with Secretary of War Jefferson Davis, future President of the Confederacy, who was not exactly a fan of liberated slaves, even symbolically. Crawford was compelled to trade the cap for a crested Roman battle helmet, representing America's victory over tyranny.

After a near-sinking on the way from Italy, the 19-foot statue was set in place in December 1863 as the final touch on the dome, which Lincoln had insisted be completed, despite the Civil War, as a symbol of the continuing Union. If you see the lantern just below Freedom lit, it means that the House or the Senate is in night session.

modestly bills itself as the "center of Irish hospitality in America." Popular with lobbyists and tourists because of its prime location near Union Station, the Capitol, and the Union Station Metro stop, the hotel offers 150 upscale rooms and suites. Irish hospitality obviously extends downstairs; on the hotel's ground level is the *Dubliner Pub,* where the exuberant scene, ably assisted, if not inspired by Messrs. Guinness and Bass, attracts lots of Irish expats along with zillions of Irish wannabes. The fun really heats up every night at nine with the live entertainment, either professionals or customers who, after a few drinks, think that standing in front of an open mike and belting out "McNamara's Band" is perfectly normal. That might be you. The Dubliner will supply the nourishment in the form of Irish comfort food like shepherd's pie and corned beef and cabbage. Phoenix Park Hotel, at 520 North Capitol Street; 638–6900 or (800) 824–5419; www.PhoenixParkHotel.com. The Dubliner, 737–3773, at the same address, is open every day for breakfast from 7:00 to 10:00 A.M. and for lunch and dinner from 11:00 A.M. to 3:00 A.M. No reservations. Inexpensive to moderate.

And if this isn't enough flaunting of the green, next door to the Dubliner there's yet another Irish outpost, *Kelly's Irish Times,* at 14th and F Streets. A sign over Kelly's door invites "your thirsty, your famished, your befuddled masses" to drop in this no-nonsense pub with a formidable bar and a selection of sandwiches and salads. Call 543–5433. Open Sunday through Thursday 11:00 A.M. to 1:00 A.M. and Friday and Saturday until 2:30 A.M.

You don't have to be a stamp collector to enjoy the *National Postal Museum,* located across from Union Station in what was once the former sorting room of Washington's City Post Office. The monumental Post Office building

Hill Street Mews

Capitol Hill is also where you can still find some of Washington's famous (or notorious) alleys, which were built into the original city plan to provide tradesmen with backdoor access to substantial homes and mansions. But after the Civil War, the alleys became festering slums where freed slaves squatted and worked under substandard conditions. Some of the few remaining alleys have now been gentrified and turned into smart mews homes for the affluent. Georgetown's Pomander Walk is a good example, but on the Hill, three of the best examples of alleys that have become tiny, tony streets, are Miller's Court, which you can find by following the directional sign in front of the Douglass House at 316 A Street NE; Rumsey Court, off D Street SE, opposite the exit from the Capitol South Metro station; and Terrace Court, just off A Street behind the Supreme Court. Another hidden beauty is Library Court, reachable by the alley next to 315 A Street SE, just behind the Library of Congress's Adams Building.

itself dates from 1914, but the museum only goes back to 1993, when it opened as part of the Smithsonian's network. In it you'll find exhibits that trace the history of America's mail system from its Colonial days down to the present.

A major crowd-pleaser is the series of exhibits called *Moving the Mail,* tracing the growth of postal technology, which leads off with a replica of a 1915 railway post office car, where clerks sorted letters and parcels to drop off at stations up the line; a film interviews the few remaining post office veterans who worked in these cars. Next door, a 1930 Ford Model A delivery vehicle painted in the old post office green illustrates how urban mail was delivered once it left those trains. And overhead, vintage planes from the U.S. Airmail Service hang from the ceiling to dramatize the beginnings of what is now the standard way of carrying the mail.

The museum is also the home of the Smithsonian's priceless collection of eleven million U.S. and foreign stamps, which can be viewed in a series of sliding vertical files. Your visit will probably end with a stop in the museum shop, which is crammed with books on stamps and stamp collecting, plus the usual branded mugs and T-shirts. The National Postal Museum, at First Street, and Massachusetts Avenue NE, 357–2991, is open daily from 10:00 A.M. to 5:30 P.M. One-hour tours begin daily at 11:00 A.M. and 1:00 P.M. For group tour information phone 633–5534; www.si.edu/postal. The museum also contains the world's largest philatelic research library; if you're a serious philatelist and want to visit, phone 633–5544. The museum's Discovery Center has hands-on learning activities for children and adults on the third Saturday of every month. Web site: www.si.edu/postal/collections/ustamp.htm.

If you're looking for any of the U.S. government's over 12,000 publications, you'll find them at the ***U.S. Government Bookstore,*** at 710 North Capitol Street behind the Postal Museum. The bookstore carries publications that will help you get accepted at college, plant your crops, or read all about the findings of the special prosecutors. If you have access to industrial-strength No-Doz, you can also pick up the latest federal budget or the president's latest economic report to Congress. The bookstore is open Monday through Friday 8:00 A.M. to 4:00 P.M.; 512–0132.

Washington's ***Union Station*** is hardly off the beaten path; with twenty-three million visitors each year, it's the city's most visited site. Most visitors pass through on their Amtrak visits to the District without taking a close look at this monumental Beaux Arts structure patterned after Rome's Baths of Diocletian, with its soaring, vaulted ceilings and, in the magnificent main waiting room, forty-six elaborate statues of Roman legionnaires—one for each state in 1908, when this masterpiece opened. But this glorious restoration has also become one of Washington's most vibrant places, where travelers and locals alike shop, take in a movie, buy a book at one of the five well-stocked bookstores, or dine at one of the station's forty restaurants and cafes. While lots of *mangiare* goes on at the twenty restaurants in the lower-level food court, some of the better choices are located upstairs on the main level and mezzanine and listed on pages 61–62.

Although the Capitol Hill area includes all four of the city's quadrants, it is also the gateway to the Northeast section, which includes the community known as Brookland. The Northeast is itself diverse, ranging from quiet suburban streets to gritty industrial districts, but it is also, in its Brooklands neighborhood, about the closest thing you'll find to Vatican on the Potomac. About sixty Catholic organizations cluster in Brooklands, which is said to be the highest number in

Union Station

one area outside of Rome; the most significant structure is the ***Basilica of the National Shrine of the Immaculate Conception.***

As soon as you spot the Basilica's brightly colored mosaic dome, flanked by a bell tower that seems straight out of Venice's Piazza San Marco, you know that you're in a special place where the operative word is "immense." This is the largest Catholic church in the hemisphere: It can hold 6,000 worshipers in its upper church and 400 in the crypt below, which is modeled after the Roman catacombs. This magnificent church, rich in marble mosaics, is a mix of the Byzantine and the Romanesque, with thirty-two chapels in the upper church that gleam with the vivid colors of their 200 stained glass windows. The effect of the interior can be overwhelming, so don't forget to look in on the Basilica's quiet gardens, especially the restful Mary's Garden, all in white with restful pools and fountains.

The shrine also has an excellent gift shop and bookstore, plus a cafeteria, which can come in handy in this restaurant-free zone. The Basilica of the National Shrine of the Immaculate Conception, 400 Michigan Avenue NE (526–8300; www.nationalshrine.com), is open daily 7:00 A.M. to 7:00 P.M. Mass is celebrated several times a day. Guided tours are given Sundays from 1:30 to 4:00 P.M. and weekdays from 9:00 to 11:00 A.M. and 1:00 to 3:00 P.M. The cafeteria is open from 8:30 A.M. to 2:00 P.M. (until 3:00 on Sunday). If you're interested in a group tour—and there are a lot of them at this national shrine—call 526–8300 and ask for the Pilgrimage Department. Metro: Brookland (red line).

A much lesser known feature of Northeast's "Little Rome" is the ***Franciscan Monastery***—modeled on the famed Hagia Sofia church in Istanbul—where Franciscan priests and brothers are trained for work protecting the Holy Land's religious sites and helping its needy. You don't have to spring for a passport or become a martyr to jet lag to visit the Holy Sepulcher or the Grotto of Bethlehem. They, along with reproductions of other Holy Land shrines like the grotto of Gethsemane, are right here in little old Washington, in the monastery's lush rose gardens. There's also a detailed and spooky reproduction of a frescoed Roman catacomb to give you an idea of what early worshipers were up against in the real Rome. The Franciscan Monastery, 1400 Quincy Street NE (526–6800) is open 9:00 A.M. to 5:00 P.M. daily. Tours by Franciscan brothers are given Monday through Saturday on the hour (except at noon) from 9:00 A.M. to 4:00 P.M., and hourly on Sunday from 1:00 to 4:00 P.M. The gift shop is open daily 9:00 A.M. to 5:00 P.M.

One of the mid-Atlantic's dance meccas is ***Dance Place,*** a 200-seat center of contemporary and avant-garde dance. Every weekend, all year long, Dance Place presents programs of original, often experimental dance by top American and international companies. Every June it hosts a "Dance Africa Festival" that attracts large numbers of African and African-American dancers and dance lovers. During the day, Dance Place offers a number of modern and African dance classes for children and adults. Dance Place is located at 3225 Eighth Street NE. Call 269–1600 or visit www.danceplace.org. Metro: Brookland (red line).

Even if your interest in flowers surfaces only every Valentine's Day, you'll have to agree that the ***U.S. National Arboretum*** is one of Washington's "must visit" sites. The Arboretum, which is run by the U.S. Department of Agriculture as a research and education facility and as a living museum, is located on the city's outskirts, not far from an industrial zone and the high-octane, high-decibel roar of New York Avenue, a.k.a. U.S. 50. But once inside this 444-acre ministate, there's a great sense of beauty and tranquillity.

Most of the Arboretum's main attractions are reachable via the 10 miles of roadways within the park, but start off at the Administration Building for a map, then stroll outside to begin your tour at a large pond dense with lilies, where kids are feeding some of the biggest koi you've ever seen. Move on to the National Herb Garden, with its 2½ acres of 800 herbs, including lavender, sweet bay trees, rosemary, and a formal sixteenth-century knot garden with dwarf evergreens. Visiting the National Bonsai and Penjing Museum, a few steps away, is like entering a corner of Asia, where quiet gardens with stone lanterns showcase ferns, chrysanthemums, and a superb collection of bonsai trees from Japan, China, and North America. The North American contingent is made up of miniature cypress, cedar, and juniper, while the Asian pavilions are lined with 200-year-old yews and wisteria. The area's "Special Exhibits Wing" is located in a Chinese house with an exquisite Chinese scholar's studio in

National Arboretum

the style of the sixteenth century; nearby you'll find row after row of splashy bonsai azaleas.

You can continue by car or "tram tour" to the outlying displays, such as the dogwood, azalea, and conifer collections; check at the information desk to see which are in flower during your visit. Picnicking is possible at the Arboretum in either the National Grove of State Trees picnic area or in the area behind the gift shop.

No matter where you go, you can't miss the National Capitol Columns, the twenty-two Corinthian columns that from 1826 to 1957 formed the East portico of the Capitol building. These columns, which looked down on the Jackson and Lincoln inaugurations, were dismantled when the building's east front was extended; they were stored at the Arboretum until 1990 when they were reerected in their former configuration.

The U.S. National Arboretum, 3501 New York Avenue NE (245–2726; www.usna.usda.gov), is open as follows: grounds 8:00 A.M. to 5:00 P.M.; Bonsai and Penjing Museum, 10:00 A.M. to 3:30 P.M.; Administration Building, 8:00 A.M. to 4:30 P.M. daily; gift shop, 10:00 A.M. to 3:30 P.M. daily. Tram Tours, the Arboretum's sightseeing trains, run from mid-April to mid-October, weekends only; tours leave at 10:30 and 11:30 A.M. and 1:00, 2:00, 3:00, and 4:00 P.M. No Metro nearby; travel by car or taxi. If you're driving, the Arboretum is reached by taking New York Avenue from the city, then following the directional sign posted just past the intersection of New York Avenue and Bladensburg Road. Because its headquarters is located very near the Arboretum's gate, Yellow Cab (544–1212) is probably the best bet for a return trip by taxi.

When you visit the **Kenilworth Aquatic Gardens,** you're standing in the District's ultimate off-the-beaten-path experience, a unique nature sanctuary that few Washingtonians have visited or even heard of. The gardens consist of twelve acres and forty-five ponds located on the wetlands of the Anacostia River, Washington's last tidal marsh and home to exotic water lilies, ferns, and lotuses; it is the only National Park Service installation devoted entirely to water plants. The gardens are also a sanctuary for a large variety of birds (including the occasional bald eagle), wetland animals from turtles to snakes and fish, which have returned in force, thanks to herculean efforts to restore the once-dead Anacostia.

As you enter you'll be tempted to go no farther, choosing instead to plop down on the porch of the nifty little visitor center and enjoy the vast ponds with lily pads, lavender water hyacinth, and primrose, all surrounded by carpets of daffodils. But press on to follow the Marsh River Trail back into the wetlands and see the riverside sites where fox, muskrat, and deer hang out and wading herons often appear among the cattails. Ranger-led tours are also available, but you must reserve in advance. Field guides and other nature publications are available at the visitor center. Kenilworth Aquatic Gardens, 1900 Anacostia Avenue NE (426–6905; www.nps.gov/nace/keaq), are open 8:00 A.M. to 4:00 P.M. There are no Metro stops or bus lines that service the gardens. Because of potential security problems, take a cab or your own vehicle to the gardens.

You're probably too young to have seen an idyllic, vintage 1870 college campus, but if you ever want to know exactly what one looked like, get in your time machine and warp yourself over to *Gallaudet University,* America's preeminent institution for the hearing impaired. There, at 800 Florida Avenue NE, you'll find, preserved like a fly in amber, a glorious collection of Victorian Gothic and Queen Anne houses gathered around a campus with grounds and gardens designed by Frederick Law Olmsted, the same nineteenth-century landscape architect mentioned earlier, who designed the Summer House here in D.C. and created New York's Central Park and dozens of other landscape masterworks.

While you'll want to see the school's College Hall and Chapel Hall, two grand examples of Victorian Gothic style, don't leave campus without visiting the 1889 statue of founder and teacher Thomas Gallaudet and his nine-year-old pupil. The sculptor was Daniel Chester French, whose most famous work is the statue of Abraham Lincoln in the Lincoln Memorial. Like the Lincoln statue, where the president is signing his initials (page 81), Gallaudet and his student are forming the letter *A* in sign language. The statue is just outside Chapel Hall.

Aside from its aesthetics and being the world's only university for the deaf, Gallaudet has a distinction that will never die as long as there are sports trivia nuts. In the nineteenth-century, Gallaudet football players noticed that opposing teams were reading and anticipating all of their plays, which were exchanged among the players in sign language. To thwart this, the team began gathering in a tight circle to sign plays without being observed, thereby inventing the football huddle.

The campus visitor center (651–5000; www.gallaudet.edu) is open Monday through Friday 9:00 A.M. to 5:00 P.M. and offers tours. To get there either drive or take a D-2, D-4, or D-6 bus from downtown.

If you're in the Gallaudet neighborhood, find out what an Italian megagrocery looks like by heading for *Litteri's,* located among the loading docks and warehouses of the Capital City Market, where the city's foods are brought and traded. At Litteri's you'll find Washington's oldest, largest, and best Italian grocery. It's a treat for the eyes and nose, and a still life of all goodies Italian, from shimmering bottles of extra virgin olive oil to thirty brands of balsamic vinegar and every known pasta shape. In the back, a deli counter serves up sandwiches, hunks of Romano and provolone cheese, and glistening slices of prosciutto. Just walking through Litteri's will cost you 300 calories, but it will save you a trip to Rome. Litteri's is at 517 Morse Street NE, near the intersection of New York and Florida Avenues. Open Tuesday and Wednesday 8:00 A.M. to 4:00 P.M., Thursday and Friday until 5:00 P.M., and Saturday until 3:00 P.M. Call 544–0183. Drive or take a D-2, D-4, or D-6 bus from downtown.

Places to Stay in Capitol Hill and Northeast

Bull Moose B&B,
101 Fifth Street NE; 547–1050 or (800) 261–2768; www.bullmoose-b-and-b .com
In case you're wondering, the Bull Moose in question is the breakaway third party founded by Teddy Roosevelt in the early twentieth century. T. R. would have felt right at home in this turreted Victorian mansion with high ceilings and lots of wood paneling. The Bull Moose's eighteen guest rooms all have Rooseveltian themes. The "Kermit on Safari Room," named for his son, is decorated in early twentieth-century safari style with weathered gladstone bags stacked in a corner. Other rooms also echo the president who inspired the "Teddy bear" (there are a few of them around as well). Inexpensive. Metro: Union Station (red line) or Capitol South (orange and blue), but it's about a 6- or 7-block walk from each.

Capitol Hill Suites,
200 C Street SE; 543–6000, fax 547–2608.
It's not just a great location—a two-minute walk from the Capitol and the Supreme Court, and across the street from the Library of Congress—that makes this former apartment house so appealing. The 152 suites, studios, and efficiencies, each with a kitchen or cooking facilities, were all remodeled in mid-2000 and the prices are moderate. Judging from the photos and endorsements that line the lobby walls, this is also a big favorite of the congressmen who work just across the street. Moderate. Metro: Capitol South (orange and blue lines).

Hotel George,
15 E Street NW; 347–4200 or (800) 576–8331; www.hotelgeorge.com
The sleek, contemporary lobby of glass and stainless steel is your introduction to a boutique-chic, New Yorky world of neomodern rooms and dramatic paintings by Steve Kaufman, a disciple of Andy Warhol. The George's 139 rooms offer intimacy and style along with state-of-the-art in-room communications with the outside world. Downstairs, the George's hip French restaurant, Bistro Bis,

is in a class by itself; reservations are a must, especially for the memorable Sunday brunch. This all comes at a price, but the George offers some surprisingly low weekend deals. Expensive. Metro: Union Station (red line).

Places to Eat in Capitol Hill and Northeast

Aatish,
609 Pennsylvania Avenue SE; 544–0931.
This storefront near Eastern Market is a neighborhood favorite for its fresh, well-prepared Pakistani dishes, its relaxed, friendly atmosphere, and its low prices. Try the clay oven chicken or shrimp tandooris (my personal favorite: the shrimp kebab tandoori). Open Monday through Thursday 11:30 A.M. to 2:30 P.M. and 5:00 to 10:00 P.M., until 10:30 on Friday and Saturday. Inexpensive. Metro: Eastern Market (orange and blue lines).

America,
Union Station;
682–9555.
Everyone wants to be in America, which sports a large menu of regional specialties from all over the United States, including New Mexico's Navaho fry bread, Cincinnati's chili, and Cobb salad, first produced in Hollywood. There's even something called a fluffernutter sandwich from Las Vegas, which I'm not sure I'll ever order. And is the Reuben sandwich really a "Nebraska specialty"? What happened to New York's Lower East Side? Open 11:30 A.M. to 9:30 P.M. everyday. Moderate.

Barolo,
223 Pennsylvania Avenue SE;
547–5011.
With its movie-set view of the Capitol dome from the second floor of a Capitol Hill town house, Barolo may be one of Washington's most romantic restaurants. Barolo's specialty is northern Italian cuisine, with rich pastas and appetizers like bagna cauda and roasted artichoke hearts. True to its name, Barolo also has an impressive wine list that stresses those opulent Piedmontese wines. Open Monday

through Friday from 11:30 A.M. to 2:30 P.M. and Monday through Thursday from 5:30 to 10:00 P.M. and until 10:30 on Friday and Saturday. Reservations essential.

B. Smith's,
Union Station;
289–6188.
Located in the station's former presidential waiting room, this restaurant is a luxurious reminder of the days when presidents traveled only by train. The watchword here is Southern cooking— jambalaya, deep-fried catfish, fried green tomatoes, and a potent seafood gumbo. Feeling adventurous? Order the "Swamp Thing," a wonderful dish of mustardy mixed seafood over collard greens. Try the desserts before you waddle over to your train. Open Monday through Friday 11:30 A.M. to 4:00 P.M. and 5:00 to 10:00 P.M., Saturday 11:30 A.M. to 4:00 P.M. for brunch and evenings 5:00 P.M. to 1:00 A.M., Sunday brunch 11:30 A.M. to 3:00 P.M. and dinner is 3:00 to 9:00 P.M. Expensive.

Bread and Chocolate,
666 Pennsylvania Avenue SE;
547–2875.
See page 48 for full description.

Cafe Berlin,
322 Massachusetts Avenue NE;
543–7656.
One of Washington's few German restaurants, and a good one. Springtime is definitely asparagus time at the Berlin, but all year long you can order up schnitzels, goulash, sauerbraten, and all those other Teutonic temptations. The lunch menu also offers up soups, salads, and sandwiches. Open Monday through Thursday 11:30 A.M. to 10:00 P.M., Friday and Saturday 11:30 A.M. to 11:00 P.M., and Sunday 4:00 to 10:00 P.M. Moderate. Metro: Union Station (red line).

Dubliner Pub,
520 North Capitol Street;
737–3773;
See page 53 for full description.

East Street Cafe,
Union Station;
371–6788.
This bright and cheerful cafe, on the station's mezzanine level, calls itself "a culinary journey of the East" because of its offerings of tempuras, curries, Pad Thai, and other classics from eight Asian nations, including seldom seen dishes from Malaysia. If you're in a hurry, try a one-meal noodle or rice dish.

AUTHOR'S FAVORITE PLACES TO EAT IN CAPITOL HILL AND NORTHEAST

La Colline

Bistro Bis

Pete's Diner

Market Lunch

Montmartre

Open Monday through Friday 11:00 A.M. to 8:00 P.M., Saturday and Sunday 1:00 to 8:00 P.M. Moderate.

Jimmy T's,
East Capitol and Fifth Streets;
546–3646.
See page 45 for full description.

Il Radicchio,
223 Pennsylvania Avenue SE;
547–5114.
One of a chain of reasonably priced trattorias around the District run by one of Washington's top restaurateurs. The rules are simple: all the spaghetti you can eat for $6.50 and you pay extra for each helping of one of the twenty sauces available. Also thick Italian panini and great pizza. No reservations. Open Monday through Thursday 11:30 A.M. to 10:00 P.M., until 11:00 on Friday and Saturday. Inexpensive. Metro: Capitol South (orange and blue lines).

Kelly's Irish Times,
14th and F Streets;
543–5433.
See page 53 for full description.

La Colline,
400 North Capitol Street NW;
737–0400.
See page 49 for full description.

Market Lunch,
225 Seventh Street SE;
Located at the Eastern Market. See page 46 for full description.

The Monocle,
107 D Street NE;
546–4488.
See page 49 for full description.

Montmartre,
327 Seventh Street SE;
544–1244.
See page 48 for full description.

Park Cafe,
106 Thirteenth Street.
See page 46 for full description.

Pete's Diner,
212 Second Street SE;
544–7335.
Pete's is the quintessential neighborhood hangout that draws lots of local families and single Hill staffers who love its combination of good food and low prices. It can't be because of the decor, which is 50s Quirky, sporting Chinese banners on the wall next to an award and photograph from the Kiowa tribe and Hong Kong calendars. Otherwise Pete's looks like a typical lunchroom, with stools and a formica counter, a row of no-nonsense (i.e., beat-up) wooden booths, and in the middle, a communal table. At first blush the menu seems pretty much standard diner—sandwiches, steaks, pot roast, omelettes, grits, and lasagna—until you get to the part about the Asian vegetarian combo (excellent), the bok choy, and the smattering of Chinese dishes and soups. Like a milk shake to go with that

wild ginger soup? Open Monday through Friday 5:00 A.M. to 4:00 P.M., Saturday 6:00 A.M. to 3:00 P.M. and Sunday 7:00 A.M. until 3:00 P.M. Inexpensive. Metro: Capitol South (orange and blue lines).

Thunder Grill,
Union Station;
898–0051.
Decorated in adobe and turquoise, Thunder Grill offers classic Southwestern U.S. dishes such as burritos, fajitas, and tacos, along with the house specialty, chicken enchiladas with mole sauce. You'll also be offered a wide selection of margaritas served by the yard in a 48-ounce glass, after which you may not even care about getting on that train. Open daily 11:30 A.M. to 10:00 P.M. Moderate.

Two Quail,
320 Massachusetts Avenue NE;
543–8030.
Local restaurant critics invariably rank Two Quail among Washington's most romantic restaurants because of its comfy, hidden corners and eclectic, intensively decorated surroundings. The menu is also eclectic, ranging from Pad Thai to Muscovy duck and, yes, stuffed quail (with bacon and cheese). Reservations essential. Moderate. Metro: Union Station (red line).

The Waterfront and Anacostia

Washington owes its very existence and its role as our capital to its riverfront location at the head of navigation on the Potomac, at the point where it meets the Anacostia River. In selecting this site, George Washington hoped that the new capital, then a Maryland swamp "on the easterly bank of the Potomac," would be one of the young republic's major deepwater ports, a transfer point between ocean transport and the planned canal system that led back into Ohio and other frontier regions. Although the Seventh Street wharf, the current site of the Washington Marina, was one of the country's busiest ports in antebellum days and the Washington Navy Yard occupied an important role in the life of the city until well into the nineteenth century, Washington's long riverfront has slipped into disuse. That said, the banks of the Anacostia and the Potomac have some terrific opportunities for anyone exploring off-the-beaten-path Washington. What they do not offer, however, is a wide selection of places to stay.

Start your waterfront experience by taking the Metro to the L'Enfant Plaza stop (all lines except red) and walk 4 blocks to the ***Maine Avenue Fish Market,*** located well off the beaten path on the Potomac's Washington Channel in the shadow of

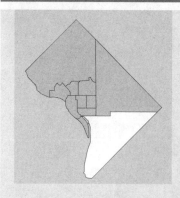

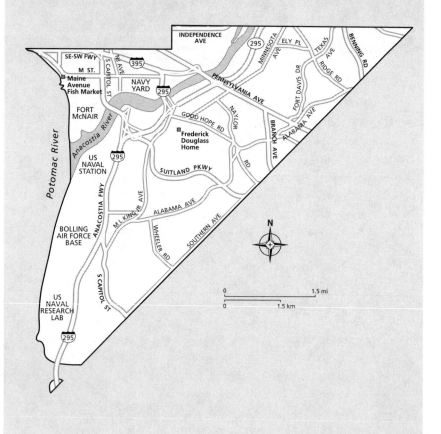

The Awakening

East Potomac Park, located just across the Potomac from the Maine Avenue Fish Market on Hains Point, is a great rest stop and perfect for an urban picnic. But if you go, you'll see one of the city's most unusual pieces of urban statuary, which in a town crowded with statues and monuments like Washington, is really saying something. Even though you're now warned, you'll still do a double take when you first spot the cast aluminum *Awakening,* or as many Washingtonians call it, *The Giant,* which depicts a bearded face, knee, hand, and arm of a man struggling to free himself from the ground. It's very dramatic and more than a little weird, but that doesn't keep kids from using the giant's huge body parts as slides. If you decide you don't like the *Awakening,* you can always gaze out at the Potomac or watch tennis at Hains Point's nineteen courts. But if you do like the sculpture, you'll find more of these "life castings" by J. Seward Johnson also along the Potomac at Washington Harbour in Georgetown.

the 14th Street bridge. Here you'll stroll into an open-air, high-protein scene to find the bounty of the Chesapeake spread out before you on barges, where aproned vendors preside over rows of glistening, freshly caught rockfish, catfish, bluefish, and carp. And since we're talking Chesapeake Bay, there are bushel baskets crammed with oysters and that Eastern Shore delicacy, blue crab. Open daily 7:30 A.M. to 8:00 P.M., the market draws a large number of customers searching for finny friends from other lands and a cadre of chefs from local Asian restaurants.

If all of this triggers a hunger pang or two, no problem. You'll find a number of possibilities for highly informal dining in the market at places like ***Captain White's,*** where a seafood combo of oysters, shrimp, scallops, and fish tops the bill, and ***Jessie Taylor Seafood*** for steamed crab legs and shrimp, plus a nifty raw bar. Both are open from 8:00 A.M. to 9:00 P.M. Another option

TOP ATTRACTIONS IN THE WATERFRONT AND ANACOSTIA

Maine Avenue Fish Market	Marine Museum
Arena Stage	Marine Barracks
Washington Navy Yard	Cedar Hill
Navy Museum	

is **Custis and Brown,** open from 8:00 A.M. to 9:00 P.M., which modestly advertises "The Best Hot Cooked Crabs in Town."

You can explore the waterfront area very nicely and have a picnic in the process by picking up some Fish Market take-out and following the riverside promenade that begins behind Le Rivage and runs along the Washington Marina for several blocks. As you'll learn, the riverside walk is a favorite with fishermen and sightseers who enjoy the views across the Potomac to Hains Point Park and its municipal golf course and, beyond that, the shores of Virginia and Arlington Cemetery. Your stroll will also take you past some of the many luxury powerboats and sailboats that anchor there regularly and a colony of elaborate houseboats, where a number of lucky Washingtonians enjoy life on a permanent cruise on the Potomac.

When you reach Sixth Street, the round (polygonal, actually) building on the left is the **Arena Stage,** a multitheater complex that enjoys a massive local and national reputation for the quality of its productions and of its resident theater company. Of the Arena's three stages, the 827-seat Fichandler (named for one of the Arena's 1950 cofounders), reflects the Arena's origins as theater-in-the-round. Its neighbor, the Kreeger Theatre, which seats 500, is fan-shaped, and the more intimate Old Vat is configured for cabaret. All three serve up a rich schedule that includes contemporary plays, experimental works, and even some musicals. Call 488–3300, visit www.arenastage.org, or consult either the

capitalquote

"It is very unhealthy. Few people would live in Washington who were not obliged to reside there."

Charles Dickens
—*American Notes,* 1842

Washington Post or *City Paper* to see what's playing when you're in town. The Arena Stage complex is located at 1101 Sixth Street SW. Parking is available. Metro: Waterfront (green line).

Friday night may mean fish for some, especially over at the Maine Avenue market, but at the **Westminster Presbyterian Church,** at 400 I Street SW, it means great live jazz. Every Friday from 6:00 to 9:00 P.M., some of Washington's top musicians jam at Westminster. There's also a buffet served from 6:00 to 8:30 P.M. Admission is $5.00 for adults; if you're under sixteen it's free; 484–7700; www.westminsterdc.org.

To the left of the Arena stage, in a charming park vibrant with azaleas, is one of Washington's oldest structures, the **Thomas Law House,** built in 1796 by a wealthy, eccentric land speculator who married into Washington and American nobility when he wed Eliza Custis, Martha Washington's granddaughter. This marriage was not made in heaven, and it ended in 1804 with

Washington's first power divorce, but that didn't keep the miserable couple from having President John Adams and King Louis Philippe of France over for dinner in their splendid Federal mansion. Today Eliza would probably cringe at learning that her Washington home is *(a)* named after her disagreeable husband and *(b)* also known as the "Honeymoon Cottage." The Law House is located at 461 North Street SW and is not generally open to the public. For an appointment to visit the house and its selection of period antiques, call 554–4844 between 9:00 A.M. and 5:00 P.M. Monday through Friday. Metro: Waterfront (green line).

The riverside walk will take you past the piers at Sixth and Water Streets, home port to a pair of the District's leading dinner and sightseeing cruise lines.

Spirit Cruises operates the *Potomac Spirit* and the *Spirit of Washington* on lunch and dinner cruises featuring live entertainment, ample buffets, dancing, and a chance to see the District's waterfront and landmarks from an entirely new angle. The company also offers special cruises downriver to visit Mt. Vernon. For schedules and prices, call (866) 211–3811 or 484–2320; or visit www.spiritofwashington.com.

Odyssey Cruises operates *Odyssey III,* a mammoth version of the glassed-in *bateaux mouches* that take visitors to Paris up and down the Seine. Dancing and live music, plus lunch, dinner, and a Sunday jazz brunch. And for all of you romantics, there's also a moonlight cruise available. Call 488–6000 or visit www.odysseycruises.com.

After passing the docks you'll see the **Titanic Memorial,** an impressive statue dedicated to the gentlemen who lost their lives by giving up their lifeboat seats to the ladies in that 1912 disaster. The 18-foot figure forms a forward-leaning crucifix. Don't look now, but isn't that exactly the pose struck by Leonardo DiCaprio, a.k.a. King of the World, and Kate Winslet on the prow of the *Titanic* in the movie of the same name?

A left turn leads to the entrance of **Fort Leslie J. McNair,** strategically located on the Potomac to defend the city, which is why it was part of L'Enfant's original plan and one of Washington's first military bases when it opened

AUTHOR'S FAVORITES IN THE WATERFRONT AND ANACOSTIA

Friday Evening Parade	Cedar Hill
Navy Museum	Arena Stage

in 1791 as an arsenal; it is also one of the most beautiful locations in the city. Despite all that fancy strategic planning, the British had no trouble torching the arsenal during their occupation of Washington in 1814, and Fort McNair has gone through many renovations ever since. Today its broad lawns and Beaux Arts buildings are best known as the site of the *National War College,* where military and foreign affairs leaders, in a one-year sabbatical, take courses to improve their professional skills and take a fresh look at their world and its culture.

Fort McNair is a great place to stroll along the river past "Generals Row," the white-columned officers' houses that conjure up memories of those Hollywood frontier forts with their broad parade grounds and tidy military housing. Over by the tennis courts, at the north end of the fort, you'll find a historical marker recording that four of the Lincoln conspirators were hanged on that spot in July 1865. The building next to the courts is all that remains of the 1826 Federal Penitentiary, where the plotters were held until their execution. Fort Mc Nair is located at 103 Third Street SW. Since the events of September 11 visitor access to Fort Mc Nair has been suspended, but call 685–3196 to see if it will be possible during your visit.

Once America's largest shipyard, the *Washington Navy Yard,* which dates back to America's earliest days, was burned to prevent its falling into British hands during the War of 1812. Rebuilt in classic Victorian red brick, the yard is now the home of two terrific military museums. The yard is a twenty-minute walk from the Eastern Market station (orange and blue lines). Parking is available. Security considerations have led Navy Yard authorities to close the former main gate at 901 M Street SE and open a visitor gate at the corner of 11th and O Streets SE. The only visitors admitted to the yard will be those who have made a prior reservation to see the Navy and Marine Museums. To reserve, phone the Navy Museum at 433–6897 or the Marine Museum at 433–3534 at

The Reprint Bookshop

Although L'Enfant Plaza has the Loew's L'Enfant Plaza Hotel and a major-league Metro station (all lines but red), there's also an extensive underground shopping promenade that few visitors see. The promenade has several fast-food outlets, something good to know about in this restaurant-free zone. Also within the promenade you'll find *The Reprint Bookshop,* which carries a heavy schedule of book signings, many of them by well-known writers and celebrities. Despite its name, the Reprint also carries lots of contemporary bestsellers and children's books. 554-5070; www.reprintbookshop.com. Open Monday through Friday 8:00 A.M. to 6:00 P.M.

Kayaking the Monuments

For a unique look at some of Washington's best-known places, take one of Atlantic Kayak's guided kayak tours of the District's waterside monuments. The tour glides past magnificent views of the Washington Monument, the majestic white colonnades of the Lincoln Memorial, the Kennedy Center, and the Chrysler Airflow swirl of the Watergate. Your guide will also take you for a close-up look at seldom-visited Roosevelt Island, a ninety-acre wilderness park in the middle of the Potomac that was once a farm, then a Union Army camp, and now an urban oasis of wildlife and wildflowers. You'll then cross the Potomac for a water-level tour of the historic waterfront in Georgetown, once one of America's great ports and now a magnet for visitors seeking an eclectic combination of stately Federal mansions and hip street life. And along the way you'll probably cross wakes with rowing teams from local universities, one more sign that recreation is alive and well on the Potomac.

Wherever you've spent the day, you'll find another perspective on the Potomac by paddling over to Georgetown's Washington Harbour complex for a sundowner on the terrace overlooking the river. **Atlantic Kayak,** 1201 North Royal Street, Alexandria, VA, (703) 838–9072, www.atlantickayak.com.

least twenty-four hours before your intended visit; you'll have to furnish the names of everyone in your party.

Once inside, head for the **Navy Museum** in the old Naval Gun Factory, which covers every aspect of U.S. naval history, from the Revolution right down to Vietnam. Exhibits range from the gun deck from *Old Ironsides* to a replica of Admiral Byrd's hut from the Antarctic Expedition of 1933. The museum's vast collection of hands-on World War II exhibits includes film shows, electronic reconstructions of key naval battles, and nostalgic displays of life on the 1942 home front. Even though they might never have seen John Wayne save democracy, visitors can tour the destroyer *Barry,* another artifact of World War II, which is permanently anchored nearby. Or you could experience life on a submarine, with operating periscopes so kids can track enemy carriers to their hearts' content. The Navy Museum, in building 76, is open Monday through Friday 9:00 A.M. to 4:00 P.M., Saturday and Sunday 10:00 A.M. to 5:00 P.M.; www.history.navy.mil. Call 433–4882 to reserve.

The yard's **Marine Museum,** also housed in a Victorian-era factory building, uses a "time tunnel" of uniforms, weapons, and battle memorabilia to guide visitors chronologically through the Corps' glorious history. Dioramas show scenes from some of the Marines' most gallant and critical battles in World Wars I and II, Korea, and Vietnam, along with an explanation of the strategies and tactics behind each engagement. One high point: the collection

Visiting the Voice

Although not many Americans ever tune in to their country's official radio station, a lot of other people do. *The Voice of America,* known to all as the VOA, transmits 24/7/365 in fifty-three languages to a worldwide audience of ninety-three million, informing them by radio and television about the United States, its policies, culture, and society. This fascinating tour will begin with a brief video, then show you around the studios and newsrooms of this major international broadcaster. As a bonus, before your tour leaves VOA's C Street lobby, look up at the great Ben Shahn murals representing and dramatizing themes and accomplishments of Franklin Roosevelt's presidency in fighting the Depression. VOA tours are given Monday through Friday at 10:30 A.M. and 1:30 and 2:30 P.M. Reservations are essential. To get them call 619–3919. The VOA Web site is www.voa.gov. The Voice of America is located at 330 Independence Avenue SW. Metro: Federal Center (orange and blue lines) and L'Enfant Plaza (every line except red).

of Marine treasures that includes the famous flag raised on Mt. Suribachi on Iwo Jima. The Marine Museum is located in building 58 and is open Monday through Friday 10:00 A.M. to 4:00 P.M. Call 433–3534 to reserve.

The Navy Yard is a rich oasis of military history located in a restaurant desert, but you won't need to call in the Marines to fight hunger. You'll find William III, an upscale deli with thick sandwiches in building 36 near the Marine Museum, open 6:30 A.M. to 2:30 P.M. If you want a more elaborate lunch, head for the former Officer's Club in building 101 (11:00 A.M. to 1:30 P.M.), and if fast food will do, Mc Donald's, in building 184, is open 5:00 A.M. to 5:00 P.M.

The *Marine Barracks,* located at Eighth and I Streets, were built in 1801 on a site personally selected by President Thomas Jefferson because of its strategic defensive situation between the Navy Yard and the Capitol. Although its military significance has long vanished, this massive, walled quadrangle—"The Oldest Post of the Corps"—remains the epicenter of Marine tradition and spectacle. This is the home of the Marine Commandant, who lives in an 1805 house on the Parade Ground and the ground zero of Marine history. It is also the headquarters of the Marine Band, which will always be identified with its legendary leader, the world's "March King," John Philip Sousa.

Well before Sousa's day, its perfectly manicured Parade Ground was the scene of the Corps' most hallowed rituals. You'll definitely want to see the most stirring of those ceremonies, the Friday Evening Parade, an inspiring patriotic pageant with precision drills, brilliant uniforms, flashing sabers, martial fanfares, and enough Sousa marches to set the most ardent pacifist ablaze. Speaking of the March King, Sousa Hall, which looks across the Parade Ground at the Commandant's House, is the sanctum sanctorum for the legions of Sousaphiles throughout the world. Here, at the headquarters of the Marine Band, you'll see a wealth of Sousiana, including a library of his original sheet music, personal mementos, and a large hall where today's band members practice under a large portrait of Sousa himself.

Guided tours of the barracks leave regularly from the main gate at Eighth and I Streets between 8:00 A.M. and 4:00 P.M. daily; all you usually need to do is turn up. Admission to Sousa Hall is also possible, but because of the regular morning Marine Band practice, tours are usually possible only between noon and 4:00 P.M. For information about this and the Friday Evening Parade, call 433–4073.

The Friday Evening Parade is given only from May through August and starts at 8:45 P.M. Reservations for the parade should be made in advance, either online at the Barracks' nifty Web site, www.mbw.usmc.mil, or by writing to: Protocol Office Attn.: PARADES, Marine Barracks, Eighth and "I" Streets SE, Washington, D.C. 20390–5000.

Your request should include the names of your party, your return address, and a point of contact with a telephone number; you should also specify an alternate parade date in case your preferred date is unavailable. That said, you'll stand an excellent chance of getting in by joining the general admission line which forms at the main gate on Friday evenings, but since seating is first come, first served, plan to arrive at 7:00 P.M. and certainly not after 8:00 P.M. Another thing: Don't drive. Either take a cab or walk over from the Eastern Market Metro, which is on the orange and blue lines.

If you attend the Friday Evening Parade and are looking for a pre- or postceremonial dinner, you'll find the Marine Barracks neighborhood isn't exactly brimming over with dining opportunities. Your best bet is the nearby **Starfish Cafe,** at 539 Eighth Street SE; 546–5006. This cozy, attractive neighborhood storefront serves up a wide range of seafood, including grilled fish, crab and shrimp salads, and sandwiches and the prices are reasonable. Open Monday through Friday 11:30 A.M. to 2:30 P.M., Monday through Saturday 5:00 to 10:30 P.M., Sunday 5:00 to 9:30 P.M.

An eclectic group from every era of American history is buried in the **Congressional Cemetery,** a quiet corner of the capital where American notables have been interred since 1807. The cemetery is the final resting place of military leaders of all wars since the Revolution, as well as Declaration of Independence signer Elbridge Gerry, Pushmataha (the son of Apache chief Cochise), and Civil War leaders from both sides. Many of the cemetery's Congressional

Furniture Frenzy

If you'd like to do some megashopping, even if it's just the window variety, or if you're looking for some decorating ideas, stop off at one of the East's top design showcases, the *Washington Design Center,* which brings together dozens of major manufacturers of furniture, textiles, and kitchen and bath equipment under one roof.

Although this sumptuous collection is aimed at designers and the trade, the public is welcome in many, but not all, showrooms from 9:00 A.M. to 5:00 P.M. Monday through Friday and from 10:00 A.M. to 3:00 P.M. on Saturday. Purchases, however, can be made only by design professionals.

Having said that, if you've found something you absolutely must have, you can get it by hiring a designer on the spot. The center's front desk will help you find one ASAP. Washington Design Center, 300 D Street SW. Call 646–6118; www.merchandisemart .com/dcdesigncenter. Metro: Federal Center (orange and blue lines).

guests are buried under peculiar, mushroomlike monuments that prompted one U.S. senator to comment that "the prospect of being interred under these atrocities brings a new terror to death."

The Congressional Cemetery has its share of interesting graves. Between the main gate and the chapel you'll find the obelisk dedicated to noted writer and historian Ruth Ann Overbeck, who was also a teacher. You can tell that when you see "look it up" inscribed where the dates of birth and death usually go. And beyond the chapel a bench on the main road bears the poignant inscription, "Poopsie and Baby Pie. A lifetime together wasn't enough."

After the John Philip Sousa plot, the cemetery's most visited graves include those of Lincoln photographer Mathew Brady, J. Edgar Hoover, and Belva Lockwood, the first woman to run for president. And every November 6, Sousa's birthday, the Marine Band visits his grave to lay a wreath and play his marches in musical tribute to its former leader. A self-guided tour brochure is available at the office. The Congressional Cemetery, at 1801 E Street SE (543–0539; www.congressionalcemetery.org), is open daily from dawn to dusk. Metro: Stadium-Armory (orange and blue lines).

It's not easy finding a lunch spot near the Congressional Cemetery. Your best bet is to head up to Pennsylvania Avenue. where *Mangialardo and Sons* at 1317 Pennsylvania Avenue SE, serves fifteen kinds of whopping submarines Monday through Friday from 7:30 A.M. to 3:00 P.M.; 543–6212; the Web site says it all: www.subshop.net. Metro: Eastern Market (orange and blue lines).

Across the Anacostia River from the Navy Yard is the section known as Anacostia. Because of its crime rate, out-of-town visitors should exercise caution, especially at night. Its historic significance, however, makes the area worth a visit. An early guidebook called Anacostia "the eastern slice of Washington . . . a place that developed slowly and independently." Because of its physical separation by the river from the rest of the District, Anacostia from its earliest days had a life of its own, starting as a collection of stand-alone villages within the District. Today's Anacostia is an almost entirely African-American residential and commercial community, but in the nineteenth century, Anacostia brought together residents of many backgrounds in settlements like Uniontown, a mainly white community; Stantontown, where free blacks lived; and other villages where German immigrants prevailed.

On a knoll in Anacostia stands **Cedar Hill**, the Victorian frame home of African-American leader Frederick Douglass. Born a slave in 1818, Douglass, after teaching himself to read and write, became a publisher, bank president, diplomat, musician, fiery orator, and the author of hundreds of books, monographs, and speeches; he somehow also found time to learn seven languages and serve as the American Minister to Haiti. This Renaissance man's greatest achievements, however, were in the political arena as an eloquent advocate of abolition, women's rights, and racial justice, and as a trusted adviser to Abraham Lincoln on these issues.

Visitors to Cedar Hill wander through rooms filled with mementos of Douglass's extraordinary life, including his beloved Stradivarius, Abraham Lincoln's cane (a gift from Mary Lincoln), and a leather rocking chair given to Douglass by a grateful Haitian people. The dining room stands ready for one of the formal dinners Douglass gave for fellow members of the Washington power grid of the 1880s, while his library bursts with more than 1,100 books and a massive rolltop desk covered with papers. A visit to Cedar Hill will also give you a spectacular hilltop panorama of the Capitol and other Washington landmarks. Cedar Hill is located at 1411 W Street SE. The House and its adjoining National Park Visitor Center, where you can view a film of Douglass's life, are open from 9:00 A.M. to 5:00 P.M. in the summer, until 4:00 P.M. the rest of the year. Tours are scheduled throughout the day. No Metro.

anacostia farmers' market

If you're in Anacostia and hankering for fresh produce, the Anacostia Farmers' Market convenes every Friday between June and November in the parking lot of the Union Temple Baptist Church, 1225 W Street SE, Hours: 4:00 to 6:30 P.M.

Another showcase of African-American history and culture is the **Anacostia Museum and Center,** located in a former school at 1901 Fort Place SE. The museum reopened in 2002 after a two-year, $8 million overhaul, and the results are well worth the wait. The exterior is now a curvy brick facade with drumlike columns. Inside, the exhibition spaces have been greatly improved, which will enhance your appreciation of the museum's busy schedule of African-American sculpture and art and collections reflecting black cultural history. The museum also displays materials borrowed from private collections of African-American art and artifacts in the D.C. area. The museum is open daily from 10:00 A.M. to 5:00 P.M. No metro or bus stops; however in past summers the Smithsonian has run a weekday shuttle bus from its main building on the National Mall out to Anacostia. Call 287–3306 for tour information or visit the museum's Web site, for further information; www.si.edu/anacostia.

Places to Eat in the Waterfront and Anacostia

Captain White's,
in Main Avenue Fish Market, Washington Channel at Fourteenth Street bridge; see page 65 for full description.

Custis and Brown,
in Maine Avenue Fish Market, Washington Channel at Fourteenth Street bridge; see page 66 for full description.

H2O,
800 Water Street SW;
484–6300;
www.h2odc.com
You'll have lots of company along with great river views at this Washington landmark that has recently undergone a major overhaul. H2O prides itself on its crab cakes, lobster, clambakes, and the mammoth Captain's Platters. Check the Web site for H2O's special events and parties, which include major-league dancing to DJs on Friday and Saturday nights. Open Monday through Wednesday 5:00 to 10:00 P.M., Thursday through Saturday 5:00 to 9:00 P.M., Sunday for brunch 11:00 A.M. to 3:00 P.M. Expensive.

Jessie Taylor Seafood,
in Main Avenue Fish Market, Washington Channel at Fourteenth Street bridge; see page 65 for full description.

Mangialardo and Sons,
1317 Pennsylvania Avenue;
543–6212;
www.subshop.net;
see page 72 for full description.

Maine Avenue Fish Market,
Washington Channel at Fourteenth Street bridge. See page 63 for full description.

Phillips Flagship,
900 Water Street SW;
488–8515.
Takes the self-serve approach, with huge seafood buffets at reasonable prices. Phillips is popular with tour groups, especially for Sunday brunch, which is practically overwhelming. Open Monday through Thursday 11:00 A.M. to 11:00 P.M., Friday 11:00 A.M. to midnight, Saturday noon to midnight, and Sunday 10:30 A.M. to 10:00 P.M. Moderate.

Starfish Cafe,
538 Eighth Street SE;
546–5006; see page 71 for full description.

AUTHOR'S FAVORITE PLACES TO EAT IN THE WATERFRONT AND ANACOSTIA

| H2O | Maine Avenue Fish Market |

Foggy Bottom

Although Foggy Bottom is the home of the State Department, it did not get its name from the torrents of bafflegab and diplo-speak that gush forth daily from America's Foreign Policy Headquarters, known locally as "the fudge factory." This neighborhood was originally named Funkstown for Jacob Funk, the German immigrant who founded a small industrial community on the Potomac that clearly would have trouble meeting today's pollution standards. In addition to scads of smoke and pollutants, Herr Funk's riverfront slum also suf-fered from the gases and other emanations of its surrounding swamps, adding up to a perpetual haze that gave this OSHA paradise its picturesque name. That said, the State Department hasn't helped much.

Today's Foggy Bottom gives new meaning to the term "mixed use." Its tenants include large government agencies, embassies, the Watergate, the Daughters of the American Revo-lution, and major institutions such as the grandiose Kennedy Center and sprawling George Washington University, along with more human-scale neighborhoods where narrow nineteenth-century row houses line leafy residential streets.

On Pennsylvania Avenue, about 2 blocks from the White House, stands the massive World Bank building and the

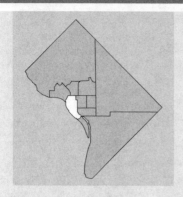

M ST
M ST
23RD ST
NEW HAMPSHIRE AVE
21ST ST
L ST
L ST
26TH ST
K ST
K ST
WASHINGTON CIRCLE
25TH ST
PENNSYLVANIA AVE
I ST
18TH ST
17TH ST
22ND ST
I ST
24TH ST
H ST
GEORGE WASHINGTON UNIVERSITY
G ST
20TH ST
19TH ST
Watergate
F ST
F ST
John F. Kennedy Center for the Performing Arts
The Octagon
N.Y. AVE
VIRGINIA AVE
Corcoran Gallery
18TH ST
E ST
D ST
Dept. of State
23RD ST
21ST ST
C ST
DAR Constitution Hall and Museum
C ST
22ND ST
CONSTITUTION AVE
50
Vietnam Veterans Memorial
HENRY BACON DR
17TH ST
Reflecting Pool
Lincoln Memorial
Korean War Veterans Memorial
INDEPENDENCE AVE
West Potomac Park
N
Potomac River
OHIO DR
Franklin D. Roosevelt Memorial
Tidal Basin
Jefferson Memorial

0   1/4 mi
0   1/4 km

Infoshop, the Bank's well-stocked bookstore. The store carries a huge collection of books on international affairs, especially global development issues, along with Bank country reports to prepare you for your next overseas jaunt. This is also the place where foreign affairs mavens can pick up that World Bank polo shirt they've always hankered after. After the Infoshop, at 701 18th Street NW, is open from 9:00 A.M. to 5:00 P.M. Monday through Friday; 458–4500; www.worldbankinfoshop .org. Metro: Farragut West (orange and blue lines) or Farragut North (red line).

The *Breadline,* at 1751 Pennsylvania Avenue NW, has great early morning choices, including a memorable breakfast croissant, along with a lunchtime assortment of imaginative sandwiches and the best lemonade in town. That's probably why you're likely to find lots of White House staff folks and World Bankers perched on those stools, and maybe a few Famous Faces as well. The Breadline also has outside tables that turn Pennsylvania Avenue into Via Veneto (assuming you're into serious self-deception). Open 7:30 A.M. to 3:30 P.M. Monday through Friday; 822–8900. Inexpensive. Metro: Farragut West (orange and blue lines) or Farragut North (red line).

Foggy Bottom is also home to another significant international financial institution, the International Monetary Fund, which serves 183 countries. While

funky bottom

Jacob Funk and Funkstown may be ancient history, but their Zeitgeist lives on at Foggy Bottom's United Church, at 1920 G Street NW, which regularly offers services in German.

TOP ATTRACTIONS IN FOGGY BOTTOM

The Octagon	Watergate
Corcoran Gallery	Arts Club
Daughters of the American Revolution Museum and Genealogy Library	Franklin Delano Roosevelt Memorial
	Vietnam Veterans Memorial
Department of the Interior Museum and Indian Craft Shop	Lincoln Memorial
	Korean War Veterans Memorial
Federal Reserve Bank	National Academy of Sciences
State Department Diplomatic Reception Rooms	

you wouldn't want to troop around the Fund's corridors even if you could, its **IMF Center,** at 720 19th Street NW, has permanent exhibits related to the global economy, the work of the IMF, and money, almost everyone's favorite subject. A recent show at the center featured exhibits of the objects such as shells, beads, and weapons that once served as currency in Africa and coins from the Silk Road, the Mediterranean, and other historic trade routes. The center also has a global finance-oriented bookstore and a gift shop. Open 10:00 A.M. to 4:30 P.M., Monday through Friday; 623–6869; www.imf.org/external/np/exr/center/index.htm. Metro: Foggy Bottom (orange and blue lines) or Farragut North (red line).

Your next stop is at Foggy Bottom's most elegant home. **The Octagon,** known in its day as "The Palace of Washington," must have seemed wildly out of place among the crude shacks and muddy streets of the young capital. Built by Col. John Tayloe in 1801, this grand Federal town house was designed by William Thornton, the architect of the U.S. Capitol. Jefferson, Monroe, Adams, and Andrew Jackson all passed through the Octagon's circular entrance hall to visit the Tayloes in their splendid home. The Octagon added an entirely new and unwelcome chapter to its history when for six months it served as the Executive Mansion for President Madison after the British burned the White House during the War of 1812. After a long period of decay as a tenement, the Octagon was rescued and restored in 1902 by the American Institute of Architects. The American Architectural Foundation now maintains it as the oldest museum in the United States devoted to architecture.

The Octagon

Your guided tour will start in the drawing room, once covered with 4 feet of trash, where you'll see the priceless stone mantel that somehow survived those years of neglect. You'll pass through the dining room, with its Chippendale breakfront and Gilbert Stuart portraits of the Tayloes, before climbing the splendid oval staircase. Check out the ivory "amity buttons" on the handrail, which indicated that the house was paid for, an early American custom that few could follow today. Upstairs in the oval study stands the English rent table where Madison signed the Treaty of Ghent, which ended the war with Great Britain. The house's bedrooms, which are regularly occupied by traveling historical and architectural exhibits, are reportedly haunted by the ghosts of two Tayloe daughters who threw themselves down the staircase when told by their father they could not marry the men of their choice. Odd noises, swaying chandeliers, and mysterious footsteps are not included in the tour.

Down in the basement where President Madison stashed the presidential wine and servants toiled in the large kitchen, this magnificent home shows its human side. The restored (and euphemistically named) "servant's hall" is where the Tayloe's African-American slaves ate and did their household chores, then slept in shifts under impossibly cramped conditions in the small bedroom next door. As you'll see from drawings and cross sections, extensive archaeological research and reconstruction have restored all the original walls and structures of the basement rooms.

The Octagon, 1799 New York Avenue NW (638–3221) is open Tuesday through Sunday 10:00 A.M. to 4:00 P.M.; closed Monday; www.archfoundation.org. Admission is $5.00 for adults, $3.00 for students and seniors. Metro: Farragut West and McPherson Square (orange and blue lines) or Farragut North (red line).

The headquarters building of the **American Institute of Architects,** at 1735 New York Avenue, behind the Octagon, offers regular architectural exhibits in its lobby. The building and its shop, which carries a broad selection of books on architecture, are open Monday through Friday 8:30 A.M. to 5:00 P.M.; www.aia.org.

Although the **Corcoran Gallery of Art** is on a lot of people's "must-see" lists, it's also slightly off the beaten path because it's *(a)* off the Mall, *(b)* generally not as well known as the more publicized National Gallery of Art, and *(c)* one of the few great Washington museums not part of the Smithsonian family. The Corcoran Collection moved to its splendid Beaux Arts building in 1897, when it outgrew what is now the Renwick Gallery. Before entering, take a look at the imposing rotunda and the facade frieze bearing the names of great painters and you'll see why the Corcoran was Frank Lloyd Wright's favorite building in Washington.

Inside you'll find a large, distinguished, and eclectic permanent collection of classic and contemporary American and European art. Here the luminous work of French impressionists mingles with American works such as Albert Bierstadt's epic *The Last of the Buffalo,* the famous Gilbert Stuart portrait of George Washington seen on the $1.00 bill and even a thirteenth-century stained glass window from Soissons Cathedral. Although the Corcoran's famous statue *The Greek Slave* scandalized Victorian-era visitors, who gazed on it in gender-segregated viewings, nobody gives it a thought today, especially anyone who's

Corcoran Gallery of Art

been to the movies since 1970. The museum also has numerous special exhibits of contemporary American art and photography.

But for me the star of the Corcoran show is the gilded *Salon Dore,* imported from a Parisian town house. With golden paneling, mirrored walls, and flower garlands, it gives visitors the sense of being transported to a sumptuous, eighteenth-century garden. Our last visit occurred during one of the museum's periodic "family days," which featured performances of Colonial music and dance, children's art lessons, and "appearances" by Abraham Lincoln and a crinkly Benjamin Franklin, who told stories to the kids. The museum shop, well-stocked with art and photography books, is a real treat. So is the Cafe Des Artistes in the museum's double atrium, which offers light fare Wednesday to Monday 11:00 A.M. to 2:00 P.M., until 8:00 P.M. on Thursday; closed Monday and Tuesday. There's a Cajun-influenced gospel brunch every Sunday 10:30 A.M. to 2:00 P.M., cost $23.95, $10.95 for children. Every Wednesday 12:30 to 1:30 P.M. a free program of live jazz is presented in the museum's Hammer Auditorium.

The Corcoran, at 500 17th Street NW (639–1700; www.corcoran.org), is open daily 10:00 A.M. to 5:00 P.M.and until 9:00 P.M. on Thursday. The museum is closed on Tuesday. Docents lead forty-five-minute tours at noon on weekdays, and on weekends at noon, and 2:30 P.M. Admission is $6.75 for individuals, and $4.75 for seniors and students, $12.00 for families. Metro: Farragut West (orange and blue lines).

Inside the national headquarters of the ***American Red Cross,*** at 1730 E Street NW, you'll find a visitor center and small museum with exhibits of the Red Cross's many achievements and services, including its response to September 11. Others demonstrate the organization's work with the armed forces and in nursing. Both are open Monday to Friday from 8:30 A.M. to 4:00 P.M. And

Memorial Walk

The best way to see the off-the-beaten-path Franklin Delano Roosevelt Memorial and four other important memorials is by taking a half-day stroll that meanders across the National Mall, through the park and polo fields along the Potomac, and winds up at the Jefferson Memorial for a look at the cherry trees around the Tidal Basin.

From the Foggy Bottom Metro exit, turn right on 23rd Street and walk past the State Department to Constitution Avenue, where a left turn takes you to the most poignant spot in Washington, the *Vietnam Veterans Memorial,* with its wall of black granite bearing the names of the 58,000 Americans who died in that war. Offerings, flowers, and mementos of the fallen are often left at the wall and the emotions of their surviving buddies, relatives, and ordinary visitors are always close to the surface.

At the *Lincoln Memorial* at the end of the National Mall, the magnificent Daniel Chester French statue symbolizes Lincoln's greatness. But this memorial is loaded with other symbolic touches. The thirty-six exterior Doric columns represent the number of states in the Union when Lincoln was shot, while the fifty-six steps up to the statue mark Lincoln's age at the time of his death. Then take a close look at Lincoln's hands; one is clenched and the other open, which reputedly represents both his will to preserve the Union and act with openness and compassion. Probably so, but they are also signing his initials, **A** with the left and **L** with the right.

To the right of the Lincoln Memorial you'll pass the *Korean War Veterans Memorial,* which honors the fighting men and women who served in one of America's bloodiest and most frustrating conflicts. The memorial's centerpiece is the group of nineteen stainless steel statues depicting a squad on patrol and the images on black granite of more than 2,400 servicemen and women.

Signs will direct you across Independence Avenue to Ohio Drive and a walk along the Potomac through West Potomac Park, past soccer fields, baseball diamonds, and even Washington's only polo fields.

At the *Franklin Delano Roosevelt Memorial* you'll walk through four granite-walled spaces, one for each of Roosevelt's four administrations. On the walls are inscribed memorable phrases from FDR's speeches; sculptures dramatize the challenges Roosevelt and other Americans faced in each of his terms. In the first room, haggard and hungry men stand in a Depression breadline for handouts; in another sculpture, a man listens to a radio for inspiration from one of Roosevelt's "fireside chats." In the third room the wartime president sits with his dog Fala and in the fourth, a statue of Eleanor Roosevelt commemorates her role as First Lady and champion of human rights.

Exiting the FDR Memorial you'll be next to the Tidal Basin and ready to continue your stroll among the cherry trees to the *Jefferson Memorial,* a few yards away. Then head for the Smithsonian Metro stop and your next off-the-beaten-path destination.

on Tuesdays and Fridays at 9:00 A.M. you can take a special escorted tour of the headquarters building and its grand Louis Tiffany windows. For details call 636–3300 or visit www.redcross.org. Metro: Farragut West (orange and blue lines) or Farragut North (red line).

The block-square **Daughters of the American Revolution** (DAR) complex includes a museum, a genealogical reference library, and a series of richly furnished rooms depicting typical upscale American rooms during the period 1770–1840. It also includes one of the city's finest auditoriums, the 4,000-seat Constitution Hall. The DAR may have a fusty image in some areas, but its museum comes up with snazzy displays of American decorative art, most recently an exhibit of colorful and intricately made quilts from colonial times right down to the present. A collection of early American ceramics includes useful medical equipment such as a handsome leech jar to hold the friendly little critters that will happily cleanse that pesky bile from your blood, and you know how important that can be. After all, if it was good enough for (the late) George Washington, it's good enough for you.

Docents also take visitors to the DAR's "period rooms" on tours that depart every forty-five minutes. Among the standouts are the New Jersey Room, with walls paneled in walnut retrieved from a ship that sank in 1777; the California Room, which faithfully reproduces a room of the whaling station in Monterey as it appeared in the early 1800s; and a Maryland Room with wallpaper depicting Baltimore in 1770 that was discovered in a Paris antiques shop by a DAR member.

If you're interested in tracing your colonial-era ancestors, the DAR's vast genealogical library, located in Continental Hall, the building's elaborate theater, is one of the best research sources anywhere. A $5.00 fee will start you off with one of the in-house professional genealogists and a computer to track down your family.

The DAR also offers a "Colonial Adventure" tour: Costumed guides take five- to seven-year-olds on a travel in time back to colonial America, where they play eighteenth-century games, attend a period tea party, and learn what it was like to be a child in pre-Revolutionary days.

The **Daughters of the American Revolution Museum,** 1776 D Street NW; 879–3241; www.dar.org/museum. Open Monday through Friday 8:30 A.M. to 4:00 P.M. and Saturday 9:00 A.M. to 5:00 P.M. Closed Sunday. Tours of the period rooms are offered Monday through Friday 10:30 A.M. to 2:30 P.M. and Saturday from 9:00 A.M. to 5:00 P.M. The genealogical library is open from 8:30 A.M. to 4:00 P.M. and Saturday 9:00 A.M. to 5:00 P.M. Closed Sunday. Colonial Adventure tours are given the second and fourth Saturday of every month at 1:00 P.M. and 3:30 P.M. Admission is free, but reservations are essential and, because of the tour's popularity, should be made early by calling Kelly Scott at 879–3240.

The ***Organization of American States (OAS),*** once known as the Pan-American Union, is an international organization where diplomats from the United States and thirty-four other Western Hemisphere nations come together to promote hemispheric peace, political stability, and social progress. Aside from its many cultural and educational projects and a long list of political initiatives throughout our hemisphere, the OAS's ornate headquarters building, "The House of the Americas," at 17th Street and Constitution Avenue, is a good place to know about if you're walking the neighborhood in any season. In summer, its sumptuous interior courtyard—a shady Spanish colonial patio with a tinkling fountain—is a Latin oasis that's ideal for cooling off and escaping Washington's sizzling temperatures. This sparkling loggia, with tropical flowers, lovely blue tiles, and walls bearing Inca, Maya, and other early Latin American motifs, also makes a great refuge that brightens those winter greys and chills. But there's more. Upstairs you'll see the "Hall of the Americas," the grand meeting room where the OAS Permanent Council gathers under splendid Tiffany chandeliers, and the "Hall of Heroes," with busts of Latin America's greatest figures. The Organization of American States offers guided and self-guided building tours Monday through Friday from 9:00 A.M. to 5:30 P.M. Photo ID is needed. Call 458–3927; www.oas.org.

Behind the OAS you'll find the ***Aztec Garden,*** with guava, coffee, date, and other exotic plants collected from all over Latin America. Behind the garden, but facing 18th Street, stands the ***Art Museum of the Americas,*** in a charming Spanish colonial building that was once the official residence of the secretary-general of the OAS. The museum showcases contemporary art of Latin America and the Caribbean. You'll always find exhibits of vibrant works from its extensive permanent collection, usually accompanied by at least one

All About GWU

George Washington University originated in the dream of both Washington and L'Enfant to establish a national university in the District somewhere near the current intersection of 23rd Street and Virginia Avenue. Washington, in fact, held stock in the Potowmack Canal Company, which was founded to create both the university and the C&O Canal. Long story short, Congress never voted to create a national school, but the idea morphed into Columbian College, founded in 1824, which became today's GWU. After the federal government, the university is the largest single private landholder in the city and growing every year.

Caught in the Crossfire

Political buffs in the District and all over America tune into CNN's *Crossfire* at 4:30 to 5:00 P.M. every Monday through Friday to watch political warriors from both parties duke it out over the political issues of the day. *Crossfire* actually takes place here in Foggy Bottom in George Washington University's Media and Public Affairs Building at 805 21st Street NW. If you'd like to attend *Crossfire,* and maybe even participate in the show, contact CNN at cnn@gwu.edu or phone 994–8266 well in advance of your visit to get an idea of ticket availability dates and to make your reservations. Standby tickets, also free, are available at 3:30 P.M. weeknights at the box office. Doors open at 3:30 P.M. and close by 4:10 P.M.

Across the street George Washington's *Lisner Auditorium* offers regular and extensive programs of music and dance. To learn more, visit www.gwu.edu/~lisner/performances or phone 994–6800.

temporary exhibit presenting an established or emerging artist from somewhere in the hemisphere. Although the art is always special, be sure to see the fascinating loggia in the back of the museum where two stories of blue and terracotta tiles replicate Aztec figures, legends, and folk themes. Art Museum of the Americas, 201 18th Street NW; 458–6301, fax 458–6021; www.museum.oas.org. Open Tuesday through Sunday 10:00 A.M. to 5:00 P.M. Metro: Farragut West (blue and orange lines).

Although it looks pretty dull from the street, behind its New Deal Modern facade, the Department of the Interior offers visitors a pair of unique places. Exhibits in the **Department of the Interior Museum,** trace the Department's main areas of activity, which include the protection of wildlife, mine safety, and western lands. The real crowd pleasers, however, are the colorful Bureau of Indian Affairs exhibits of Native American culture, crafts, and heritage. If you're impressed by the exhibits, across the hall there's an authentic off-the-beaten-path find: The **Indian Craft Shop,** one of Washington's top gift shops, has a nifty collection of woven goods, pottery, and jewelry from forty-five tribal groups. The intricate Alaskan carvings from walrus ivory are in themselves worth a visit. The Department of the Interior Museum (208–4743, www.indiancraftshop.com) and its craft shop (208–4056) at 1849 C Street NW, are open Monday through Friday 8:30 A.M. to 4:30 P.M. and the third Saturday

capitalquote

"If you want to have a friend in Washington, better buy a dog."

—President Harry S. Truman

of every month from 10:00 A.M. to 4:00 P.M. Photo ID required for entry. Metro: Farragut West (orange and blue lines).

If hunger strikes while you're visiting the Interior Department, one floor down from the craft shop and museum there's a cafeteria that serves breakfast, snacks, and lunch at reasonable cost.

Let's be clear—if you take the weekly tour of the ***Federal Reserve Bank,*** Alan Greenspan is not going to come out to brief you personally about his innermost thoughts on interest rates or the direction of the stock market. What you will get is a well-organized tour of one of America's and the world's most powerful institutions, which directly influences the health of the economy and interest rates (important only if you're one of the few with a car loan, mortgage, or credit card). You can sample the rarefied air of the Fed's headquarters, with its templelike pillared entrance hall, by visiting the Federal Reserve Board Gallery, a tasteful exhibit of nineteenth- and twentieth-century paintings and sculpture; a recent show featured imaginative sculptures and sketches based on banknotes.

But for a complete look at America's cathedral of cash, take the weekly tour, which visits the gallery, then ascends the graceful stairway to the holiest of holies, the huge Board of Governor's Boardroom. Here, around a 27-foot, two-ton granite table, the world's most influential banker and his colleagues make big decisions that affect you. In fact, you can watch the excellent film describing the Fed's workings from Greenspan's chair and think about getting that mortgage paid off. As a souvenir of your visit, your guide will even give you some money, a little bag of shredded cash. (Here's a tip for parents: If the kids are getting fidgety or bored, you can keep them amused for a decade or two by asking them to reassemble the bills). And, oh yes, there's a pay phone outside where you can call your broker. Individual tours of the Federal Reserve building, once given every Thursday at 2:30 P.M., have been suspended since the September 11 attacks. The bank, however, can accommodate tour groups of ten or more. Call the Fed's visitor center at 452–3126 or 452–3324 for an update and more information. You can still visit the Fed's art exhibits by pre-registering at least twenty-four hours in advance by calling 452–3778 and giving them your Social Security number and date of birth. The visitor's entrance is on 20th Street NW, between C Street and Constitution Avenue. You'll find more information at www.federalreserve.gov.

Someone (I think it was me) once described the huge ***Department of State building*** at 22nd and C Streets NW as "a '50s insurance office without the charm." You definitely wouldn't want to tour the rabbit warren offices on the first six floors, and even if you could visit the rarefied seventh floor (which you can't), you'd find that even the secretary of state's suite suffers from the klunky boardroom decor so cherished on Planet Eisenhower.

But the eighth floor **Diplomatic Reception Rooms** are a very different story. Here you'll find an unparalleled collection of eighteenth-century American furniture, paintings, and decorative arts that is one of the city's best-kept secrets. The world leaders, foreign diplomats, and other dignitaries that attend receptions and dinners in these opulent rooms wine and dine surrounded by treasures such as Thomas Jefferson's mahogany desk, where he wrote portions of the Declaration of Independence; the secretary on which the Treaty of Paris was signed in 1783, ending the American Revolution; and a large collection of Philadelphia Chippendale chairs. Portraits of John Jay and the Washingtons by Gilbert Stuart look down from the walls, while George Washington's dinner service is displayed in a massive breakfront. The secretary of state's intimate dinners for 250 are held in the vast Franklin dining room, where the carpet is so large that it had to be helicoptered in.

capital quote

"Don't forget, even paranoids have enemies."

—Secretary of State
Henry Kissinger

Forty-five-minute guided tours of the reception rooms are conducted Monday through Friday at 9:30 and 10:30 A.M., and 2:45 P.M. and leave from the flag-filled lobby you've seen on every network TV news show. No admission charge, but reservations are required; get them by calling 647–3241 or faxing 736–4232. Summer tours are fully booked up to three months in advance, so you must plan ahead. Children under twelve discouraged. For an advance peek at some of America's greatest treasures visit www.state.gov. Metro: Foggy Bottom (orange and blue lines).

You don't have to be a rocket scientist to appreciate the **National Academy of Sciences** headquarters building at 2100 C Street NW. The academy's stunning Great Hall, with a four-story ceiling of gold and blue mosaics depicting great moments in the history of science, is similar in form and appearance to a small medieval church. A Foucault pendulum, which illustrates spinning of the earth on its axis, dangles from the center of the dome. The hall and its surrounding corridors usually house small art shows; free chamber music concerts are frequently given under the "Arts in the Academy" program.

Downstairs, the academy's small, health-conscious cafeteria makes a good lunch stop. Afterward, head for the building's gardens on Constitution Avenue, where you'll find a giant bronze statue of the great scientist Albert Einstein. A celestial map, showing the heavens as they were on April 22, 1979, the day the memorial was dedicated, is spread at Einstein's feet. In his left hand is a paper with mathematical equations that summarize his most important contributions: the theory of relativity, the photoelectric effect, and the equivalence of energy

Jazz at the "KenCen"

Although you've surely heard about the Kennedy Center's world-renowned schedule of operas, dance, musical comedy, and classical music, you probably don't know that the center also sponsors a terrific program of live jazz in its very own nightclub. The recently formed KC Jazz Club convenes several times a month from September to May to listen to jazz greats like Cleo Laine, Cassandra Wilson, and the Billy Taylor Trio. The setting is a dimly lit, intimate nightclub in the center's roof-level Terrace Gallery where, aside from great music, you'll also find a buffet table and bar.

KC Jazz Club, John F. Kennedy Center for the Performing Arts, 2700 F Street NW, Washington, D.C. (800) 444–1324 or 467–4600. You'll also find a schedule at www.kennedy-center.org/programs/jazz/jazzclub/home.html. Tickets are $25.

and matter. To round out your visit, offer to explain all three to your spouse and children. The academy (334–2000) is open Monday through Friday 9:00 A.M. to 5:00 P.M. The cafeteria is open 7:00 to 10:30 A.M. and to visitors for lunch from 12:45 to 2:00 P.M. For information on concerts, call 334–2436. Metro: Foggy Bottom (orange and blue lines).

Watergate, where a botched break-in of Democratic party headquarters triggered the investigation and cover-up that led to Nixon's resignation and added a new word to our language, takes its name from the tiers of granite steps still visible along the Potomac just to the north of Memorial Bridge. The steps were originally envisioned as a ceremonial "water gate" where foreign dignitaries would arrive by barge, Cleopatra-like, for a formal welcome to the capital. It never happened. Instead, Washingtonians gathered here on the steps or in canoes for summer evening concerts by the Marine Band and other orchestras playing on a bandshell anchored on the river.

namesake

In 1791 a special panel, acting without the president's concurrence, changed the name of the capital city from "Territory of Columbia" to "the city of Washington." Even though he selected the site and his name is over the door, the ever modest George Washington never called the capital Washington, preferring instead to call it "The Federal City."

The apartment-office-hotel complex, which resembles a Mussolini-era Italian luxury liner that has mysteriously run aground on the banks of the Potomac, later gave part of its name to the continuing and unfortunate habit of making every minor scandal or passing illegality a "gate" of some kind. But another, real Watergate scandal came along during the '90s when it was the address of Monica

The American Meridian

At the corner of 24th and H Streets NW a plaque on the George Washington University campus marks the imaginary north-south line that once was, at least for Americans, zero longitude, which separated the Eastern and Western hemispheres. And, as the center of America's world from 1848 to 1884, the meridian was used to survey the boundaries of the western states.

The American Meridian was an invisible line that ran through the dome of the U.S. Naval Observatory, which you can see (but not visit) on its hilltop a few blocks away on "Navy Hill" at 24th and D Streets NW. Back when 24th Street NW divided the planet, a drive to the Virginia suburbs meant changing hemispheres, which is possibly one reason that, in 1884, America joined the rest of the world in recognizing the Greenwich, England, observatory as the prime meridian. Metro: Foggy Bottom (orange and blue lines).

Lewinsky; the apartments are also home to her neighbors, presidential candidates Robert and Elizabeth Dole.

The office building where Tricky Dick's "plumbers" broke in is at 2500 Virginia Avenue, while the Howard Johnson across the street that was used by their lookouts is now a George Washington University dorm. Behind the office building, the posh Swisshotel Watergate Hotel contains Aquarelle—an equally pricey restaurant—and a mediocre health club. If hunger strikes in this virtually restaurant-free zone, you could get a loan and head for Aquarelle, but a more reasonable choice would be to take the escalator down to *Chen's,* a small walk-in restaurant in the Watergate's interior shopping mall, where you'll find out why Bob and Liddy go there for the lemon chicken. Chen's is located at 2542 Virginia Avenue NW. Call 965–4104. Inexpensive.

There are at least two good reasons to visit the *Arts Club of Washington,* an organization founded to promote the appreciation of art through a broad range of cultural programs and exhibits. The parlors and public rooms of the club's headquarters exhibit paintings by local, national, and international artists

Concerts, Compliments of the Kennedy

Although you'll want to join the many who tour the *Kennedy Center,* try to time your visit for 6:00 P.M. That's when, every day, there's a free concert given in the Center's Grand Foyer, and it could be almost anything from ballet to jazz. As Woody Allen once said about life itself, "all you have to do is turn up."

The West End

Just north of Washington Circle, where Georgetown, Foggy Bottom, Downtown, and Dupont Circle all intersect, is the area known as the West End. Once a wasteland of used car lots and warehouses, the West End has become a major center for hotels, most of them pricey, and a variety of restaurants for all pocketbooks. Alas, there's not a lot to see in the West End, but you can't beat the location for lodging or dining. The hotel selection includes upmarket names like the Ritz Carlton (1150 22nd Street NW; 835–0500), the Fairmont (2401 M Street NW at 24th Street; 429–2400), and the Park Hyatt (1201 24th Street NW; 789–1234). However, a less expensive possibility is the moderately priced Best Western New Hampshire Suites at 1129 New Hampshire Avenue NW; 457–0565.

Good restaurant choices in the West End include:

Agua Ardiente,
(translation "firewater")
at 1250 24th Street NW,
833–8500.
Has the decor of a Latin American country church, but this is a hip chapel with soft light and textures and walls decked out with South American church and Indian art. The Nuevo Latino food includes tapas of pork, chicken, and shrimp and empanadas, those tasty little meat turnovers from the Andes.
Try the potent "guarapos" of rum, fruit juice, and sugar. Open for lunch Monday through Friday and daily for dinner. Live music Wednesday through Saturday 833–8500. Moderate.

Blackie's,
1217 22nd Street NW;
333-1100.
Once a mere steakhouse, but now one of the city's top restaurants, with a French chef, a 3,500-bottle wine cellar, and a plush decor. Expensive.

Courtyard Cafe,
BNA Building
1227 25th Street NW;
785–1388.
For more modest fare when you're wandering the West End, try this self-service cafe where you can choose from a mammoth salad and fruit bar and a zillion sandwich possibilities. Breakfast too. Open Monday through Friday from 7:00 A.M. to 5:00 P.M. Inexpensive.

Grillfish,
1200 New Hampshire Avenue NW;
331–7310.
Casual with very well-prepared seafood. Moderate.

Marcel's,
2401 Pennsylvania Avenue NW;
296–1196.
This award-winner combines French subtlety with Belgian robustness, especially in its rich game dishes. After your pre-performance dinner, Marcel's limousine will whisk you to the Kennedy Center, then bring you back for a sumptuous dessert. Expensive.

Meiweh,
1200 New Hampshire Avenue NW;
833–2288.
Excellent Chinese at a moderate price.

Metro: Foggy Bottom (blue and orange lines).

Dining at the Kennedy Center

Although most of the restaurants in this chapter, especially Marcel's and the others on Pennsylvania Avenue, are well located for dining before performances at the Kennedy Center, don't overlook the center's two in-house possibilities. All are located on the center's Roof Terrace level, which will give you a million-dollar view of Washington and the Potomac:

The Roof Terrace,
416–8555.
Dining in New American style. This sleek, newly redecorated restaurant is usually open only Thursday, Friday, and Saturday from 5:30 to 10:30 P.M., but when performances are given on other evenings pretheater dinners are served from 5:00 to 8:00 P.M. Since the restaurant is often also used for special occasions, it is sometimes closed to the public. The restaurant's renowned Kitchen Brunch is served Sunday from 11:30 A.M. to 2:30 P.M. Reservations recommended. Expensive.

KC Cafe,
416–8560.
Lighter fare, with salad, coffee, and dessert bars plus gourmet sandwiches and the Chef's Table, which offers daily special dishes. Open daily from 5:00 to 8:00 P.M., making it pretheater only. 416–8560. Moderate.

In good weather you'll see lots of folks picnicking outside on the lower-level terrace overlooking the Potomac. You can join them by either picking up a sandwich from one of the food carts in the Grand Foyer or by brown bagging it from your favorite food shop.

and are the scene of a wide range of cultural programs that include literary readings and concerts. The house also contains period furnishings and an old-shoe, book-lined library that will take you back to 1916 when the club was founded. The club offers a free concert series at noon every Friday.

The club's headquarters, located in the Monroe House, one of the capital's oldest and most historic structures, is alone worth a visit. Built in 1806, this handsome Georgian mansion, later expanded to include the house next door, was the home of Secretary of State James Monroe in 1814; in 1817, when Monroe became president, this became the *de facto* White House until restoration of the Executive Mansion could be completed after the fire of 1814. The house was later the British Legation, until the club moved there in 1916.

The Arts Club, 2017 I Street NW (331–7282 www.artsclubofwashington .com) is open Tuesday through Friday 10:00 A.M. to 5:00 P.M., Saturday 10:00 A.M. to 2:00 P.M.; closed Sunday. Metro: Foggy Bottom or Farragut West (orange and blue lines).

The **B'nai B'rith National Jewish Museum** covers the totality of the Jewish experience from antiquity down to the present. The museum's rare and beautiful displays of Judaica include the 1790 corrspondence between George Washington and the sexton of the first American synagogue in Newport, Rhode Island, sixteenth-century European torahs, and collections of historic ritual objects. Other exhibits trace Jewish history, explain dietary laws, and illustrate Jewish holidays and traditions.

There's even "Stars of David," the Jewish American Sports Hall of Fame, a collection of sports memorabilia honoring athletes such as Sandy Koufax, Hank Greenberg, and Mark Spitz. Aside from these exhibitions from its permanent collection, the museum often hosts special shows of Jewish culture, art, and history. The B'nai B'rith National Jewish Museum is located at 2020 K Street NW. Tours are given by appointment between 10:00 A.M. and 4:00 P.M. from Monday to Thursday and can be arranged by calling 857–6583; www.bnaibrith.org. Metro: Foggy Bottom or Farragut West (blue and orange lines).

Places to Stay in Foggy Bottom

The George Washington University Inn,
824 New Hampshire Avenue NW; 337–6620 or
(800) 426–4455,
fax 298–7499;
www.gwuinn.com
This well-furnished and well-run hotel is nicely positioned on a residential street close to both the Kennedy Center and the Foggy Bottom Metro stop. Its ninety-five rooms are split between suites and regular guest rooms. Moderate. Metro: Foggy Bottom (orange and blue lines).

Hotel Lombardy,
2019 Pennsylvania
Avenue NW;
828–2600 or
(800) 424–5486;
www.hotellombardy.com
Unless you're looking for

it, you might miss this European-style urban inn between downtown and Georgetown. Once an apartment house, the Lombardy has 127 well-appointed suites and guestrooms, many with kitchenettes and dining areas; the best rooms are on the renovated floors. As a bonus, it has the only attendant-operated, door cage elevator you're likely ever to find. Moderate. Metro: Foggy Bottom (orange and blue lines).

Melrose Hotel,
2430 Pennsylvania
Avenue NW;
955–6400;
www.melrosehotel.com
This European-style hotel predictably attracts many international visitors as well as performers who like its proximity to the Kennedy Center. Both Georgetown and downtown are a short walk away. Also check out the Melrose's clubby little bar, The Library, and its bistro-

style restaurant The Landmark, which is long on big salads and fish. Moderate. Metro: Foggy Bottom (orange and blue lines).

Suite or Apartment Hotels
Conventional hotels attract the most visitor attention, but don't overlook the District's many suite hotels, especially if you're traveling with kids or like the idea of returning to the comfort of your own space after a long day of work or sightseeing. Some of the best are conveniently located in Foggy Bottom. All of the following offer well-appointed suites with kitchens. Prices are moderate, but ask about weekend and other special rates, of which there are many.

One Washington Circle Hotel,
One Washington Circle NW;
872–1680 or
(800) 424–9671,
fax 887–4989;
www.thecirclehotel.com

Overlooks Foggy Bottom Metro. The hotel's moderately priced restaurant, The Circle Bistro, (293–5390) routinely draws praise from local food critics for its creative dishes. The cafe is open daily for breakfast, lunch, and dinner.

River Inn,
924 25th Street NW;
337–7600 or
(800) 424–2741,
fax: 337–6520;
www.theriverinn.com
e-mail riverinn@erols.com
Don't be surprised if you find your fellow guests lugging tubas and cellos (this is where it pays to be a flutist); the River Inn is a favorite long-term hideaway for musicians, actors, and other performers at the Kennedy Center just up the street.

State Plaza Hotel,
2117 E Street NW;
861–8200 or
(800) 424–2859;
www.stateplaza.com
Convenient to the State Department, George Washington University, and the Kennedy Center. The hotel's moderately priced Garden Cafe, a definite find with an outdoor patio and top-notch American cuisine, is popular with American and foreign diplomats. Open Monday through Friday 7:00 A.M. to 3:00 P.M. and 5:00 to 10:00 P.M., Saturday and Sunday 8:00 to 11:00 A.M. and 5:00 to 10:00 P.M., Sunday brunch 10:00 A.M. to 2:00 P.M.

Washington Suites,
2500 Pennsylvania Avenue NW;
333–8060;
www.washingtonsuites
hotel.com

This 124-suite hotel is handy to the Foggy Bottom Metro (orange and blue lines), the World Bank, and downtown. Georgetown is only a five-minute stroll away. Moderate.

Places to Eat in Foggy Bottom

Agua Ardiente,
1250 24th Street NW;
833–8500;
See page 89 for full description.

Blackie's,
1217 22nd Street NW;
333–1100.
See page 89 for full description.

Breadline,
1751 Pennsylvania Avenue, NW;
822–8900.
See page 77 for full description.

Chen's,
2542 Virginia Avenue NW;
965–4104.
See page 88 for full description.

Courtyard Cafe,
1227 25th Street NW;
785–1388.
See page 89 for full description.

Dish,
924 25th Street NW;
338–8707;
www.theriverinn.com/dining
Located in the River Inn, and not far from the Kennedy Center, Dish serves classic comfort food with a big difference in its ultra-chic

quarters. Chef Ronald Reda signs every dish personally in balsamic syrup, and well he should. This is an all-American menu with an elegant touch, including great buttermilk fried chicken and pork chops. George Clooney, like everyone else, loves the meat loaf sandwich; we don't know what he thought about the classic Wegman photographs of Weimaraners on the walls. Open for breakfast Monday through Friday from 7:30 A.M. to 10:30 P.M. and weekends 8:00 to 10:30 A.M. Lunch Monday through Friday from 11:30 A.M. to 2:30 P.M. and dinner every day from 5:00 to 10:30 P.M. Moderate. Metro: Foggy Bottom (orange and blue lines).

Grillfish,
1200 New Hampshire Avenue NW;
331–7310.
See page 89 for full description.

KC Cafe,
2700 F Street NW;
416–8560.
See page 90 for full description.

Kinkead's,
2000 Pennsylvania Avenue NW;
296–7700.
One of America's top food authorities recently wrote that when in Washington he could eat every meal at Kinkead's. That's no exaggeration—this American brasserie consistently makes the top of most everyone's list of places to dine in the capital. Everything is great, but Chef Robert Kinkead specializes in seafood dishes like Scandinavian salmon stew, baked halibut with crab

and Virginia ham, or maybe something from the extensive raw bar. Sinful desserts, Sunday brunch, and a world-class wine list too. Reservations essential. Expensive but worth it. Open daily 11:30 A.M. to 2:30 P.M. and 5:30 to 10:30 P.M. Metro: Foggy Bottom (orange and blue lines).

Marcel's,
2401 Pennsylvania Avenue NW;
296–1196.
See page 89 for full description.

Marshall's,
2524 L Street NW;
333–1155.
A neighborhood hangout that visitors find handy for dining before and after performances at the Kennedy Center. Mainly American food—burgers and salads—along with a nice selection of Italian dishes. Upstairs an English pub serves drinks, ESPN, and food. Open Monday through Thursday 11:00 A.M. to 2:00 A.M., Friday and Saturday until 3:00 A.M., Sunday until midnight. Inexpensive. Metro: Foggy Bottom (orange and blue lines).

Meiweh,
1200 New Hampshire Avenue NW;
833–2288.
See page 89 for full description.

Nectar,
824 New Hampshire Avenue NW,
298–9095;
www.gwuinn.com/nectar
Although it's just a short stroll from performances at the Kennedy Center, Nectar is worth a visit for breakfast, lunch, or dinner any time. Located in the George Washington Inn, this intimate and highly rated restaurant offers up a "modern American" menu of seafood and game, including tuna tartare at lunch and imaginatively prepared grilled fish and veal dishes at dinnertime; game, including pheasant with morels and asparagus, is usually a possibility. All this and a widely praised wine list too—that's probably why it's called Nectar. Courtyard dining in good weather. Nectar has room for only forty-two, so reservations are usually essential, especially on performance evenings. Open for breakfast Monday through Friday 7:00 to 10:00 A.M. and

Saturday and Sunday 8:00 to 10: 30 A.M. Lunch: Monday through Friday 11:30 A.M. to 2:30 P.M. Dinner: Sunday through Thursday 5:00 to 10:00 P.M.; Friday through Sunday 5:00 to 11:00 P.M. Expensive. Metro: Foggy Bottom (orange and blue lines).

The Roof Terrace,
2700 F Street NW;
416–8555.
See page 90 for full description.

The Venetian Room and Cafe Lombardy,
2019 Pennsylvania Avenue NW;
828–2600.
The intimate Venetian Room and the bright and informal Cafe Lombardy, both located in the Hotel Lombardy, are well worth visiting even if you're not a guest. Open daily 7:00 to 10:30 A.M., 11:30 A.M. to 2:30 P.M., and 5:30 to 9:30 P.M. Moderate. Metro: Foggy Bottom (orange and blue lines).

AUTHOR'S FAVORITE PLACES TO EAT IN FOGGY BOTTOM

Kinkead's

Dish

Marcel's

Grillfish

Nectar

Blackie's

Cafe Lombardy

Georgetown

A mix of smart shops, historic homes, and hip street life have made Georgetown one of Washington's liveliest and most desirable neighborhoods. But Georgetown was there first: Almost a century before the District of Columbia was created, Georgetown had a life of its own as a wealthy but inelegant Maryland river port that was the commercial gateway to the "west" (i.e., Ohio). In the eighteenth and early nineteenth centuries, an era that saw the founding of Georgetown University, Georgetown was also a slave-trading center and a key player in the tobacco trade at a time when tobacco was the lifeblood of the economy. The decline of the Chesapeake and Ohio Canal siphoned off the once-profitable Western trade and Georgetown fell on hard times, becoming, strange as its now seems, a smelly industrial town and one of Washington's worst slums. Georgetown was rescued in the 1930s when it was rediscovered and rehabilitated by officials of Roosevelt's New Deal. In the 1960s Georgetown was rediscovered all over again when President Kennedy's administration made it their headquarters and an enclave that became nationally known for a glittering lifestyle with chic dinner parties where Important People gathered to make Important Decisions.

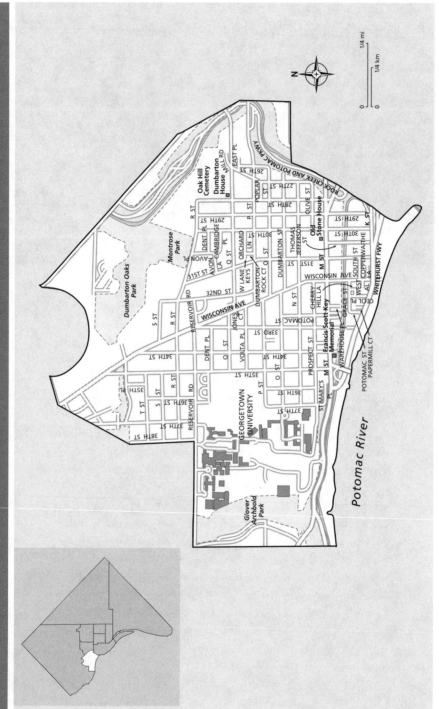

Potomac River

Oak Hill Cemetery
Dumbarton House
Montrose Park
Dumbarton Oaks Park
Old Stone House
Thomas Jefferson
Francis Scott Key Memorial
Glover Archbold Park
GEORGETOWN UNIVERSITY

N

0 1/4 mi
0 1/4 km

Georgetown was a town in its own right until 1871, when it was incorporated into Washington, D.C., and its historic and evocative street names were lettered, numbered, and made part of the city's grid. Georgetown is not integrated into the city's Metro system, however, having opted out to avoid the congestion and crowds that residents thought the Metro would bring. Bad decision—both arrived anyway. Given the problems of parking on Georgetown's narrow streets, when you visit, either walk from the nearest Metro station, which is Foggy Bottom/GWU (it'll take about twenty minutes), take a cab, or hop a Metrobus. Any of the 30-numbered buses (30, 32, 34, 35, 36) will take you from downtown to Georgetown; you can also transfer to these Metrobus routes from the Metro at 24th Street and Pennsylvania Avenue, near the Foggy Bottom stop. If you're coming from Dupont Circle, catch a D-2 or G-2 bus from 20th and P Streets.

The Georgetown Metro Connection, a privately operated bus service, makes it even easier for visitors to reach Georgetown from Dupont Circle, Foggy Bottom, and northern Virginia. The Connection's Line one runs from the Foggy Bottom/GWU Metro station past the Georgetown waterfront and then follows Wisconsin Avenue uphill as far as the Naval Observatory. Line two connects the Dupont Circle Metro station with the Metro station in Rosslyn, Virginia, just across the Potomac, making several stops in Georgetown's M Street shopping areas along the way. You can transfer between the two lines where they intersect at Wisconsin Avenue and M Street. Fares are $1.00 one-way, 35 cents with a Metrorail transfer. Buses run every ten minutes Monday through Thursday between 7:00 A.M. and midnight, Friday from 7:00 A.M. to 2:00 A.M., Saturday 8:00 A.M. to 2:00 A.M. and Sunday 8:00 A.M. to midnight. Stops are clearly marked with a blue sign. Call 625–7433; www.georgetowndc.com.

Although its main streets—M Street and Wisconsin Avenue—are definitely among Washington's well-worn tracks, this historic district offers a number of opportunities for visitors to leave the usual tourist treadmill behind and explore some often overlooked places that exude American culture and history.

TOP ATTRACTIONS IN GEORGETOWN

Dumbarton Oaks	The Old Stone House
Tudor Place	Chesapeake and Ohio Canal
Dumbarton House	Smith Row
Riggs Riley House	

One of them is **Dumbarton Oaks,** whose ultratraditional Georgian facade conceals a surprising trove of pre-Columbian, Roman, and Byzantine treasures assembled by career diplomat Robert Woods Bliss and his wife, Mildred. In the mansion's pre-Columbian wing, dazzling Inca masks, necklaces, and plates of hammered gold from ancient Peruvian tombs compete for attention with radiant displays of Aztec artifacts of solid gold and jade. Incidentally, the museum building, designed by Philip Johnson, is itself a gem—an octagonal structure of glass, marble, teak, and bronze surrounding a lovely little garden and fountain.

Other rooms contain a priceless collection covering more than eleven centuries of Byzantine art: luminous bronzes, mosaics, and ivories that turn their display cases into jewel boxes. Its centerpiece is the magnificent Sion Treasure, a collection of liturgical silver from sixth-century Constantinople that lay hidden for fourteen centuries.

Most of Dumbarton Oaks is given over to staff offices and research libraries for Byzantine and pre-Columbian studies that are administered by Harvard, which was deeded the house, gardens, and collections in 1940. Visitors may, however, wander through the house's sumptuous music room, with El Greco's *Visitation,* tapestries, and memories of the 1944 Dumbarton Oaks Conferences, where the Allies planned and shaped the United Nations.

Lovers of fine gardens will also want to stroll through Dumbarton Oaks' ten acres of formal gardens, among America's best, and one of Washington's truly special places. The gardens unfold downhill on a series of broad terraces with colorful blooms that change with the seasons. Better yet, lots of tree-shaded walks and benches make the gardens an inviting R&R stop, but picnics are out. Be sure not to miss **The Orangery,** a joyous collection of orange and lemon trees attached to the main building. The Orangery, which dates back to 1810, also houses jasmine trees and creeping fig. The Museum at Dumbarton Oaks, 1703 32nd Street NW; 339–6401; www.doaks.org, is open Tuesday through Sunday 2:00 to 5:00 P.M.; donations accepted. The garden entrance is at 31st and R Streets; open April through October 2:00 to 6:00 P.M.; November through March 2:00 to 5:00 P.M. Garden admission $6.00 for adults, $4.00 for children and seniors.

Back in 1816, when **Tudor Place** was completed, Georgetown was a thriving but noisy and disheveled tobacco port that Abigail Adams dismissed as "a dirty little hole." She could get pretty nasty, that Abigail, and she sure wouldn't say that today. While traffic and tumult may have lurked outside the massive gates of Tudor Place for nearly two centuries, this yellow stucco neoclassic mansion and its formal gardens have always been an oasis of urbanity and tranquillity.

AUTHOR'S FAVORITES IN GEORGETOWN

Dumbarton Oaks

Chesapeake and Ohio Canal

Martin's Tavern

Clyde's

Wisconsin Avenue Shops

Tudor Place was designed by William Thornton, the architect of the Octagon and the Capitol, for his friend Thomas Peter, a wealthy tobacco merchant and relative of Martha Washington. The Peter family then proceeded to make this estate their home for almost 200 years, which must be some kind of record for nomadic Americans. Through all of those years, Tudor Place was a distinguished home with distinguished visitors, including Robert E. Lee (also a Peter relative), Lafayette, and Henry Clay. Although it is one of Washington's finest Federal homes, Tudor Place is far from being a period house. The Peter family's long ownership and discerning tastes have created there a continuum of rarities acquired throughout the span of their occupancy, ranging from George Washington's furniture, silver, china, and other memorabilia to rare Oriental rugs and glass paintings collected in this century by Armistead Peter, the last of the family to reside there.

Before entering to start your guided tour, take a few minutes to see the mansion's historic North Garden, where, in azalea season, secluded walks lead to outbursts of showy whites and fiery pinks. But this southern formal garden, with its English boxwood hedges, also holds many year-round pleasures, including colorful magnolias, sprawling oaks that saw the mansion's first days, and an elliptical bowling green that dates back to the early 1800s.

Once inside, you'll surely be taken by the elegant simplicity of the "Saloon," a sitting room with a two-story wall of concave windows and a staggering view out over the Potomac and Virginia. Outside, overlooking the south lawn, a columned rotunda creates a templelike porch that is Tudor Place's signature architectural feature.

Although the drawing rooms and parlors, with their priceless portraits and Colonial-era furniture, are splendid indeed, your real favorite is likely to be the mansion's handsome dining room, where chairs that once belonged to George Washington grace a grand mahogany table set with gleaming silver and period china. Upstairs all visitors, especially those from the other side of the Potomac, are thrilled to see the guest room and four-poster that Robert E. Lee used on

Pleased as Punch

A plaque on the wall at 1054 31st Street commemorates Herman Hollerith, hardly a household name, but this gifted inventor launched the computer age from his workshop on this site. In 1880 Hollerith invented the punch card tabulating machine, after getting the idea of storing data on punched cards by watching a train conductor punch tickets. His machines took off in a big way, especially when the government used them to replace hundreds of clerks and save months of labor in tabulating the 1890 census. Still wondering why you should be interested in all this? To help you sort it out, I'll just mention that, in the early 1920s, Hollerith's Computer Tabulating Machine Company changed its name to International Business Machines.

his frequent visits. Tudor Place is located at 1644 31st Street NW; 965–0400. The Tudor Place Web site, www.tudorplace.org, carries a schedule of special events, including lectures and art exhibits. House tours, which last forty-five to sixty minutes, are Tuesday through Friday at 10:00 and 11:30 A.M. and at 1:00 and 2:30 P.M. Saturday tours are given on the hour from 10:00 A.M. to 3:00 P.M. Sunday on the hour from 10:00 A.M. to 3:00 P.M. No tours on Mondays or major holidays. The garden is open Monday through Saturday 10:00 A.M. to 4:00 P.M. and Sunday noon to 4:00 P.M. Suggested donations: $6.00 for the house, $2.00 for the garden.

Back on R Street you'll find two other oases of tranquility. ***Montrose Park*** is a preferred outdoor destination for Georgetowners looking for a little urban R&R—a primo place for dog walking, Frisbee flipping, sunbathing, or just getting the kids out of the house. Tennis courts are also available, but you can't reserve. And then there's ***Lover's Lane,*** a quiet walking path along the wall that separates the park from Dumbarton Oaks. Although it definitely has romantic connotations, Lover's Lane also has its practical side. If you follow it to the end, then walk through Dumbarton Oaks Park and follow the path upward, you'll surface near the Italian Embassy on Massachusetts Avenue and will have discovered a nifty (and scenic) shortcut between Georgetown and Embassy Row.

Farther along R Street, ***Oak Hill Cemetery*** may be a little too restful for some, but it has an elaborate redbrick gatehouse that looks like an Italian villa and a gorgeous little Gothic chapel that dates from 1850, but looks like it was built in the thirteenth century; both are easily reachable from the main gate at 30th and R Streets. For a map of the cemetery and the graves of the many notables that are buried there, visit the superintendent's office in the gatehouse.

Visiting hours; Monday through Friday 10:00 A.M. to 4:00 P.M. Closed evenings and weekends.

On your way down 28th Street, crane your neck to get a glimpse through the boxwoods and azaleas of *"Evermay,"* at number 1623. This Georgian mansion was considered the most elegant house in the city when it was built between 1792 and 1794, and it still is. Although no visitors are permitted except once a year as part of the Georgetown Garden Tour, a bronze plaque outside the entrance will fill you in on the history of this grand estate and the distinguished families that have lived there.

Architectural historians view **Dumbarton House** (not to be confused with Dumbarton Oaks) as a perfect example of the great Georgian manor houses built by wealthy Washington and tidewater Virginia merchants during the late 1700s. Dolley Madison fled to Dumbarton House when the British torched Washington in 1814. However, you'll probably remember it more for its wonderful collection of American cabinetry and furniture-making. In the library there's a gleaming secretary bookcase from 1775 New York, flanked by a pair of English globes showing the world of 1800. And if you want to see what Georgetown's busy port looked like in 1789, take a look at the background of the Peale portrait of the Stoddert children in the dining room.

In the music room, where women guests were exiled after dinner while husbands talked serious stuff, a 1795 Pembroke table is set for tea, consolation, perhaps, for missing all that early American guy talk; across the room a harp, piano, and violin of the same era stand ready for an eighteenth-century musicale.

In the upstairs bedroom you'll see that Washington political kitsch didn't begin with those Jack and Jackie drugstore plates when you spot the allegorical print of *America Paying Homage to France,* showing a native American princess in full headdress saluting an elegantly reclining France. This print was, *naturellement,* made in Paris. In addition to its elegant furnishings, Dumbarton House is the headquarters of the National Society of Colonial Dames. Dumbarton House, 2715 Q Street NW (337–2288; www.dumbartonhouse.org), conducts forty-five-minute tours Tuesday through Saturday at 10:15 and 11:15 A.M., 12:15 P.M., and 1:15 P.M. Admission is $5.00.

Next to Dumbarton House, tucked away on the grassy space behind the apartment house at 27th and Q Streets, is **Mt. Zion Cemetery,** the oldest predominantly black burial ground in Washington. The property originated in 1809 as a cemetery for slaves and freedmen, as opposed to the ritzy whites-only Oak Hill Cemetery visible next door. Mt. Zion was neglected for years, and its wooden markers disappeared; trustees, however, have removed most of the remaining grave markers, which have been recorded and stored pending eventual restoration of this historic site as a memorial to the historic and large black presence in Georgetown. If you look carefully at the back of the cemetery, you'll find the redbrick underground vault used as a hideout for slaves escaping north to freedom on the Underground Railroad.

The *Mt. Zion United Methodist Church,* at 1334 29th Street NW (www.forministry.com/church/home), is the oldest African-American congregation in the District, having been organized in 1816 by slaves and freedmen of Georgetown's thriving black community that were subjected to segregation by their original, mainly white church. The first Mt. Zion Church, which was a major stop on the Underground Railroad, burned down in 1880. Over the years many of the black parishioners either had moved away or were, before that, "sold to Georgia traders," but Mt. Zion retains its unique character. Its historic role in Georgetown's African-American community is commemorated in its *Heritage Center,* a cozy English cottage built in 1810 and located just around the corner at 2906 O Street. Admission to the Heritage Center and its archives is by appointment only; to set up a visit call 234–0148.

As you wander around on the east side of Wisconsin Avenue, you'll find plenty of mansions and row houses you'd like to wrap up and take home, but keep an eye out for some really special places such as the *Colonial House,* at 1305 30th Street, home of Miss Lydia English's tony finishing school for wealthy young women until the Civil War, when the army threw out the girls and brought the wounded of Bull Run there to recuperate. The building was later turned into an apartment house, which it is today.

Cooke's Row, which extends from 3007–3027 Q Street, is a cluster of four duplexes built in 1868 in, atypically for Federal Georgetown, the Italian style. These grand and luxurious Victorians, with their ornate dormers, mansard roofs, and bay windows, were patterned after an Italian villa and are among Georgetown's grandest homes.

The "Social Safeway"

The seemingly standard mega-grocery at 1855 Wisconsin gets its nickname from the Washington notables who flock there. Where else are you going to routinely find cabinet officers squeezing the lemons, pundits prowling the produce, or a certain very well-known TV news anchor sniffing the cantaloupe? The Safeway is also a meeting place for zillions of single Georgetowners who over the years have met, not really by chance, among the cleansers or condiments, then made plans for dinner, a movie, and who knows what else. I once spotted Elizabeth Taylor shopping at the Social Safeway and still haven't gotten over it. Visiting hours: 6:00 A.M. to 11:00 P.M. daily. Black tie optional.

Camelot on the Potomac

Jack Kennedy loved Georgetown and lived there in five different houses. As a freshman congressman, the future president established bachelor quarters at 1528 31st Street, then, after his 1950 election to the Senate, moved to 1400 34th Street. As newlyweds, Jack and Jackie set up their first Georgetown home at 3321 Dent Place. Later in his senatorial term the Kennedys rented the house at 2808 P Street. Jack and Jackie's longest residence in Georgetown was at 3307 N Street, where they lived from 1957 until they moved to 1600 Pennsylvania Avenue. The doorstop of the N Street house became famous as the place where the president-elect announced his cabinet choices. Across the street, on the wall at 3302 N Street, you'll see the plaque presented to the owner by a White House press corps grateful for the shelter, coffee, and doughnuts she supplied them during their long waits for Kennedy's appearances during the icy winter of 1960–61.

In the backyard of **2726 N Street,** you'll find a large and beautiful Chagall mosaic on the back wall of the garden. The story is that Marc Chagall was a close friend of the owner and, after a visit, bestowed this wonderful gift on his host. You and I should be so lucky. The mosaic is best viewed from the 28th Street sidewalk. The house also has a handsome bronze sculpture in its front garden.

The houses at **2806–2812 N Street** represent three of the finest examples of Federal architecture in Georgetown. All three were built between 1813 and 1817; number 2812 is where Susan Decatur, the widow of naval hero Stephen Decatur, lived after her husband was killed in a duel.

The **Riggs Riley House** at 3038 N Street is a splendid Federal home built in 1816 by a prominent banker, but better known more recently as the home of Averell Harriman and his wife, Pamela. The Harrimans turned the house over to their friend Jackie Kennedy after President Kennedy's assassination. After living there a month, she bought the house across the street at 3017 N Street.

At the corner of N and 30th Street, you'll visit a medical compound from Washington's Civil War days, when Georgetown was an important center for treating thousands of the wounded. Those bright, narrow little row houses from 2916 to 2924 N were nurses' housing for the hospital across the street at 2929 N, now a private residence. Down the block, the nicer houses, starting at 2903 N, were reserved for the hospital's doctors.

At 1220 31st Street, you can browse through one of the city's most distinguished collections of antique prints and maps from all over the world at the **Old Print Gallery.** The gallery specializes in city views and maps from the nineteenth century and earlier, including Brooklyn in 1816 and a bird's-eye view of Abraham Lincoln's Washington of 1861 and a spectacular 1720 city map of

Rome. 965–1818; www.oldprintgallery.com. Open Monday through Saturday 10:00 A.M. to 5:30 P.M.

The **Old Stone House,** at 3051 M Street, is Washington's oldest dwelling. The house started out in 1765 as a cabinetmaker's workshop, after which it was used variously as either a private home or place of business. It's now run by the National Park Service, which uses it as a small house museum of pre-Revolutionary life, with the spinning wheels and furniture of the period; check to see about taking in one of the frequent craft demonstrations. The house's garden/orchard makes a great place to take it easy or even picnic with the locals. Open Wednesday through Sunday 9:00 A.M. to 5:00 P.M.; 426–6851; www.nps.gov/rocr/oldstonehouse.

Washington's legendary **Blues Alley,** true to its name, is tucked away off the alley at 1073 Wisconsin Avenue. World-class jazz artists like Wynton Marsalis, Benny Green, and Nancy Wilson have performed there, which is one reason that the *New York Times* called it "the nation's finest supper club." The food is almost as good as the music, which is saying a lot. With all this good stuff going on, you must reserve by calling 337–4141 or visiting www.blues alley.com. Open seven days a week, with nightly shows from 8:00 to 10:00 P.M. and a third show at midnight on Friday and Saturday. Dinner from 6:00 P.M.

With a little historical imagination, you can get a sense of the long-vanished port of Georgetown at the corner of Wisconsin Avenue and K Street, which 200 years ago was the heart of the town's busy waterfront. This cluster of redbrick commercial buildings is the Old Dodge Warehouse, which was built in 1800 next to the Potomac docks as warehouses for Havana "seegars," Cuban molasses, Santo Domingo coffee, and the other cargoes of a busy port.

Washington Harbour, on the Georgetown waterfront at 3000 K Street, between 29th and 31st, is a major residential and office complex, which will interest you chiefly for its lively restaurant scene and riverside promenade. In good weather it's great fun to dine outside next to the Potomac and gaze out

Black History Tour

One weekend a month a guided walking tour takes visitors on a stroll to places that dramatize Georgetown's long and rich African-American heritage. One of these is "Herring Hill," the large black enclave between Rock Creek Park and 29th Street, that was named after the fish that residents used to catch in the creek. Mt. Zion and other local churches are also on the itinerary. Tours leave from the Old Stone House; call 426–6851 for dates and times. You can get a preview and a map for a self-guided tour by logging on to www.nps.gov/rocr/olst/black.htm.

Art and Antiques on M Street

You'll find some of Washington's top galleries and antiques stores along M Street, in the blocks between 28th and 30th Streets. Among the best:

American Studio+,
2906 M Street;
965–3273.
For the latest from Alessi and other cutting-edge U.S. and European designers of tableware and ceramics. Also the latest in zoomy watches and pens. Monday through Saturday 11:00 A.M. to 6:00 P.M., Sunday 1:00 to 5:00 P.M.;

Grafix,
2904 M Street;
342–0610.
For vintage posters and an encyclopedic collection of *New Yorker* and *Fortune* covers dating back to the '20s. Ask to see the posters for the long-vanished transatlantic luxury liners of the '30s and '40s. Thursday through Saturday noon to 7:00 P.M., Sunday noon to 6:00 P.M.

Janis Aldridge,
2900 M Street;
338–7710.
Specializes in rare botanical and architectural prints, along with antique European silver and furniture. Tuesday through Saturday 11:00 A.M. to 5:00 P.M.

Spectrum Gallery,
1132 29th Street;
333–0954.
www.spectrumgallery.com
For colorful posters and prints, along with a selection of nice oils and photographs. Tuesday through Saturday, noon to 6:00 P.M.; Sunday noon to 5:00 P.M.

Justine Mehlman,
2824 Pennsylvania Avenue;
337–0613.
The place to find antique jewelry of all kinds, along with Art Deco ceramics from Paris and art nouveau picture frames and candlesticks. Open Monday through Saturday 10:00 A.M. to 6:00 P.M., Sunday noon to 5:00 P.M.

Bridge Street Books,
2814 Pennsylvania Avenue;
965–5200.
One of those book stores every neighborhood should be so lucky to have. This one's for lovers of serious nonfiction; heavy on politics, literature, history, and film; remainders table out front. Open Monday through Thursday 11:00 A.M. to 10:00 P.M., Friday and Saturday until 11:00 P.M.; Sunday noon to 6:00 P.M.

at the Lincoln Memorial, the Kennedy Center and, across the way, Theodore Roosevelt Island, now a wooded park but once an important Civil War encampment used for the defense of Washington. But it's the river that's the big attraction for diners, who enjoy the nonstop aquatic pageant of racing sculls from Georgetown and other schools, frequent sightseeing ships, and a luxury yacht or cabin cruiser tied up across the way. The Washington Harbour restaurants are *Sequoia,* with a large glassed-in dining room with great river views and lots of action at the outside bar and tables, *Tony and Joe's* with seafood specialties (none from the Potomac), and *Bangkok Joe's* (no relation) for Thai street food with an elegant twist. All serve great Sunday brunches Sequoia, 944–4200, is open Monday through Saturday from 11:30 A.M. to 3:30 P.M. and Sunday from 5:30 to 11:30 P.M.; weekend brunch 10:00 A.M. to 3:30 P.M. Tony and Joe's, 944–4545, is open daily from 11:00 A.M. to 10:00 P.M. Bangkok Joe's, 333–4422, is open Sunday through Thursday 11:30 A.M. to 11:00 P.M. until midnight Friday and Saturday.

Washington Harbour is also home port or a stop for the fleet of sightseeing boats that cruise the Potomac, giving passengers a unique look at some of Washington's best-known places. Boat tours of the District's waterside monuments glide past magnificent views of the Washington Monument, the majestic white colonnades of the Lincoln Memorial, the Kennedy Center, and the Chrysler Airflow swirl of the Watergate. Some will also take you for a close-up look at seldom-visited Roosevelt Island, a ninety-acre wilderness park in the middle of the Potomac that was once a farm, then a Union Army camp, and is now an urban oasis of wildlife and wildflowers. Some will take you downriver to historic Alexandria, Virginia, and its Old Town of stately Federal mansions and lively street life. Cruises run from April 1 through October. For information about *Capitol River Cruises,* which offers narrated fifty-minute trips within the District only, phone (800) 405–5511 or visit www.capitolrivercruises.com. Adults $10.00, children $5.00.

Boats of the Alexandria-based *Potomac Riverboat Company* (703–548–9000; www.potomacriverboatco.com), call at Washington Harbour, then cruise past the District's monuments on their way back to Alexandria. Some boats continue from Alexandria to Washington's home at Mt. Vernon. Prices range from $8.00 to $26.00 for adults, $5.00 to $13.00 for children, depending on the route you choose. Potomac Riverboat operates cruises on weekends only in April and October and up to six daily from May through September. Both lines sell refreshments aboard, but think about bringing your own lunch or snacks from one of Georgetown's patisseries. You'll find more information about both lines at the ticket booth on the water at the foot of 31st Street NW.

If you're on a spring visit, you should know that Washington Harbour is the best place to watch the annual *Dragon Boat Festival,* one of Washington's most exciting and colorful spectacles. The boats themselves are worth the trip—these are ornate boats in red, blue, green, yellow, and other shades, with dragon's heads on the prow, dragon's scales on the side and a forked tail at the end. And they're 45-feet long, with a crew of twenty who paddle in unison, plus two members who mark the strokes with a drum. About forty-five teams compete in a series of heats over a 1,500-meter course between the Key Bridge and Thompson's Boathouse. The race continues an ancient tradition that began in the third century B.C. and begins when the dragonheads are brought to life symbolically by dotting the eyes with paint. The ceremony is held on the fifth day of the fifth month of the lunar calendar. If your terrestrial calendar doesn't stretch that far, find the exact dates and more details by going to www.dragon boatfestivaldc.com, or phoning the Georgetown Visitor Center for information at 333–1600. Hint: In 2004 this was the third week in May. The races are held over a weekend on Saturday from 10:00 A.M. to 5:00 P.M. with the finale the following day from 10:00 A.M. to 4:00 P.M.

In season, which is April to November, you won't want to miss the *Georgetown,* a replica of an early canal boat, for a ride on the **Chesapeake and Ohio Canal,** which is now a National Historic Park. During these hour-long mule-drawn excursions, you'll pass through locks and hear from period-costumed guides. You'll also see some of the canal's original warehouses, built in 1828 and now reincarnated as sales and office space, and you'll envy the Washingtonians who jog, bicycle, or amble along the towpath. The *Georgetown* hurtles along at speeds reaching 4 miles per hour, so fasten those seat belts! Although you'll enjoy the leisurely pace, the slow speed is the reason that the canal, which was conceived as a 185-mile freight artery connecting the port of Georgetown with the West, never panned out commercially, losing out to the railroads despite the political and financial support of heavy hitters like George Washington and Thomas Jefferson. No reservations, but to hear more, call the Park Service at 653–5190 for sailing times, which vary during the season. Get your tickets at the visitor center at the rear of 1057 Thomas Jefferson Street: $8.00 for adults, $5.00 for children. The visitor center is open in season from 9:00 A.M. to 4:30 P.M. and from November to March on weekends only 10:00 A.M. to 4:00 P.M.

On your walk up Wisconsin Avenue, you'll find a profusion of stores with the usual names offering the usual running shoes, designer jeans, and legible clothing. But if you look selectively, you'll be rewarded with visits to the fine specialty shops and restaurants for which Georgetown has long been renowned.

Start just below the intersection of Wisconsin and M at **Ching Ching Cha,** a corner of perfect repose and serenity on busy Wisconsin Avenue, Ching Ching Cha, a Chinese tea house, has everything for the lover of fine teas and the ancient rituals that go with them. The shop serves and sells every kind of tea imaginable, along with tea meals of miso salmon and curried chicken, and a wide assortment of kettles, cups, and other tea paraphernalia you'll need to hold a special tea ceremony in your own home. If that's your plan, you'd better snaffle up a few of Ching Ching Cha's low rosewood tables and pillows,

Paddle Your Own Canoe

If gazing at the Potomac and the C&O Canal has started you thinking about your own nautical expedition, you're in luck. At *Jack's Boathouse,* at 3500 K Street, not far from the foot of Wisconsin Avenue, you can rent a canoe or kayak and paddle the Potomac for $10 an hour or $30 per day. Just be sure and get some river safety instructions first—the Potomac can be hazardous. Jack's is open between April 1 and November 1 from 8:00 A.M. to sunset. 337–9642.

Fletcher's Boat House is 2 miles upriver from Georgetown, so you can either drive or, better yet, walk there along the C&O Canal towpath; it'll take about forty minutes. When you arrive you'll find one-stop shopping for recreation involving the river or the canal. Fletcher's will rent you a canoe ($10 an hour, $20 per day) or rowboat ($10 and $18). Fletcher's will also rent you a bike to ride the towpath for $8.00 an hour (two-hour minimum) or $12.00 per day.

If fishing is your passion, Fletcher's is just the place for you. In 1608, near Fletcher's secluded cove, Captain John Smith (who had earlier hooked Pocahontas) reported fish "lying so thickke with their heads above water . . . we attempted to catch them with our frying pans." Well, the Potomac hasn't come back *that* strongly, so you can leave your skillet at home. Instead, let owner Ray Fletcher rent you a rowboat and sell you bait, tackle, and a D.C. fishing license so you can join the regulars and a surprising number of foreign and American visitors in fishing for white perch and fat striped bass. You can e-mail or phone Ray to find out how the fish will be running during your breakaway, especially if you're in town during the spring spawning run, when these waters teem with shad and you can watch the cormorants swoop down to dive underwater for herring. There's also a small snack bar and large picnicking area. Fletcher's does not rent fishing rods. Fletcher's, at 4940 Canal Road at Reservoir Road NW, 244–0461; www.fletchersboathouse.com. Open daily 7:30 A.M. to dusk from mid-March to Thanksgiving.

then figure out how to slip them into your car or onto the plane. Tea with sweets and dumplings is served on those tables Monday through Friday from 2:30 to 5:30 P.M. Ching Ching Cha, at 1063 Wisconsin Avenue NW; 333–8288. Open 11:30 A.M. to 10:00 P.M. daily.

Martin's Tavern has been a Georgetown tradition since it opened on the day after Prohibition was repealed in 1933, which in Washington restaurant years, is equal to being in town since the Van Buren administration. In the '50s, when they lived just up O Street, Martin's was Jack and Jackie's neighborhood hangout. The Kennedys, like today's regulars, probably liked Martin's cozy atmosphere where Tiffany glass drop lamps hang over cozy wooden booths and a real bar where patrons are just as likely to order martinis or scotch as chardonnay. So slide into a battered wooden booth, and enjoy the clubby atmosphere of a Georgetown institution. Martin's menu is also special—where else these days can you find comfort food like the elusive welsh rarebit or shepherd's pie and local specialties like shad roe and first-rate crab cakes? And the hamburgers just might be the best in the city. Also great for breakfast and weekend brunch. Martin's Tavern, at 1264 Wisconsin Avenue NW, is open from 10:00 A.M. to 11:00 P.M. Sunday through Thursday, from 8:00 A.M. to 12:30 A.M. on Friday and Saturday; 333–7370; www.martins-tavern.com.

Random Harvest is the place to find antique furniture, especially restorations of period pieces ranging from antebellum to New Deal. The selection includes American-made hutches and tables of pine, along with a wide selection of vintage prints, especially botanicals. You'll also find European armoires, commodes with wood inlaid tops, and maybe even a mega-bed with posts that look like the pillars in St. Peter's in the Vatican. Random Harvest also offers distinctive outdoor chairs, tables, cachepots, and a lot of other excuses to start furnishing your garden. Random Harvest, at 1313 Wisconsin Avenue, 333–5569, is open Monday through Thursday and Saturday 11:00 A.M. to 6:00 P.M., Friday 11:00 A.M. to 8:00 P.M. and Sunday, from noon to 6:00 P.M.

Big Planet Comics, at 3145 Dumbarton Avenue NW, just off Wisconsin Avenue, is one of the city's top comic book outlets, where the motto is "we're serious about comics." This is where you'll find every comic and cartoon book you've ever heard of or remember, including my favorites, those eternal sweethearts, Archie and Veronica. Great for reliving your youth or finding out what's new in comics. 342–1961; www.bigplanetcomics.com.

The Tomb of the Well-Known Mascot

This is very weird, but you shouldn't leave Washington without knowing about that stone tablet on the wall of 1066 Wisconsin that memorializes a dog. This was not just your everyday pooch, but "Bush, the Old Fire Dog," beloved mascot of the Vigilant Volunteer Fire Company, which occupied this site in the 1860s. Bush died in July 1869 under mysterious circumstances, probably poisoned by a rival fire company in a day of cutthroat competition between the city's firefighters. Although RIP is inscribed on the tablet, the site of Bush's grave is not definitely known; a recent *Washington Flyer* story speculates that the murdered mutt was buried by his bereaved owners under the firehouse, minus his tail, which for years was reverently kept in the firehouse in a glass case. The building is the oldest firehouse in the city; over the door you can still see the "V" for Vigilant. Today it is home to Papa Razzi, a popular Italian restaurant. If you ask about Bush's tail, they will smirk, then deny knowing anything about it. Obviously, this is another Washington cover-up.

"Georgetown Bazaar"

Although the neighborhood is much more suitable for Harper's Bazaar, rather than the Algiers version, you'll find strongholds of collective bargaining scattered among Georgetown's tony shops. All along Wisconsin Avenue, especially at the corners of N and Potomac Streets, street merchants with folding tables will offer you their wares, mainly knockoff Kate Spade handbags, Gucci purses that never saw Rome, and Swiss Army watches crafted with care in New Jersey.

If you shop at **Baldaquin** you'll not only sleep better, but you might (no offense meant) even smell better. Downstairs you'll find imported linens, duvet covers, and sheets from upscale European producers such as Frette and Porthault. Upstairs, Baldaquin offers choices for your table, such as Herend china and Baccarat crystal. Owner Lisa Mullins Thompson will also sell you the bed of your dreams (so to speak), perhaps one handmade and carved by Simon Horn, said to be England's top bedmaster (if that's a real word). To round out all of this pampering, Baldaquin also sells a definitely upscale line of French bath oils and gels. And if all this nighttime luxury is making you think harder about marriage, Ms. Thompson will happily help you assemble your wedding list because "Baldaquin is changing the way Washingtonians are getting married," a goal not to be snoozed at. Baldaquin, 1413 Wisconsin Avenue NW; 625–1600, fax 625–1631, is open Tuesday through Saturday 10:00 A.M. to 6:00 P.M.; www.baldaquin.com.

georgelivesonin georgetown

At the corner of 33rd and Prospect Streets you'll find a former police call box that has been rescued, repainted, and remade into a brightly colored mini-shrine to Beatle George Harrison.

Although Baldaquin specializes in European craftsmen, next door, at **Appalachian Spring,** the emphasis is strictly all-American, with works by homegrown designers and craftspeople. This is the place to find a huge assortment of cutting boards and other housewares of hand-carved woods, along with handmade designer pottery and ceramics. Appalachian Spring's artisan collection also features textiles, including colorful place mats, quilts, and rag dolls for the kids. Appalachian Spring, 1415 Wisconsin Avenue NW; 337–5780. Open Monday through Friday 10:00 A.M. to 8:00 P.M. Saturday 10:00 A.M. to 6:00 P.M., Sunday noon to 6:00 P.M.

For a smallish shop, **Phoenix,** at 1514 Wisconsin Avenue NW, carries an astonishing and vibrant array of quality Mexican jewelry, Latin American ceramics, and contemporary clothing in natural fibers by noted designer Eileen Fisher. Local diplomats and lots of savvy Georgetowners flock to this local landmark every time owner Sharon Hays returns from Mexico with her usual haul of silver, antiques, and fine art. Find out why from 10:00 A.M. to 6:00 P.M. Monday through Saturday. Sunday hours in winter are noon to 5:00 P.M. and in summer from 1:00 to 6:00 P.M.; 338–4404.

Amid all of these tough choices, you might want to wander across the street into **Marvelous Market,** at the corner of Wisconsin and P for a little R&R and give your credit card a chance to cool off. Essentially an upscale grocery and bakery, the market has a battery of coffee machines ready to re-caffeinate you with the most exotic concoctions along with the croissants, Danish, and other goodies you'll need to go with them. The market also offers a variety of pizzas

Hollywood on the Potomac

If you get a sense of déjà vu on your wanderings through Georgetown, it's probably because this charming and photogenic neighborhood has appeared in many Hollywood films.

The best-known film location of all are the *The Exorcist* steps, from that memorable scene where Father Damien takes a fatal header down a steep flight of ninety-seven stairs. You'll find these steps, now used by students and seekers of cardiovascular perfection, at Prospect and 36th Streets NW, next to the Victorian D.C. Transit car barn. *The Exorcist* also included other scenes shot on the nearby Georgetown campus and at Holy Trinity Church at 3513 N Street NW.

Some of the many other films with Georgetown footage:

Suspect, in which Cher and Dennis Quaid investigate a murder in Georgetown's waterfront parking lot along K Street.

No Way Out, in which Kevin Costner jogs along the Chesapeake & Ohio Canal and later bails out of a moving car on the Whitehurst Freeway (involving Kevin in a fall of at least 100 feet), then heads for the equally fictitious "Georgetown metro station" (actually Georgetown Park Mall).

Georgetown Park Mall was also used in several scenes from Governor Arnold Schwarzenegger's *True Lies* and in Jean Claude Van Damme's *Time Cop.*

And let's not forget TV's *West Wing,* which often films in Georgetown, including Josiah Bartlet's mawkish commencement speech on the Georgetown campus.

Flea Market, Georgetown Style

Addicted to flea markets? Georgetown's may not be the cheapest you've ever seen, but it's probably one of the toniest and most socially acceptable. This is just the place to pick up Muffy and Jason's castoffs, along with a lot of other stuff. You'll find it across from the "Social Safeway," natch, in the schoolyard at the corner of Wisconsin and 34th. Open Sunday 8:30 A.M. to 5:00 P.M.

---

and some great in- and outdoor people-watching tables. 3217 P Street NW; 333–2591. Open from 8:00 A.M. to 9:00 P.M. Monday through Saturday, 8:00 A.M. to 8:00 P.M. Sunday.

Proper Topper, at 3213 P Street NW, gives new meaning to the word eclectic. True to its name here you'll find hats of every era—cloches, fedoras, and lids from your favorite '30s movies. But there's also an exciting assortment of hip and imaginative gifts, women's dresses from the Roaring Twenties, great jewelry, retro sunglasses, and books. Call 333–6200; www.propertopper.com. Open Monday through Friday from 10:00 A.M. to 8:30 P.M., Saturday 10:00 A.M. to 7:00 P.M., Sunday noon to 6:00 P.M.

A few steps from Wisconsin Avenue, at 3241 P, you'll find the ***Bryn Mawr Lantern Bookshop,*** which lives up to its name by operating for the benefit of the famous college. This bright and attractive shop is well-stocked with lightly used books and well-run by volunteer staff, all of whom would be happy to see you walk in with a few hundred books to donate to their favorite cause. Call 333–3222; www.his.com/~lantern. Open Monday through Friday 11:00 A.M. to 4:00 P.M., Saturday 11:00 A.M. to 5:00 P.M., Sunday noon to 4:00 P.M.

Just Paper and Tea, across the street at 3232 P, sells just that—luxurious stationery, invitations for classy weddings, exotic teas, and a wide selection of Florentine paper seldom seen this far from the Arno. Call 333–9141.

Back on Wisconsin Avenue, you'll find a slew of great antique and decorative arts shops in the blocks between Q Street and Reservoir Road. ***August Georges,*** at 1523 Wisconsin Avenue, will sell or show you everything you'd want for your home, from sixteenth-century prints to upscale bed linens from Pratesi and even some snazzy, belt-driven "architectural fans." Wonderful furniture, too; just check out the George Smith chairs and the other top-quality, top-designer pieces. Call 337–5110; www.augustgeorges.com. Open Monday through Friday 9:00 A.M. to 5:00 P.M. and Saturday 11:00 A.M. to 4:00 P.M.

Gore-Dean is another treasure trove of museum-quality antiques, with an eclectic collection of nineteenth-century French mirrors, Asian ceramic figures, and Chinese lacquer tables. Pratesi bed linens and garden furniture, too. 1525 and 1529 Wisconsin Avenue NW. Open Monday through Friday 9:30 A.M. to 5:30 P.M., Saturday 10:00 A.M. to 5:00 P.M., Sunday noon to 6:00 P.M.; 625–1776; www.Gore-Dean.com.

If you've been hankering after those vacation dinners in Ocho Rios or Kingston, look in on **Red Ginger** at 1564 Wisconsin Avenue, a Caribbean bistro with jerk chicken, chutneys, and a host of other dishes sure to bring back memories of the islands. Call 965–2009. Open 5:00 to 11:00 P.M. Tuesday through Thursday, 5:00 to 11:30 P.M. Friday, 11:30 A.M. to 11:30 P.M. Saturday, and 11:30 A.M. to 10:00 P.M. Sunday.

My vote for most beautiful shop in D.C. goes to **Marston Luce,** a storefront luminous with eighteenth- and nineteenth-century French antiques, especially pine armoires and tables. This citadel of exquisite taste will also gladly sell you a nice Provençal buffet, a lovely flowered screen from Louis Napoleon's Paris, or a peaceful French landscape painting. As a nice touch for your garden, snap up that bucket of vintage petanque balls so you'll be the first in your neighborhood to lawn bowl, French-style. Expensive, but lots cheaper than a trip to France. Marston Luce, 1651 Wisconsin Avenue NW; 775–9460. Monday through Saturday 11:00 A.M. to 6:00 P.M.

Patisserie Poupon, at 1645 Wisconsin Avenue, 342–3248, is a great place to know about for a break or a light lunch. Favorites include wonderful croissants, light salads, a plate of charcuterie, or baguette sandwiches. Open Tuesday through Saturday 8:00 A.M. to 6:30 P.M., Sunday 8:00 A.M. to 4:00 P.M. Before leaving try a slice of a chocolate cake, which will provide a sugar surge powerful enough to last until at least the next stop, which is:

Addison/Ripley Fine Art, at 1670 Wisconsin Avenue, is one of the city's most renowned galleries, with regular exhibits of contemporary art, sculpture, and photography. To find out what's on when you're in D.C., go to their Web

Stars and Fire Marks

On the walls of many old Georgetown buildings you'll spot large metal stars, which were not meant just to be decorative. Instead these "rod stars" secured the ends of iron poles that ran through each end of a building and held them together.

As you stroll through Georgetown you'll also see little oval plaques on the walls of many houses, some with a hose, tree, or eagle, each symbol representing a different insurance company. Those "fire marks" indicated to volunteer firemen that the house was insured, thus assuring them that they'd be rewarded for saving that home. History records a number of occasions when firemen allowed uninsured houses to burn or even, some say, would themselves do a little selective torching.

site; www.addisonripleyfineart.com or give them a call at 339–5180. Open Tuesday through Saturday 11:00 A.M. to 6:00 P.M.

Carling Nichols is an Aladdin's cave of rare and exotic Chinese antiques. Treasures in the classical and graceful Ming style, mostly from the eighteenth and nineteenth century, including lacquer boxes, stone statues, tables, and screens. 1675 Wisconsin Avenue; 338–5600. Open Tuesday through Saturday noon to 5:00 P.M.

And at the end of this sumptuous strip, you'll find *A Mano,* at 1677 Wisconsin Avenue, where, for a few (well, maybe more than a few) bucks, you can buy yourself the snazziest ceramics in town. True to its name, A Mano specializes in handmade tableware, especially Italian majolica and French faience; it also carries a broad selection of linens and decorative objects, including wonderful cachepots and rooster-head wine carafes from Umbrian workshops. Open Monday through Saturday 10:00 A.M. to 6:00 P.M., Sunday noon to 5:00 P.M.; 298–7200.

At 1524 33rd Street you'll find a survivor of Georgetown's earliest days, the eighteenth-century *Yellow Tavern* or *White Horse Inn,* its name depending on what year you did your drinking. Back in the 1700s, Georgetowners gathered in taverns like these, then known as "ordinaries," which were in fact the municipal centers of their times. Here colonials held town meetings, plotted to give King George III the heave-ho, and guzzled the drinks of the day, including rum punches and "flips" (ale sweetened with sugar, molasses, and rum). As a plaque points out, this tavern, back in the colonial days when 33rd Street was called Market Street, was a favored hangout for travelers, merchants, and even Thomas Jefferson. Next door you'll see the innkeeper's house, also clearly marked. Beyond that look sharp at 1528 33rd Street, where you'll discover, tucked away in a tiny courtyard, one of Georgetown's hidden houses.

For a perfect example of Georgetown's ability to come up with hidden nooks and crannies, stick your head into *Pomander Walk,* a tiny dead-end mews just off Volta Place between 33rd and 34th Streets. Pomander Walk, which consists of ten cozy row houses, each painted a different pastel color, started out as Bell's Court, a group of homes rented by African-American laborers and named for inventor Alexander Graham Bell, who lived in the neighborhood and owned a sizable chunk of nineteenth-century Georgetown. It's hard to believe now, but these charming dwellings were condemned in the 1950s; thanks to Georgetown's post–World War II housing boom, they were rescued and restored.

At 34th Street think about turning left and heading downhill to O Street, a leafy (and bumpy—the residents like it that way) cobblestone street where you'll see the peculiar tracks of Georgetown's long-vanished cable-powered

Tours for Voyeurs

If you're frustrated at not being able to peek inside all those splendid Georgetown homes, try to arrange your visit for the weekend after Easter and take the annual **Georgetown House Tour,** the only time that some of the neighborhood's finest homes open their doors to visitors. The tour takes visitors to six homes on Saturday; six more are open the following day. Tickets are $30 per person per day, but $50 buys you both days of gawking and envy; a sumptuous afternoon tea at St. John's Church is included in the ticket price. Children under ten are not permitted. To order tickets, call 333–2287, ext. 50 or fax 338–3921. Tickets may also be ordered on the Internet at www.georgetownhousetour.com.

And if you're interested in flowers, the first Saturday in May is **Georgetown Garden Day,** when self-guided tours will take you to twelve of Georgetown's finest private gardens. Garden Day hours at 10:00 A.M. to 5:00 P.M. Tickets cost $25 if purchased in advance or $30 on tour day. Get them by turning up at Christ Church, 31st and O Streets; on the day of the tour or reserve by either calling 965–1560 or e-mailing www.georgetowngardentour.com.

streetcar system. O Street is also lined with fine homes, each of which, in a place as old as Georgetown, has a past.

The gaudiest history, however, may belong to the **_Bodisco House_** at 3322 O, named for Baron Alexander de Bodisco, Russian ambassador to the United States from 1837 until 1854. Bodisco was probably a terrific diplomat and surely a credit to the czar, but is remembered today for his remarkable marriage to Washingtonian Harriet Williams. The wedding took place in this house in June 1839, when Bodisco was sixty-three ("short and stout with . . . a shining brown wig") and Harriet was lovely and sixteen. More than a few eyebrows were raised, but that didn't keep the ceremony from being a high point of the Georgetown social season, with Washington glitterati like President Van Buren, Henry Clay, and the entire diplomatic corps in attendance, proving once again that official and social Washington will turn out for almost anything. Defying all bets and leers, this April-December couple, delicately referred to at the time as "Beauty and the Beast," apparently got along very well, producing six children. The Bodisco house became a Washington social center famous for its lavish and frequent entertaining. When the baron died in 1854, he was buried in Georgetown's Oak Hill cemetery under an obelisk proclaiming his full titles. As for Harriet, she married the British military attaché, presumably another beauty, and lived happily ever after (again). Unfortunately, the Bodisco House is not open to the public.

Thomas Jefferson contributed $50 to the cost of building **St. John's Episcopal Church,** at 3240 O Street, a quintessential colonial church in the Federal style. Dolley Madison was a regular at St. John's, as was Francis Scott Key. The church building was started in 1796 and opened in 1804. Since then, the church and its adjoining parish house have undergone a few modifications, but retain their clean, classic lines and the original "pepper pot" belfry. Inside this classic, spare, high-ceilinged church are fine stained glass windows and, unexpectedly, a mosaic floor that will remind you more of Rome than of Washington. The door to the church's rustic Chapel of the Carpenter is around the corner on Potomac Street. Ring for admission.

From Potomac Street, walk down to N Street and some superb Federal-style homes, which have remained practically unchanged since the time they were built between 1815 and 1818. As you walk past **Smith Row,** from number 3255 to 3267, and **Cox's Row,** from 3327 to 3339 in the next block, take a look at the wonderful details in these elegant homes—the handsome doorways and fanlights, the dormers, and the recessed swags on each facade. John Cox, the Mayor of Georgetown who built Cox's Row, turned 3337 over to the Marquis de Lafayette during the 1824 visit when Lafayette Square was named for him. Between the two rows, at 3307 N, stands the Marbury House, where John F. Kennedy lived when he was elected president.

The Capital's first public market was built at 3276 M Street in 1795, then replaced in 1865 by the current historic landmark. The building's original fishmongers, butchers, and produce sellers have long since taken their wares to the Big Market in the Sky, but their much more genteel successors, **Dean and Deluca,** carry on in a market sure to remind you of those great European food halls and their enticing pyramids of lovely fruit and carefully arranged fish and meat. Just don't expect those 1795 prices or the veal deal that Thomas Jefferson got when he shopped here in 1806. Although he may have been a tired shopper, Jefferson didn't get to order a gourmet sandwich at the indoor/outdoor cafe, but you can.

Just beyond Dean and Deluca, at 3282 M Street, you'll find **Pizzeria Paradiso,** (337–1245), which serves up some of the best pizza in town. Your margherita, fra diavolo, and maybe even the bottarga, made of fish roe and egg, will arrive fresh from the wood-fired oven on thin, crisp crusts. And the Paradiso always uses fresh ingredients such as real mozzarella and genuine Parma ham, not the ersatz industrial substitutes found in the usual pizza inferno. There's also a good assortment of great sandwiches and desserts. Open Monday through Thursday 11:30 A.M. to 11:00 P.M., Friday and Saturday until midnight, and Sunday noon to 10:00 P.M.

Back in Georgetown's bad old days, Keady's Alley was one of its worst neighborhoods, a collection of shacks, shanties, and sheds that paralleled the C&O Canal just below M Street. Today this former slum has a spiffy new name, *Cady's Alley,* and it's lined with shops filled with some of the country's outstanding collections of home furnishings and antiques. Enter this cobblestone mews of converted nineteenth-century warehouses with exposed walls and tall ceilings at 3318 M Street NW, and then proceed to places like:

Bo Concept, for dramatic and contemporary furniture by top Danish designers. It's the cutting edge from Copenhagen. Main entrance is at 3342 M Street NW; 333–5656. Open 10:00 A.M. to 6:00 P.M. Monday through Saturday, noon to 6:00 p.m. Sunday.

Hollis and Knight, for a massive and eclectic treasury of everything from Tibetan rugs to antique grandfather clocks, exquisite crystal, and highly contemporary furniture. Enter at 3320 M Street NW; 333–6969. Open Tuesday through Saturday 10:00 A.M. to 6:00 P.M. Sunday and Monday noon to 5:00 P.M.; www.hollisandknight.com.

Ligne Roset offers urban dwellers a wide selection of cutting edge furniture from top European designers, along with lots of lamps and other accessories you'll want to make your own. You'll find them at 3306 M Street; 333–6390. Open 11:00 A.M.to 6:00 P.M. Tuesday through Saturday, noon to 5:00 P.M. Sunday; www.ligne-roset-usa.com.

Thos. Moser, to see what fine American woodworking and design is all about. Hand-crafted furniture in rich woods with simple, classical lines from master cabinet workers. They are located at 3300 M Street; 338–4292; 10:00 A.M. to 6:00 P.M. Monday through Saturday).

And there's much more to see. To preview all the Alley shops, visit www.cadysalley.com. One other thing—take money.

Places to Stay in Georgetown

The Georgetown Inn,
1310 Wisconsin Avenue NW;
333–8900,
www.georgetowninn.com
This Olde Georgetowne inn is colonial only when it comes to the decor in its rooms—four-poster beds, faux Sheraton furniture, and brass lamps—but the amenities and services are pure twenty-first century. Downstairs there's an outpost of the California-based Daily Grille, which means great salads and steaks. The inn is expensive; the Daily Grill isn't.

Georgetown Suites,
1111 30th Street NW;
298–7800,
www.georgetownsuites.com
As its name tells you, this is an all-suite hotel located just off M Street, next to bus lines that will take you everywhere you want to go, including the nearest Metro stop. Also handy to the Canal and Washington Harbour. Suites come with full kitchens, but if you don't feel like making breakfast, go down to the lobby for the complimentary continental breakfast bar. Moderate.

Hotel Monticello,
1075 Thomas Jefferson Street NW;
337–0900.
Georgetown's newest hotel, opened in early 2000, the Monticello is an intimate boutique inn with forty-seven wonderfully furnished suites and a central location in Georgetown. It won't be cheap, but if you're looking for the convenience of upscale suite hotel living with more than a whiff of a small European hotel, this is a real possibility. Expensive.

The Latham Hotel,
3000 M Street NW;
726–5000,
www.thelatham.com
This small European-style hotel is located right on Georgetown's main drag, but only a few steps from the tranquillity of the C&O Canal. No mistake about it, this is a first-class hotel with first-class service and amenities, and you'll pay accordingly. Not only that, the Latham's in-house restaurant, Citronelle, is among the best in the capital, if not the nation. Much less pricey is the

attached La Madeleine restaurant, which is a French-style cafeteria (when was the last time you visited one of those?) and a good one. The Latham is expensive.

Places to Eat in Georgetown

Bangkok Joe's,
3000 K Street NW;
333–4422.
See page 106 for full description.

Bistro Lepic,
1736 Wisconsin Avenue;
333–0111.
It's easy to imagine you're dining on the Left Bank at this small, bright restaurant lined with lively oils and prints. It's a big favorite with locals seeking super French cooking at a reasonable price. My favorite is the loin of lamb with truffles, but you might prefer the salmon in

potato crust or the beef medallions with polenta. Good wine list too. Reservations are essential. Open daily 11:30 A.M. to 2:30 P.M., Monday through Thursday 5:30 to 10:00 P.M., until 10:30 P.M. on Friday and Saturday, 9:30 P.M. on Sunday. Moderate.

Ching Ching Cha,
1063 Wisconsin Avenue NW;
333–8288.
See page 107 for full description.

Clyde's,
3236 M Street NW;
333–9180.
If there's one Georgetown restaurant that almost everybody likes it's Clyde's. This landmark restaurant gets the Oscar for longevity by staying in business since 1963, when JFK was president and nightlife on M Street consisted of a few bars like the Silver Dollar Cafe. (On amateur night, at the Silver Dollar, an elderly and none-too-sober gent in a greasy Uncle Sam suit frequently tapdanced on stilts.) Clyde's is still an outstanding neigh-

AUTHOR'S FAVORITE PLACES TO EAT IN GEORGETOWN

Bistro Lepic	Ching Ching Cha
Clyde's	Sequoia's
Martin's Tavern	La Chaumiere
Paolo's	Citronelle
Pizzeria Paradiso	

borhood saloon that also attracts a national clientele of visitors. The reason is the convivial bar and a consistently first-rate kitchen that turns out great American stuff from burgers to crab cakes and inventive salads and fish dishes, plus a notable Sunday brunch. It's a lively scene, so reserve. Open Monday through Friday 11:30 A.M. to midnight, weekends 10:00 A.M. to 1:00 A.M., Sunday 9:00 A.M. to midnight. Moderate.

La Chaumiere,
2813 M Street NW;
338–1784.
This combination of provincial French bistro and Georgetown institution has a corps of high-powered regular diners that could staff an entire administration. The price you'd pay, however, would be traces of *choucroute garni* on the treaties, onion soup stains on the legislation, and the remains of a memorable crab-filled crepe on the inaugural speech. Considering the usual quality of Washington's legislation and the exacting standards of La Chaumiere's kitchen, this would be an excellent trade-off indeed. Moderate. Reservations suggested. Open Monday through Friday 11:30 A.M. to 2:30 P.M. and Monday through Saturday 5:30 to 10:30 P.M. Moderate.

La Madeleine,
3000 M Street;
337–6975.
A French bakery and cafeteria-style cafe where lunch might be a quiche or major-league Caesar salad preceded by

the restaurant's signature tomato-basil or onion soups. At dinnertime La Madeleine shifts to roast turkey and chicken, pasta, and a tasty French version of Beef Wellington. Open Sunday through Thursday 7:00 A.M. to 10:00 P.M., Friday and Saturday 7:00 A.M. to 11:00 P.M. Inexpensive.

La Ruche,
1039 31st Street NW;
965–2684,
www.cafelaruche.com
There's a nice Gallic feel about this out-of-the-way and unpretentious "beehive" near the Potomac's left bank. You can choose between hefty salads, rich onion and other soups, and light fare, including *croque monsieur* and grilled chicken. The desserts are ethereal. Open Monday through Friday 11:30 A.M. to 11:00 P.M., Saturday and Sunday 10:00 A.M. to 11:30 P.M. Brunch is served Saturday and Sunday from 10:00 A.M. to 3:00 P.M. Inexpensive.

Martin's Tavern,
1264 Wisconsin Avenue NW;
333–7370.
See page 108 for full description.

Mendocino Grille and Wine Bar,
2917 M Street NW;
333–2912;
www.mendocinodc.com
It's hard to imagine a more cozy and chic restaurant than the Mendocino Grille, where the stylish blond wood decor and the menu justify its "California cuisine" theme. Lunch emphasizes entree salads, inventive sandwiches,

pastas, and grilled fish. Seafood also predominates on a dinner menu that often includes grilled mussels and salmon, fish chowder, oyster stew, and glazed quail. As its name suggests, the wine list is also impressive, with mainly California vintages. Open for lunch Monday through Saturday from 11:30 A.M. to 3:00 P.M. and for dinner Sunday through Thursday 5:30 to 10:00 P.M. and on Friday and Saturday until 11:00 P.M. Reservations are a good idea. Expensive.

Old Glory,
3139 M Street;
337–3406,
www.oldglorybbq.com
You'll think you've been teleported to Memphis at Old Glory, a.k.a. Georgetown's barbecue central, where cook-off winning chefs prepare award-winning ribs and pork. Check out the pulled pork or chicken and the smoky spareribs, topped by one of Old Glory's six homemade sauces. Also nice salads and desserts (non-barbecued. The ornately carved bar, which saw a lot of action at the Rendezvous Barbeque in Memphis over its 110-year life, feels right at home in D.C., especially on the weekends. Monday through Thursday 11:30 A.M. to 1:00 A.M., Friday and Saturday until 1:30 A.M., Sunday 11:00 A.M. to 11:30 P.M. Inexpensive.

Paolo's,
1303 Wisconsin Avenue;
333–7353.
The food at this trendy trattoria is billed as California-Italian. Lots of good and original pastas, including

shellfish over black pepper linguine, and imaginative salads, many of them featuring seafood and roast chicken. Paolo's wood-oven produces original pizzas such as duck confit and pesto with goat cheese. Main courses also include grilled veal chops and shrimp scampi. Paolo's also has an outside terrace for watching the Georgetown scene, but the evening scene inside is pretty lively as well. Sunday through Thursday 11:30 A.M. to 11:30 P.M., Friday and Saturday open until 12:30 A.M. Moderate.

Patisserie Poupon,
1645 Wisconsin Avenue; 342–3248.
See page 113 for full description.

Pizzeria Paradiso,
3282 M Street; 337–1245.
See page 116 for full description.

Red Ginger,
1564 Wisconsin Avenue NW; 965–2009.
See page 113 for full description.

Sequoia's,
3000 K Street NW; 944–4200.
See page 105 for full description.

Tony and Joe's,
3000 K Street NW; 944–4545.
See page 105 for full description.

Vietnam Georgetown,
2934 M Street; 337–4536.
This modest establishment always ends up on everyone's list of favorite restaurants and keeps winning local awards for food and value. Try the lemon chicken and grilled salmon. Great pho hoa too. Open Monday through Thursday 11:00 A.M. to 11:00 P.M., Friday and Saturday 11:00 A.M. to 11:30 P.M., Sunday noon to 11:00 P.M. Inexpensive.

Upper Northwest

The Upper Northwest covers a lot of territory, extending in a broad outer arc that starts along the Potomac just north of Georgetown and swings around above Dupont Circle, Adams Morgan, and Shaw, and ends at North Capitol Street, which divides Northwest from Northeast. Along the way it encompasses many of residential Washington's most agreeable neighborhoods, including Shepherd Park, the leafy area between 16th Street and Georgia Avenue, and Palisades, whose main street, MacArthur Boulevard, parallels the Potomac River. In Cleveland Park, an early twentieth-century enclave near the cathedral, media figures, senators, and lawyers live in spacious Victorian houses; their cars sport bumper stickers urging SAVE THE WHALES or even (says a reliable Washington source) DUKAKIS FOR PRESIDENT.

Upper Northwest is also home to off-the-beaten-path treasures like Rock Creek Park, the U.S. Soldiers and Airmen's Home, and the Kreeger Museum. Since this sprawling area is not all that well served by Metrorail, you'll need to take the city's Metrobus system to some of the places you want to go. In view of the distances involved, taxis or your own car are good alternatives for getting around.

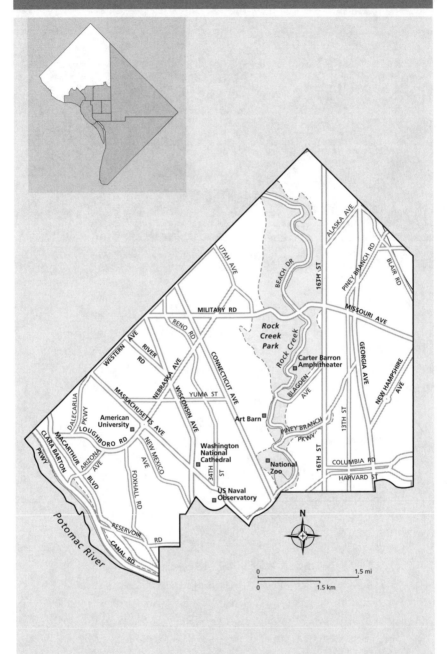

The **Washington National Cathedral** or, more formally, The Cathedral Church of St. Peter and St. Paul, is far from being an off-the-beaten- path location. Every year 800,000 visitors go to Washington's highest point to explore one of America's great churches, a magnificent fourteenth-century-style cathedral begun when Teddy Roosevelt laid the cornerstone in 1907; it was completed in 1990. It would take a book like this just to adequately cover the cathedral's architectural detail and its highlights, including the exquisite stone carvings. For information about joining one of the regularly scheduled tours or attending any of the cathedral's vast array of musical events, special programs, and observances, call 537–6200 or visit www.cathedral.org. The cathedral is best reached by bus, using one of the "30" series lines north from Georgetown and downtown or by taking the Metro to the Tenleytown station (red line) and taking one of the 30 buses south about 1½ miles to the cathedral.

While you're on the cathedral's sprawling fifty-seven-acre close, there are several eminently visitable places that are definitely off the beaten path and are not to be missed. To see them, walk down South Road, to the right of the main doors, and walk down to the **Herb Cottage.** The cottage was once the cathedral baptistry, but today it's one of Washington's top gift shops, with a nice selection of decorative china and porcelain, colorful trays and teapots, and nifty flowerpots, along with the obligatory jams and scents. There's a great selection of herbs too. The cottage is open daily 10:00 A.M. to 5:00 P.M. Call 537–8982.

Farther down South Road, an elaborately carved arch leads to the **Bishop's Garden,** which was conceived as a medieval walled garden of natural and ageless beauty to accompany a great Gothic cathedral. And that's exactly what it is. The garden is a collection of plants from historic gardens owned by

Herb Cottage, Washington National Cathedral

TOP ATTRACTIONS IN UPPER NORTHWEST

National Cathedral	Kreeger Museum
Rock Creek Park	U.S. Soldiers and Airmen's Home
Hillwood Museum	Naval Observatory

Washington and Jefferson, while the "Hortulus" or "little garden" is planted with herbs found on a plant list created by Charlemagne in 815. The garden also includes ancient boxwoods, beds of fragrant herbs, and colorful seasonal blooms (hint: if it's tulips you're after, try April or May; roses appear in June). The garden's "Shadow House," a gazebo-like stone structure, makes a perfect spot to rest and reflect. During the growing season (April 1 to October 31) guided walk-in tours of the garden leave from the Herb Cottage every Wednesday at 10:30 A.M. Group tours can also be arranged by calling 244–0568.

Below the Bishop's Garden, behind the equestrian statue of Washington, is **Olmsted Woods,** five acres of peaceful urban forest with footpaths great for taking a quiet walk among the black squirrels and songbirds. The woods are an ongoing effort by the Cathedral's All Hallows Guild to restore this oak and beech woodlands to its original pristine condition. The statue of Washington is more than just decoration; in the late eighteenth century these forests are where the first president used to ride horseback. Guided walks in the woods are given regularly and leave from the Washington statue. Call 537–2319 to get the exact dates.

Refreshed and back on South Road, you're perfectly positioned for a shopping excursion in the cathedral's **Museum Store,** a cavernous and eclectic collection of everything from books and CDs with religious and secular themes to guidebooks and reproductions of the cathedral's gargoyles, grotesques, and other carvings. Definitely off-the-beaten-path is the store's stealth snack bar; it's along the shop's south wall. Open daily 9:30 A.M. to 5:00 P.M. Call 537–6267.

Farther down South Road are the **Cathedral Greenhouses,** which grow and sell hundreds of varieties of herbs, annuals, and perennials. Even if you're not buying, it's fun to walk around, see the plants, and chat up the young employees who obviously love their work and the flowers. The greenhouse also has occasional special programs, including workshops, lectures, and children's events. For more information about them, call 537–6263. Open Monday through Saturday 9:30 A.M. to 5:00 P.M., Sunday 10:00 A.M. to 5:00 P.M.

One of the city's least-known treats for kids is the cathedral's hands-on **Medieval Workshop,** where children don aprons and gather around work

Church Suppers

Because the Washington National Cathedral is in Cleveland Park, an overwhelmingly residential neighborhood, the selection of nearby restaurants is not large. However, the shopping area 2 blocks to the right as you exit the cathedral has three good choices:

Cafe Deluxe,
3228 Wisconsin Avenue NW;
686–2233,
www.cafedeluxe.com
Every neighborhood should have a restaurant this good. The Deluxe will remind you of a bright and bustling French cafe, but the food is largely American: burgers, great sandwiches, and the zenith of American comfort food, a top-notch meat loaf. Other favorites include pastas, grilled fish, and excellent desserts. There's also sidewalk dining in good weather, but the restaurant takes no reservations. Open Monday through Thursday 11:30 A.M. to 10:30 P.M., Friday and Saturday 11:30 A.M. to 11:30 P.M., Sunday 11:00 A.M. to 10:00 P.M. Moderate.

2 Amys Neapolitan Pizzeria,
3715 Macomb Street NW;
885–5700.
One of the city's top pizzerias is owned by Peter Pastan, the owner of Dupont Circle's Obelisk, one of D.C.'s best Italian restaurants. The 2 Amys will remind you of your last visit to Naples, and by that I don't mean everything's drenched in heavy-duty red sauce. This is where pizzas are fresh, slim, and perfectly cooked in a huge, oak-fueled oven. Everyone likes the vongole pizza with clams in the shell, anchovies, and hot peppers and the puttanesca, with anchovies, garlic, and black olives. For traditionalists there's also a classic margherita with tomatoes and mozzarella. And amid all this pizza perfection don't overlook the antipasti, least of all the deep-fried rice balls that the Italians call *suppli a telefono* because of the "cords" of hot, melted cheese that hang down from the center of the rice. Open Tuesday through Sunday from 11:00 A.M. to 11:00 P.M. Inexpensive.

Cactus Cantina,
3300 Wisconsin Avenue NW;
686–7222.
The *Washingtonian's* estimable food critics recently called the Cactus Cantina one of the best restaurants in Upper Northwest, and they're absolutely right. This is the place to go for high quality Tex-Mex, especially the fajitas, grilled shrimp, and fat tamales. Believe it or not, the Cantina also has a "Cowboy and Indian Museum." So if you happen across a collection of cowboy hats, a Sioux "puberty bag," a figure of Chief Split Horn, and other Western curiosities, you'll know that it's not those eight or ten margaritas you ran through before dinner. Open Sunday through Thursday 11:30 A.M. to 11:00 P.M., Friday and Saturday 11:30 A.M. to midnight. Sunday brunch is served from 11:30 A.M.to 3:00 P.M. Inexpensive.

benches to engage in supervised medieval crafts like molding gargoyles in clay, piecing together stained-glass windows, and making brass rubbings. The workshops are held Saturdays from 10:00 A.M. to 2:00 P.M. No reservations are needed for groups of fewer than ten, just show up with your tots at the cathedral's crypt level. The charge is $5.00 per participant.

Another off-the-beaten-path possibility is the ***Gargoyle Tour,*** which combines a slide lecture with a close-up visit to some of those 107 often funny little carvings made by Italian craftsmen that parade around the cathedral's exterior, concealing waterspouts as they go. After the slide show, you'll go outside for a look at some gargoyles they never thought of in the Middle Ages, including a dog named Kiddo and Darth Vader, done by a Nebraska student as part of a national competition. Darth and Kiddo are pretty far up there, so binoculars are recommended. The tour costs $5.00. Reservations are needed; to make yours, call 537–2934.

Most people are so charmed by the cathedral and the lovely enclave that surrounds it that they'd like to stay on. With a little luck, that just might be possible. The ***College of Preachers,*** on the grounds at the rear of the cathedral, mainly offers rooms and conference space to church leaders and other individuals attending retreats, meetings, and other events at the cathedral, but opens its rooms to the public on a "space available" basis. It's a lovely experience. The college's Tudor-era building makes every visit feel something like a stay with Henry VIII, especially in the refectory, where the long tables, beamed walls and ceilings, and fabulous stained glass windows would make His Majesty (or Charles Laughton) feel right at home. Nearby there's a quiet, book-filled library and a cloistered garden with fountain. The rooms, most with shared bath, are bright and comfortable. The College of Preachers is located at 3510 Woodley Road NW. Call 537–6380, fax 537–5650, or e-mail kgilliam@ cathedral.org; www.collegeofpreachers.org.

Not far from the back of the cathedral grounds is the ***Vice President's House.*** The best way to see what the Secret Service will allow is to stand at the corner of Massachusetts Avenue and 34th Street. Here you can gaze upon the massive white 1893 Queen Anne mansion that was once the home of the superintendent of the Naval Observatory, located next door, and, after that, "Quarters A," the residence of the Chief of Naval Operations, the Navy's top officer. But since 1974, this has been the official residence of the vice president. If you're not invited in, rest assured that it's spacious, comfortable, and just the place you'd want to live when *you* become vice president. Until then, keep standing on that corner.

One of the most fascinating but least known off-the-beaten-path excursions in Washington is the nighttime tour of the ***U.S. Naval Observatory,*** which is strictly off-limits to the public except on Monday evenings, when it opens its gates to outsiders. The observatory is the nation's main celestial tracker, supplier of astronomical data, and keeper of the United States Master Clock. The observatory's sensitive data is essential for accurate navigation and support of communications on earth and in space, so don't touch anything on your tour!

The tour includes a show-and-tell about the Master Clock and discussions with staff astronomers. Best of all, you'll be able to gaze skyward through the great 26-inch telescope that was used in the discovery in 1877 of the two moons of Mars. If the night sky is clear, you'll be invited to look through the historic 12-inch refracting telescope built in 1892. You will not, however, be invited to turn those lenses on the vice president and his family, who live in the big house next door.

The U.S. Naval Observatory is at Massachusetts Avenue at 34th Street NW; 762–1467; www.usno.navy.mil. Tours are given every other Monday evening from 8:30 to 10:00 P.M. You must reserve well in advance for these tours, either online or by phoning 762–1438. And you'll have to check in at the tour's departure point at the Observatory's South Gate (on Observatory Circle opposite the New Zealand Embassy) by 8:00 P.M., armed with photo ID. Since you'll be walking outside at night, and sometimes over rough ground, consider bringing along a small flashlight and walking shoes. Cameras are permitted. No Metro.

Glover Archbold Park, a slender, 3-mile-long, 183-acre park runs through some of northwest Washington's best neighborhoods and most secluded woodlands. Although it is less well known and smaller than Rock Creek Park, it also makes a great place for an urban ramble or jog.

To reach Glover Archbold, take the Metro's red line to Tenleytown, then walk south several blocks on Wisconsin Avenue to Van Ness Street. A right turn will take you 1 block to a grassy park on the left where a sign marks the northern end of the park. The trail ends at a stone tunnel under the C&O Canal (one

AUTHOR'S FAVORITES IN UPPER NORTHWEST

Bishop's Garden	Kreeger Museum
Hillwood	2 Amys Neapolitan Pizzeria
Cafe Deluxe	

A River Runs Through It

The *Italian Chancery,* at 3000 Whitehaven Street NW, pays tribute to two world cities, Florence and Washington.

As you can see when you view the building's Massachusetts Avenue façade, the chancery, made of 42,000 pieces of Italian red stone, is a modern and highly dramatic version of a renaissance-era Florentine palazzo. But there's more. If you could see the building from the air you'd find that it is square, reflecting the shape of the original one-hundred-square-mile plot of Washington before the Virginia part was returned to that state. That four-story glass atrium that bisects the chancery represents the Potomac River, which cuts through the building exactly the same way it divided Washington's original layout.

of the canal's original structures), which opens on to the canal towpath about a ten-minute walk from Georgetown.

The little red schoolhouse on MacArthur Boulevard, not far from the Potomac, was built in 1864, making it the oldest one-room schoolhouse in the District. Now it's the home of **Discovery Creek,** a children's museum and activity center designed to help kids, especially ages four to eleven, experience and respect the natural environment. The museum is lined with terraria containing lizards and reptiles, plus other exhibits where kids can learn about wildlife and nature. Using the school as a base, Discovery Creek sponsors an extensive year-round program of outdoor adventures and other science- or nature-oriented programs either in the schoolhouse or at other area locations. The school is located on the edge of Palisades Park, which makes nature hikes and other big-league explorations a breeze. Discovery Creek, the Children's Museum of Washington, is at 4954 MacArthur Boulevard NW. Call 337–5111, fax 337–5344, or visit www.discoverycreek.org. Open Saturday 10:00 A.M. to 3:00 P.M., Sunday 11:00 A.M. to 3:00 P.M. Children's groups can be booked by calling 337–5111.

A short walk from Discovery Creek, just up Chain Bridge Road from the intersection with MacArthur Boulevard, you'll find one of the District's least known and most touching places, **The Union Burial Society of Georgetown Cemetery,** a two-acre burial ground for former slaves and their descendants at 2616 Chain Bridge Road. Except for the community's former schoolhouse, which still stands at 2820 Chain Bridge Road (not open to the public), this 200-year-old cemetery is almost the last vestige of a small black settlement that inhabited the residential area now known as the Palisades. It is well cared for by a descendant of one of the families buried there. The cemetery is usually open during the day, but has no fixed hours.

Although this part of the District, known as Palisades, is not exactly brimming over with restaurants, it boasts one of Washington's favorite neighborhood hangouts, the **Starland Cafe,** at 5125 Macarthur Boulevard NW. The food at Starland is New American Casual, with a menu of big salads, blackened and grilled fish, and top-notch burgers. Since it's co-owned by Grammy-winning songwriter and performer Bill Danoff of the Starland Vocal Band, music is important at Starland. Every Friday at 9:00 P.M. there's live jazz featuring prominent local groups; no cover charge; call 244–9396. Lunch Monday through Friday 11:30 A.M. to 3:00 P.M., Sunday 11:00 A.M. to 3:00 P.M. Dinner Sunday through Thursday from 5:30 to 9:30 P.M., Friday and Saturday 5:30 to 10:00 P.M. Moderate.

Another Palisades option is **Bambu,** a sleek and attractive Asian (Thai-Japanese-Chinese) restaurant at 5101 Macarthur Boulevard NW. At lunchtime order one of Bambu's bargain bento boxes, which pair sushi with Thai or Chinese dishes. Seafood and shellfish are always good options at Bambu; try the standout scallops or fried oysters any time. Pad Thai and soups with noodles and fish are other specialties. Call 364–3088. Hours are Sunday through Thursday. 11:00 A.M. to 10:00 P.M., Friday and Saturday. 11:00 A.M. to 10:30 P.M. Moderate.

And if you're touring the upper reaches of the Palisades near Sibley Hospital, it's good to know about **DC Boathouse,** where you'll find a lunch menu focused on sandwiches, salads, and great soups (be sure to try the minestrone). At dinnertime some good choices include crab cakes and ribs. DC Boathouse, at 5441 Macarthur Boulevard (362–2628) is open daily for lunch and dinner. Moderate.

Despite its current tranquillity and affluence, Chain Bridge Road was, in the eighteenth and nineteenth centuries, a busy and much traveled highway leading to Chain Bridge, one of the earliest (and still standing) bridges across the Potomac. If you go a little farther up this sunken road you'll arrive at **Battery Kemble Fort,** very agreeable for walks and picnics. Although it is now a totally suburbanized city park, Battery Kemble was once a keystone of the "circle of forts" that defended the District during the Civil War. You'll also gaze upon the houses of the rich and famous that line Chain Bridge Road, which is now one of Washington's very best addresses.

The **Kreeger Museum** displays the art and sculpture collection of David Lloyd Kreeger, insurance mogul, philanthropist, and art collector extraordinaire, in an intimate atmosphere. In fact, just a glance at the museum itself, a 1967 design by famed architect Philip Johnson, tells visitors that they have arrived at a special place. To get the idea, imagine an architectural wedding of classical and Renaissance—a sprawling Roman villa in white travertine with soaring neo-Palladian windows that expose its exhibit walls to warmth and sunlight. A trip to this small, private museum is like visiting the home of a wealthy friend blessed with exquisite tastes in both art and architecture.

The two-story atrium of the museum's Great Hall showcases impressionist masterpieces including Picassos and van Goghs, while the Kreeger's former dining room now serves up a feast of Monets. Across the atrium, Mondrian's *Mill on the River* presides over a teak-lined library.

The Kreeger's downstairs rooms lack the spacious feel of the Great Hall, but compensate with more Picassos, Miro etchings, a Frank Stella, and works by other abstract expressionists. Somewhat incongruously, there's also a fascinating collection of African wood carvings and tribal masks. The Kreeger Museum is at 2401 Foxhall Road; 337–3050, fax 337–3051. The Kreeger hosts conducted, ninety-minute tours twice a day, at 10:30 A.M. and 1:30 P.M. Tuesday through Friday, for which reservations are required. However, you will not need reservations for tours given during the Kreeger's Saturday afternoon Open Hours, which run from 10:00 A.M. to 4:00 P.M. The museum is closed the month of August. Children under twelve not admitted. Reservations are essential and should be obtained well in advance by phoning 338–3552; www.kreeger museum.com. Suggested donation is $8.00 for adults, $5.00 for seniors and students. Since the Kreeger is far from public transportation, a personal vehicle or taxi is best; free parking on the grounds.

As Truman Capote said about Venice, a visit to **Hillwood** is a great treat, "like eating an entire box of chocolate liqueurs all at one go." This forty-room mansion of cereal heiress Marjorie Merriweather Post is one superlative after another, especially when describing its wealth of Russian decorative art, a collection that began when one of Mrs. Post's four husbands, Joseph E. Davies, served as the American ambassador to Moscow in the late '30s. Among Hillwood's riches, the high point is the Icon Room, which gleams with enamel and gold Fabergé eggs and clocks, a dazzling diamond tiara worn by the last empress, and masses of jewel-encrusted gold and silver chalices. The Russian porcelain room is special too, chiefly for the four dinner services that once belonged to Catherine the Great and some pieces from the personal dinner service of Empress Elizabeth I made in the late 1750s.

Hillwood's Russian art is rivaled only by its array of French antiques. A portrait of Empress Eugenie and hangings of Gobelin tapestries look down on Hillwood's French drawing room, where the wood paneling comes from a French château and the rolltop Roentgen desk is a marvel of marquetry. In the dining room Mrs. Post's guests banqueted by the light of Russian Imperial candlesticks on Russian Imperial porcelain; the room's Aubusson carpet once belonged to the Emperor Maximilian. After exploring Hillwood, don't forget to saunter through the estate's formal gardens and look in on the excellent collection of Native American arts gathered in the Indian Building. The estate's *dacha,* a modest one room Russian log cabin, is now used for small exhibitions of Russian art.

Docent-led and audio-guided tours of Hillwood Museum, at 4155 Linnean Avenue NW, are given regularly Tuesday through Saturday between 9:30 A.M. and 5:00 P.M. Closed in February. Hillwood's Web site is www.hillwoodmuseum.org. Since Hillwood admits a maximum of 250 visitors per day, reservations are required. Call 686–5807 or (877) 445–5966 to get them. Suggested donation: $12.00 for adults, $10.00 for seniors and $5.00 for children six to eighteen. Hillwood's Cafe is open for breakfast, lunch, and afternoon tea from 9:30 A.M. to 4:30 P.M.; reserve for lunch by phoning 686–8505. The Museum Shop, located in the visitor center, will sell you handsome books, gifts, and other mementos of this Washington treasure. Hillwood is about 1 mile from the Van Ness Metro station (red line) and from all Connecticut Avenue bus routes.

Rock Creek Park is one of America's oldest, largest, and most beautiful urban parks and one of Washington's great treasures. This wedge-shaped, 2,800-acre wilderness follows Rock Creek, a rushing rural stream, for 6 often secluded miles right through the heart of a busy city, starting at the Kennedy Center and ending at the District's border with Maryland, passing the National Zoo as it winds along. And unlike New York's Central Park, Rock Creek is hilly, a gorge with ravines and hidden pockets of heavily wooded forests and running brooks. It's so nice that, after the Civil War, a commission formed to find a "healthier situation" for a new Executive Mansion to replace the White House gave this in-town oasis serious consideration.

Rock Creek was made a national park in 1890 when Congress set it aside as "a pleasuring place for the enjoyment of the people of the United States"; ever since, Washingtonians have happily headed there to bicycle, walk its 29 miles of foot trails, ride the 13 miles of bridle paths, and even play golf. Picnicking too—within this city forest there are dozens of clearings with picnic tables that during the spring and summer are the scenes of family gatherings and softball games. Picnicking in some

capitalquote

"Rock Creek has an abundance of all the elements that make up not only pleasing, but wild and rugged scenery. There is, perhaps, not another city in the Union that has on its very threshold so much natural beauty and grandeur."

—Naturalist and author
John Burroughs

areas requires permission; call 673–7646 about permits. Presidents also have been big Rock Creek fans, including Teddy Roosevelt, who loved the park and hiked there often, and Ronald Reagan, who often rode at the stables. The Park Service Web site for Rock Creek is www.nps.gov/rocr.

The park remains a hidden corner for many visitors without their own automobiles, in part because there are no Metro stations in the park and no buses roll along Rock Creek Parkway and Beach Drive, its two main thoroughfares. Nevertheless, it's not all that difficult to enjoy the park and its excellent facilities.

One way is to start at the corner of Rock Creek Parkway and Virginia Avenue NW across from the Watergate and simply follow the path next to the parkway back into the park. Along the way you'll pass under Embassy Row and behind the zoo before you reach Tilden Street, where the park's most scenic area begins with Peirce Mill.

Another way of getting to Peirce Mill involves taking the Metro's red line to the Cleveland Park station, then walking up Connecticut Avenue 2 blocks north to Rodman Street; at the corner you'll see an inviting little woods with signs directing you down the Melvin Hazen Trail. The trail leads a short distance down to Rock Creek where a left (north) turn on West Ridge Trail takes you, after a few minutes, to the mill.

Peirce Mill, named for the family that built and ran the mill in the early nineteenth century, was one of eight mills that lined Rock Creek in the 1820s and used its waterpower to grind corn and wheat into flour. The mill outlived its economic usefulness and was closed in 1897. But today thanks to the National Park Service, this lovely stone building, with its wooden waterwheel, is once again a functioning flour mill with antique millstones and hoppers that give visitors a fascinating view of a functioning nineteenth-century flour and cornmeal mill. Peirce Mill, at the intersection of Beach Drive and Tilden Street NW, is open Wednesday through Sunday noon to 5:00 P.M. A repair program is

Peirce Mill, Rock Creek Park

French Bench

Jules Jusserand may not be a household name today, but if you'd lived in Washington any time between 1902 and 1925, when Jusserand was the French ambassador to the United States, you'd certainly have heard about him.

One reason Monsieur Jusserand stayed in Washington for twenty-three years was his ability to befriend every U.S. president he ever met, from Teddy Roosevelt to Warren Harding; he was influential in persuading Woodrow Wilson that the United States should join the Allied side in World War I. What's more, Jusserand was also a noted scholar; his book, *With Americans of Past and Present Days,* won the 1917 Pulitzer Prize for U.S. history.

Jusserand and Teddy Roosevelt were great bird-watchers and frequently went birding together in Rock Creek Park. Jusserand is remembered today with a stone bench in the park, in the woods across Rock Creek from Peirce Mill.

in progress, so call 282–0927 to make sure the interior of the mill is visitable or check out www.nps.gov. Contributions are welcome.

Next door to the mill is the trim little "Art Barn," built in 1820 as the Peirce family's carriage house. The barn, at 2401 Tilden Street, now hosts the ***Rock Creek Gallery,*** an art gallery with a series of eleven rotating monthly exhibits by local artists along with special art programs. The gallery also offers a children's summer camp and art workshops, and poetry readings at 8:00 P.M. every Thursday. Open Thursday through Sunday noon to 6:00 P.M. The gallery is sometimes closed in July, so if that's when you're going, you'd better check first at 244–2482.

If you're on foot, at Peirce Mill you have the option of following markers along West Ridge Trail 1½ miles south to the National Zoo and its Metro stop on the red line or 2 miles north to the Park's ***Nature Center.*** The Web site is www.nps.gov/rocr/naturecenter/index.html.

The nature center is the hub of Park Service programs and activities in the park, and there are a lot of them. To get an idea of the range of flora and fauna that live here in the middle of a large city, wander through the displays, photographs, and explanatory data in the center's large exhibit area. The center also has a bevy of children's programs, including a special "discovery room" for those under eight. As the park's "information central," the center can supply checklists of birds to watch for, a road map of the bike and other trails that crisscross the park, and instructions on a self-guided walk along the Nature Center Trail, where you can see firsthand most of the plants, birds, and animals you saw mounted back at the center. The center also offers guided nature

Feeding Time near the Zoo

The National Zoo, in the 3000 block of Connecticut Avenue NW, is very much on the beaten path and is well covered in the usual guidebooks. However, if hunger strikes while you're there you'll find, close by, three restaurants they won't tell you about:

Oxford Tavern
(better known as the "Zoo Bar"),
3000 Connecticut Avenue NW;
232–4225.
A long menu of pizzas, burgers, sandwiches, and salads, plus a kids' menu. For grownups there's also a lively bar and even livelier music from 11:00 A.M. to 2:00 A.M. Sunday through Thursday and until 3:00 A.M. on Friday and Saturday. Metro: Woodley Park-Zoo (red line).

Lebanese Taverna,
2641 Connecticut Avenue NW;
265–8681.
A great place to try meze, the Lebanese equivalent of tapas, or the flavorful kebabs and broiled chicken. Open daily 11:00 A.M. to 11:00 P.M. Across from Woodley Park-Zoo Metro station (red line).

Lavandou,
3321 Connecticut Avenue NW;
966–3002.
www.lavandourestaurant.net
If you dine here, you'll be joining the locals in one of their favorite places—one they'd just as soon keep to themselves. Too bad for them, the word

is out about Lavandou's pork tenderloin, sea scallops in red wine sauce, and carbonnade, which are among the house specialties. Afterward, call for the dessert cart and forget the calories. Lavandou is a 3-block walk from the zoo gate; Metro: Cleveland Park (red line).

Firehook Bakery and Coffee House,
3411 Connecticut Avenue NW;
362–2253.
The Firehook, which has several outlets in the city, specializes in wonderful breads, with dozens of varieties ranging from designer to peasant. Your zoo break can also include a long list of coffees and scrumptious cakes and a tasty Danish to go with them. Definitely not on the Atkins-friendly list. If it's lunch you're after, the Firehook also sells French cheeses, prepared salads, and sandwiches. Open Monday through Thursday 7:00 A.M. to 8:00 P.M., Friday until 9:00 P.M., Saturday 8:00 A.M. to 9:00 P.M. and Sunday from 8:00 A.M. to 7:00 P.M. Metro: Cleveland Park (red line).

walks and a small bookshop with a well-chosen selection of publications on natural history.

Perhaps the most remarkable section of the center is its seventy-five-seat planetarium, the only one in the Park Service system, which offers regularly scheduled events that acquaint children with the elements of astronomy and relate ancient yarns about the influence of the stars and moon. Planetarium shows are given on Wednesday at 4:00 P.M. and on Saturday and Sunday at 1:00

and 4:00 P.M. The Nature Center, 5200 Glover Road NW (895–6070), is open Wednesday through Sunday 9:00 A.M. to 5:00 P.M. You can either drive to the center by following the directional signs from nearby Military Road or take the Metro to the Friendship Heights station (red line) then transfer to an E2 or E3 bus to the corner of Oregon Avenue and Military Road, at which point you're a short walk from the center. If you decide to drive, keep in mind that Beach Drive is closed to auto traffic from 7:00 A.M. Saturday to 7:00 P.M. Sunday.

The ***Rock Creek Park Horse Center,*** run by a concessionaire, is a short walk from the Nature Center. This is where you can either visit the horses or arrange to ride one and become a true urban cowboy. The horse center has large indoor and outdoor rings and offers a variety of riding programs, including pony rides on weekends by appointment for $20 for fifteen minutes. If you're interested in trail rides, one-hour rides are given Tuesday, Wednesday, and Thursday at 3:00 P.M. and Saturday and Sunday at noon, 1:30, and 3:00 P.M. at a cost of $30, reserve in advance. The horse center's office is open Tuesday through Friday noon to 6:00 P.M. and Saturday and Sunday 9:00 A.M. to 5:00 P.M. Call 362–0117 or visit www.rockcreekhorsecenter.com.

Not far from the horse center, at the corner of Military Road and Oregon Avenue NW, a footpath leads to the well-preserved gun emplacements, earth-

---

Golfing the District

If you're in town and just can't stay away from the greens, Washington has three golf courses where you can show your stuff. These courses will also rent you clubs at the rate of $6.00 for nine holes and $9.00 for eighteen. Greens fees are $15 on weekdays and $19 on weekends. And they're all open dawn to dusk year-round.

East Potomac Park Golf Club,
Hains Point and Ohio Drive
(near FDR Memorial);
554–7660.
One 18-hole championship course and two 9-hole courses. Snack bar, pro shop, and practice facility.

Langston Golf Course,
26th Street and Benning Road NE
(near RFK Stadium);
397–8638.
Regulation 18-hole, par 72 championship course. Also lighted driving range, pro shop, snack bar.

Rock Creek Park Golf Club,
16th and Rittenhouse Streets NW;
882–7332.
A hilly 18-hole, par 65 course. Pro shop, 150-yard practice hole, and snack bar.

The Club Bus

The Metro folks have added a new bus service that will help you get from Upper Northwest into the nightlife in other neighborhoods. Route 98, the Adams Morgan–U Street Link, runs between the Woodley Park Zoo/Adams Morgan Metro station and 18th Street, the heart of Adams Morgan; it then continues on to Shaw's U Street/Cardozo Metro station. The service runs every fifteen minutes between 6:00 P.M. and midnight Sunday through Thursday, 6:00 P.M. to 1:00 A.M. on Friday, and 10:00 A.M. to 1:00 A.M. on Saturday. Fare is $1.10, but with a transfer ticket from Metrorail, it's only a quarter.

works, and moats of a Civil War fortification, **Fort DeRussey,** once a crucial point in the defense of Washington during the Civil War, but now abandoned and silent in the woods of Rock Creek Park.

Despite its daytime glories, you'd be well advised not to walk in this park after nightfall.

If, after your visit to Rock Creek Park, the idea of hiking some of Washington's other trails is appealing, you've got some great walks in store. For an excellent map and overview of what else is available in the District, visit www.washdc.org/trail.html.

Not far from the nature center, you'll see the place where, in July 1864, Confederate forces led by General Jubal Early made their first and last attempt to seize Washington with a bold attack on the Union defenses that surrounded the capital. Early's 20,000 troops launched their assault by marching down the Seventh Street Road, today's Georgia Avenue, from Silver Spring, Maryland, now a Washington suburb. The Confederate forces were met and repelled at **Fort Stevens,** another one of the "circle of forts" that protected the capital in wartime, whose commander, Gen. Lew Wallace, would go on to make Charlton Heston famous by writing *Ben Hur.*

Abraham Lincoln visited Fort Stevens during the fighting and even mounted the ramparts to check out the action, exposing his lanky figure to enemy fire. When a young Union officer, said to be future Chief Justice Oliver Wendell Holmes, spotted a tall civilian peering over at the rebel forces, he shouted, "Get down, you damned fool!" Lincoln complied. The spot is marked by a boulder and plaque. You can easily visit Fort Stevens (www.nps.gov/cwdw/stevens), now a grassy park at the corner of 13th Street and Quackenbos Road NW, just off Georgia Avenue; the fort has been partially reconstructed, with its original earthworks and cannon standing ready in their emplacements and pointing north toward the Confederate lines. To reach the fort, take the Metro to Silver Spring (red line), then the 70 or 71 bus to Quackenbos Street.

Nearby, at 6625 Georgia Avenue NW, is ***Battleground National Cemetery*** (www.nps.gov/batt), where forty-one of the soldiers killed in the defense of Fort Stevens are buried. This poignant, rarely visited plot is the nation's smallest national cemetery. The cannon at the entrance gate are from Fort Stevens and were used in the Civil War battle. Inside, monuments commemorate the fallen of the 122nd New York Volunteers and other regiments; in the rear a flagpole is surrounded by a circle of headstones. Open dawn to dusk. You can visit the cemetery by taking the Metro red line to Silver Spring, then transferring to the 70 or 71 bus line and getting off at Aspen Street.

The ***National Museum of Health and Medicine*** charts the progress of medicine over the centuries, and many of its exhibits focus on pathology, the history of disease, and the development of human life. The museum also has the world's largest collection of microscopes and an internationally renowned neuroanatomical collection (read brain specimens).

The museum's visual centerpieces, however, are the exhibits of U.S. military medicine in wartime. The most extensive and interesting of these are those covering Civil War medicine, which contain some very graphic photos and wax reproductions of grievous wounds and smashed bones. Another set of models and photographs shows the reconstructive surgery used at the time to repair shattered faces and limbs and the techniques battlefield doctors used for amputations and in dealing with trauma. The museum also has casts of Lincoln's face and hands and the actual bullet that killed the president at Ford's Theatre.

After the Civil War, it's on to a medical tour of Korea's MASH units and World War II, which includes an unforgettable display of the Army's fight

History Cop

On your wanderings through Washington's historic neighborhoods you might see a young African-American woman with an investigator's badge, a digital camera, and a sheaf of day-glo stickers with "Stop Work" written in big letters. You've just run into Toni Cherry, the District's "history cop," out on her rounds. Ms. Cherry, who works for D.C.'s Historic Preservation Office, is charged with seeing that Washington's officially designated historic properties are protected from illegal or historically incompatible alterations or additions. Since there are 23,500 historic buildings to protect and only one of her, Ms. Cherry gets pretty busy, so when you see her, don't slow her down— just say "thanks" and move on.

against VD, with some photos of afflicted GIs that will definitely make you think more than twice before ever fooling around.

The National Museum of Health and Medicine is located in building 54 on the campus of Walter Reed Hospital at 6900 Georgia Avenue NW; 782–2200, http://nmhm.washingtondc.museum. Open daily 10:00 A.M. to 5:30 P.M. Reservations required two days in advance. Take the 70 or 71 bus south from the Silver Spring Metro station (red line).

Faced with the blazing heat and swampy moisture of a nonair-conditioned Washington summer, Abraham and Mary Lincoln would drive out Seventh Street NW to stay in the cool and spacious grounds of the *U.S. Soldier's and Airmen's Home* in the rural expanses of northwest Washington, making the home the first presidential Camp David.

The home was established for aging and ailing soldiers in 1851 and it is still a retirement home for 1,100 soldiers and airmen. One of its main buildings, *Lincoln Cottage,* a fourteen-room Victorian Gothic house, was originally built as a summer retreat by a wealthy banker, then made available to presidents when it was no longer needed for veterans.

Historians estimate that Lincoln spent about one-fourth of his administration living in the cottage (earlier called Anderson Cottage). It was there that he signed the Emancipation Proclamation, conferred with his generals, and spent time with his family, especially young Tad, with whom he often climbed the sprawling 300-year-old copper beech tree that once stood next to the cottage. Lincoln last visited the cottage on April 13, 1865, the day before he was assassinated, to make sure it was ready for his family's next summer visit.

Although the Soldier's and Airmen's Home grounds were an inviting refuge from tropical Washington, Lincoln Cottage has long attracted the attention of Lincoln scholars and historians. The house is still attractive, intact, and structurally sound—in many ways a time capsule where you can walk the porch where Lincoln reflected and peer through the windows at the rooms and fireplace he knew well.

In mid-2000 this little-known but historically significant house was placed at the top of the National Trust for Historic Preservation's list of endangered places needing urgent attention, which in the case of Lincoln means arresting water seepage and deteriorating woodwork. According to the trust's president, "it's probably the country's most significant Lincoln site because it is the only one associated with his presidency, and the only major Lincoln site that has not been restored." One possible use being discussed for a restored cottage is as a study center for Lincoln scholars. Just for the record, the cottage was used by three other presidents as their summer White House: Lincoln's predecessor,

James Buchanan, then Rutherford B. Hayes (1877–80) and Chester Alan Arthur (1882–84).

The gates of the U.S. Soldier's and Airmen's Home, at Rock Creek Church Road and Upshur Street NW and at 3700 North Capitol Street NW, are open from 7:00 A.M. to 4:00 P.M.; www.afrh.gov. Admission to the home's grounds to see the Lincoln Cottage, always slightly complicated, was suspended in the wake of the September 11 attacks; as of mid-2004, visitors were unable to enter the cottage because of ongoing restoration work. However, to find out if the home is open during your visit, call 730–3043 or e-mail publicaffairs@dc.afrh.gov. There is no direct Metro service, but the 60 bus from the Ft. Totten Metro station (red and green lines) will take you to the Upshur Street gate. Best of all: Drive or cab it.

If you have time, visit the nearby *Soldier's Home National Cemetery,* the entrance of which is at the corner of Rock Creek Church Road and Harewood

Grief at Rock Creek Cemetery

Rock Creek Cemetery, at Rock Creek Church Road and Webster Street NW, is one of the city's oldest burial grounds. Upon entering you'll see St. Paul's Church, which was built well before Washington was a city; it was restored after a 1921 fire, but the walls are originals that date back to 1775.

Since burials began here in 1719, Rock Creek has seen a lot of big-time funerals of leading citizens, but its most visited grave is that of Clover Adams, the wife of writer-historian Henry Adams, who committed suicide in 1885. Her memorial is Grief (1891), a deeply moving statue by noted sculptor Augustus Saint-Gaudens showing a shrouded figure, neither male nor female, its face obscured by shadows. During World War II Eleanor Roosevelt reportedly drove out here frequently to sit and meditate at this powerful memorial. Pick up a map from the box outside the office and take your own self-guided tour. The *Adams memorial* is located in section E to the right of the church. While you're at Rock Creek, take time to look at two other memorable statues. Mary Magdalene as she first recognizes the arisen Christ is the theme of the dramatic *Ffoulke Memorial* (also called *Rabboni,* or *Master*), located in section B. Sculptor Gutzon Borglum (who later carved Mt. Rushmore) pulled out all the stops in this monument to a Washington merchant.

The haunting *Kauffmann Memorial (1912),* also located in section B, reflects the union of sculpture and landscape that evolved after the ground-breaking Adams Memorial. A melancholy female sits on a large curved bench near a mourning urn in William Ordway's tribute to the owner of the also defunct *Washington Evening Star.*

The cemetery is open from 7:30 A.M. to dusk, while the office is open from 9:00 A.M. to 5:00 P.M. Monday through Friday and 9:00 A.M. to 1:00 P.M. on Saturday; 829–0585. No Metro.

Road. It was among the first to be established to hold the remains of Civil War dead and predates Arlington National Cemetery, which was created, in part, because this cemetery was filled.

If you go to the Soldier's Home you'll have both the pleasure of visiting the Lincoln Cottage, one of America's seldom visited historical treasures, and dining at the down-home ***Hitching Post,*** another off-the-beaten-path find that is also unknown even to Washingtonians. Located just opposite the Soldier's Home's gate on Rock Creek Church Road, the Hitching Post is the quintessential neighborhood restaurant, where you'll either perch on stools at the Formica counter or settle into one of four fuchsia-colored Naugahyde booths to enjoy terrific southern cooking. From their tiny kitchen, Adrienne and Alvin Carter will fix you the best southern fried chicken you've ever had, or enormous crab cakes, arguably the best in town, packed with moist crab meat, along with a side of great slaw. The menu also lists baked ham and lamb chops, which I'm saving for my next visit. The Hitching Post, 200 Upshur Street NW (726–1511), is open Tuesday through Saturday noon to midnight. Inexpensive to moderate.

Places to Stay in Upper Northwest

The Kalorama Guest House,
2700 Cathedral Avenue NW;
328–0860.
This urban bed-and-breakfast consists of two handsome 1910–12 town houses with nineteen agreeable rooms, seven of which involve shared bathrooms. And there's no beating the location, a nice residential neighborhood around the corner from the National Zoo and 2 blocks from the Metro. Inexpensive.

Omni Shoreham,
2500 Calvert Street NW;
234–0700.
This seventy-year-old Washington tradition with 812 rooms is hardly a cozy hide-

away, but it sure offers a great travel experience, with top-drawer service and a historic feel. The Shoreham is like a small, self-contained city, with restaurants, shops, and a health club. Many rooms have superb views of Rock Creek Park. The Shoreham is also handy to the Metro and the Zoo, and is only a short cab ride from Adams Morgan's lively restaurant scene. Expensive.

Savoy Suites,
2505 Wisconsin Avenue NW;
337–9700 or
(800) 944–5377.
This large (150-unit) suite hotel calls itself a Georgetown hotel, but it is in fact located close to the National Cathedral in Upper Northwest, a fifteen-minute walk from Georgetown. Some of its 150 comfortable suites have kitchens and many come with Jacuzzi tubs. The Savoy also has a bistro serv-

ing traditional Italian favorites. Moderate. No Metro, but on the route of the "30" buses.

Woodley Park Guest House,
2647 Woodley Road NW;
866–667–0218; 667–0218;
www.woodleyparkguest
house.com
Formerly known as the Connecticut-Woodley Guest House, this seventeen-room bed-and-breakfast has been both renamed and refreshed by a recent redecoration. Its moderate rates include a large continental breakfast and, at no extra charge, a great location. Although it sits in a quiet residential neighborhood, the Woodley Park is not only close to the Woodley Park-National Zoo Metro station; it's also about a block away from a major restaurant row, an easy walk from the zoo, and a ten-minute stroll to swinging Adams Morgan.

Places to Eat in Upper Northwest

Bambu,
5101 Macarthur
Boulevard NW;
364–3088.
See page 129 for full
description.

Buck's Fishing and Camping,
5031 Connecticut
Avenue NW;
364–0777.
Despite its name, Buck's
doesn't serve up campfire
specials, so don't worry
about hunkering down here
in the wilds of upper Connecticut Avenue for dinners
of greasy fish and boiled coffee. The decor may be Early
Boathouse, with a canoe
hanging from the rafters, hur-
ricane lamps, and rough-
hewn wooden tables, but the
food is anything but rustic.
This is where you'll find
noted chef Carole Green-
wood serving up unique prepared dishes such as
pan-roasted mussels, grilled
sea bass, and an ambrosial
duck pot roast. To maintain
the fishing camp atmos-
phere, Buck's also offers a
terrific fish fry, along with
wood-grilled steaks and lobsters. This high-energy
restaurant also has a short
but good wine list with reasonable prices. No reservations. Open for dinner
Tuesday through Thursday
and Sunday from 5:00 P.M.
to 10:00 P.M., Friday and
Saturday until 11:00 P.M.
Moderate.

Cactus Cantina,
3300 Wisconsin
Avenue NW;
686–7222.
See page 125 for full
description.

Cafe Deluxe,
3228 Wisconsin
Avenue NW;
686–2233.
See page 125 for full
description.

Caravela,
4615 Wisconsin Avenue NW;
537–3200
www.acaravelarestaurant
.com
This Tenleytown favorite features Portuguese cuisine.
Lots of neighbors and residents from the local Por-
tuguese and Brazilian
communities, along with
embassy types, flock to this
charming storefront. Their
reasons are many, starting
with a relaxed atmosphere,
the Portuguese oil paintings
lining the walls, and the colorful ceramic table settings.
It's what's on those plates,
however, that is the main
attraction—shellfish risottos,
grilled chicken marinated in
olive oil and Tabasco, and
a superb roast lobster
stuffed with scallops and
shrimp. The wine list is all-
Portuguese and the prices
are right. And when the live
music starts every Saturday
night, you'll think you're in
Ipanema (assuming you've
had a few liters of vinho
verde). Open for lunch Monday through Friday 11:30
A.M. to 2:30 P.M. and for dinner Monday through Thurs-
day from 5:00 to 10:00 P.M.,
Friday and Saturday until
11:00 P.M. Closed Sunday.
Moderate.

Chef Geoff's,
3201 New Mexico Avenue
NW; 237–7800;
www.chefgeoff.com
This great American bistro is
located in a tony neighborhood that needs all the
restaurant help it can get.
But Geoff would do well anywhere in the city with his
"stone pies" (a.k.a. pizza),
crab cakes, and grilled or
seared fish entrees. The
service is friendly, laid-back,
and professional, and the
wine list is both well chosen
and well priced. Open daily
11:30 A.M. to 10:00 P.M. Sunday brunch starts at 11:00
A.M. Moderate.

Colorado Kitchen,
5515 Colorado Avenue NW;
545–8280.
A lot of D.C. foodies are
trekking out to this cheerful
storefront restaurant in the
city's well off the beaten path
Brightwood neighborhood.
The reason is imaginatively
prepared comfort food by
one of Washington's top
young chefs. Don't be
fooled—this is "home cooking" of a kind you may never
see at home. On the menu
you might find "firsts" of
shrimp bisque, leek and
potato soup, or onion and
gorgonzola turnovers fol-
lowed by "big food" such as
meat loaf in black currant
gravy, roast monkfish, or a
"napoleon" made from ham
and Gruyère. The relaxed
quality is enhanced by the
Formica tables, vinyl chairs,
and a counter with stools all
against a background of '40s
music. No alcohol or wine
served and you can't bring
your own. Colorado Kitchen
keeps quirky hours: open for
memorable breakfasts

Wednesday through Friday 7:00 to 11:00 A.M. and dinner Wednesday through Sunday from 5:00 to 9:00 P.M., brunch on Saturday and Sunday from 11:00 A.M. to 3:00 P.M. Lunch is served only on Fridays. Closed Monday and Tuesday. Moderate.

DC Boathouse,
5441 Macarthur Boulevard; 362–2628.
See page 129 for full description.

Firehook Bakery and Coffee House,
3411 Connecticut Avenue NW;
362–2253.
See page 134 for full description.

Hitching Post,
200 Upshur Street NW;
726–1511.
See page 140 for full description.

Krupin's,
4620 Wisconsin Avenue NW;
686–1989
Manhattan may have lots of local Jewish delis where neighborhood folk congregate, but unfortunately they're rare in Washington.

Krupin's, located in Tenleytown, once a farm town within the District and now one of Washington's oldest localities, has that lower East Side feel, with bowls of dill pickles (imported from Brooklyn) on the table and waitresses bearing platters loaded with overstuffed sandwiches, corned beef, chopped liver, and matzo ball soup. Open 8:00 A.M. to 10:00 P.M. daily. Inexpensive.

Lavandou,
3321 Connecticut Avenue NW;
966–3002.
See page 134 for full description.

Lebanese Tavern,
2641 Connecticut Avenue NW;
265–8681.
See page 134 for full description.

Oxford Tavern,
3000 Connecticut Avenue NW;
232–4225.
See page 134 for full description.

Pesto,
2915 Connecticut Avenue NW;
332–8300.
Vincenzo Belvito, one of Washington's top chefs, holds forth at this relaxed and welcoming neighborhood favorite where, as you'd expect, you're going to find a lot of folks ordering that Genova favorite, fettucine al pesto. But the rest of his pasta repertoire, including veal tortellini and linguini with shrimp also draws raves, as do the grilled snapper and my favorite, Belvito's flavorful osso buco (braised veal shanks). The venison sausages with a balsamico sauce are great. Open Monday through Thursday 5:30 to 10:00 P.M.; Friday through Sunday 5:30 to 11:00 P.M. Moderate.

Rocklands Barbecue and Grilling Company,
2418 Wisconsin Avenue NW;
333–2558.
You'll get probably the best barbecue in the District in this modest storefront with a giant wood grill. Rocklands has a few stools for sit-down

AUTHOR'S FAVORITE PLACES TO EAT IN UPPER NORTHWEST

Lavandou	Pesto
Chef Geoff's	Buck's Fishing and Camping
Cafe Deluxe	Caravela
2 Amys Neopolitan Pizza	Colorado Kitchen
Trattoria Lilliana	

diners, but you can either eat your pork ribs or chicken standing in the corner next to the world-class collection of 120 spicy sauces and condiments or take them along on your walk through nearby Glover Archbold Park. You can make a virtual visit at www.rocklands.com, but you won't get the great smell of that wood grill. Open Monday through Friday 11:00 A.M. to 10:00 P.M., Saturday 11:00 A.M. to 10:00 P.M., and Sunday 11:00 A.M. to 9:00 P.M. Inexpensive.

Saveur,
2218 Wisconsin Avenue NW; 333–5885, fax 333–1104.
This storefront find between the National Cathedral and Georgetown has an eclectic and imaginative menu with risottos, rack of lamb, beef medallions, and crab cakes, but its real specialties are focused on game. Try the seared duck breast with duck sausage or a roast venison, maybe the best you'll ever eat, then follow up with chocolate Wellington or

another megacalorie dessert. Since chef Kao Koumtakoun frequently works the room to greet diners, you'll have a chance to tell him personally how great it is. Knowledgeable, friendly service, moderate prices, and a super-romantic atmosphere. No Metro, but the "30" buses will get you there. Expensive.

Starland Cafe,
5125 Macarthur Boulevard NW; 244–9396.
See page 129 for full description.

Tesoro,
4400 Connecticut Avenue NW; 363–6766.
This northwest trattoria does a good job on the usual Italian fare, including the better-known pastas and veal dishes. But Tesoro's menu includes some less frequently seen offerings, such as lamb shanks with vegetables and a tasty blackened salmon with pesto risotto. Inexpensive, romantic, and a nice, reasonably priced wine list—isn't that what life's really all about? Metro: Van Ness-UDC (red line).

Trattoria Lilliana,
4483 Connecticut Avenue NW; 237–0893.
Here's a rarity in Washington and many other cities—an authentic mom and pop trattoria just like the ones travelers discover and cherish on their trips throughout Italy. But since Lilliana and Maurice Dumas are from Liguria, the coastal strip of Italy near Genova, home cooking in this cheerful little storefront features regional favorites like gnocchi al pesto, cacciuco, the local fish stew, and a splendid fritto misto of fish. A reasonably priced wine list and great gelato also make this a prime choice. Lilliana is pretty cozy, so it pays to reserve. Open for lunch Monday through Thursday 11:30 A.M. to 3:00 P.M. and Saturday 11:30 A.M. to 4:00 P.M.; dinner Monday through Thursday 5:30 to 9:30 P.M. and Friday and Saturday 5:30 to 10:30 P.M. Moderate.

2 Amys Neopolitan Pizzeria,
3715 Macomb Street NW; 885–5700.
See page 125 for full description.

Dupont Circle

Dupont Circle is probably Washington's liveliest neighborhood, with a raffish street life and an intellectual reputation fueled by plenty of first-rate bookstores and cafes, several of them catering to the area's large gay community. The Circle offers visitors an abundance of house museums, art galleries, and restaurants along with a laid-back lifestyle that makes casual strolling a joy. Although the present, in itself, would make Dupont Circle an agreeable place to hang out, this neighborhood's past gives it an extra dimension that enriches any visit.

At the beginning of the twentieth century, Dupont Circle was called "Washington's Newport," one of America's most fashionable districts, where the nation's lumber barons, steel kings, and other merchant moguls built the hundreds of grand winter homes and town houses that continue to grace the area. Nowadays this neighborhood and its brownstone town houses, red-brick turrets, and Beaux Arts palaces includes the Massachusetts Avenue corridor called Embassy Row, which bristles with the flags of many nations not even dreamed of during its Victorian heyday. Behind the opulent mansions that line Massachusetts Avenue, quiet streets filter back into Kalorama, a residential neighborhood that has known elegant living in three centuries.

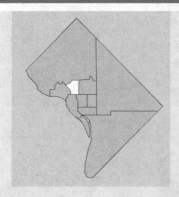

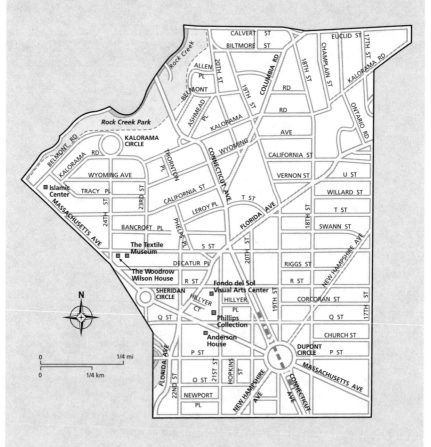

The Dupont Circle stop on the Metro's red line serves most of the sites in this chapter. Dupont Circle itself is named not for a member of the great chemical family, but after Samuel Francis Dupont, an admiral in the Union Navy. A large fountain commemorating his exploits sits in the center of the Circle, which is actually a small oasis at the intersection of three main streets: New Hampshire, Massachusetts, and Connecticut Avenues. Despite the constant traffic, the Circle has a small-town feel, with plenty of benches for checkers and conversation.

Before you leave the Circle, stop to admire three distinguished palaces that, unfortunately, cannot be visited but exemplify this historic neighborhood's elegant pedigree. That ornate white palazzo at 15 Dupont Circle is the ***Patterson House,*** built by renowned architect Stanford White in 1903 for the publisher of the *Chicago Tribune*. During the Coolidge administration, it served briefly as the interim White House while the real thing was being refurbished. It is now a private women's club. Around the corner, at 1801 Massachusetts Avenue, you'll find the stately ***Wadsworth House,*** which dates from 1900, making it one of Washington's first Beaux Arts mansions. It is now the home of the Sulgrave Club. Across 18th Street stands the ***McCormick apartment building,*** built in 1915 as one of the city's first luxury apartments. The Mellens, Phillips, and other magnates lived in the building's 11,000-square-foot apartments. In 1977 the building became the headquarters of the National Trust for Historic Preservation.

In 1892, when millionaire brewer Christian Heurich (pronounced *hy-rick*) built his thirty-one-room dream castle on New Hampshire Avenue just off the Circle, many of the other mansions that ringed Dupont Circle were built by newly minted industrial titans eager to forget their humble or distant origins. Not Heurich, who wanted his home to celebrate his German ancestry. The result is an unlikely marriage of Queen Victoria and Count von Bismarck, a ponderous brownstone home in Romanesque Revival style (or as one observer put it, "beer barrel baronial") with high-ceilinged rooms where William McKinley would feel right at home.

TOP ATTRACTIONS IN DUPONT CIRCLE

Phillips Collection	The Textile Museum
Anderson House	The Woodrow Wilson House
The Heurich House Museum	The Lindens

Embassy Cultural Events

Most visitors don't know it, but many of Washington's foreign embassies offer rich cultural programs showcasing artists and performers from their home countries. Many of these programs take place in the embassy itself or in local theaters and galleries. Among the embassies with active programs are:

Austria
895–6700;
www.austria.com

Canada
682–1740;
www.canadianembassy.org

Sweden
467–2600;
www.swedish-embassy.org

Italy
223–1125;
www.italcultusa.org

France
944–6091;
www.ambafrance-us.org

At the ***Heurich House Museum,*** you'll see the meaning of ornate, from the parlor brimming with objets d'art, to the music room with its musician's gallery, to the majestic dining room in carved walnut, with a table elaborately set for eighteen. Amid all this Gilded Age splendor you'll find German mythological scenes elaborately carved by craftsmen on the furniture, wainscoting, and the house's seventeen marble fireplaces. If the public rooms become a little too formal, lighten up by heading downstairs to the basement breakfast room, which doubled as the family *bierstube*. Here the Heurichs gathered for family meals and steins of the family product surrounded by mottoes (in German, of course) celebrating the pleasures of the glass. Since Heurich lived to be 102, maybe the suggestion that "A good drink rejuvenates" isn't such bad advice. The mansion is now the headquarters of the Historical Society of Washington, which maintains a reference library and museum shop there. The handsome little garden behind the house is perfect for a picnic or a rest. The Heurich House Museum, 1307 New Hampshire Avenue NW (429–1894; www .heurichhouse.org) is open for walk-in tours on Wednesday at 12:15 and 1:15 P.M. Group tours by reservation. Suggested donation $5.00.

Yes, it's true—at the ***Brickskeller*** you can get terrific burgers and good buffalo steaks from the Dakotas, not to mention some nice rainbow trout. But the big attraction is the Brickskeller's world-class collection of beers, totaling more than 900 brands at last count (that is, if you're sober enough to count). There are a lot of saloons in this country that make a big deal of their collection of microbrews and exotic foreign labels, but nobody, repeat nobody,

beats the Brickskeller. For proof, just check out the house collection of emp-
ties that lines the walls of this restaurant, elegantly decorated in Early American Fraternity House style. No wine list to worry about here. To spare yourself
the embarrassment of ordering the wrong beer with pierogies or other menu
choices, just ask your knowledgeable sommelier of suds to bring over the
Brickskeller's book of brews for a consultation. (Hint: A young, presumptu-
ous, and slightly spritzy San Miguel—a late harvest '97—would be perfect).
The Brickskeller is located at 1523 22nd Street NW; 293–1885; www.the
brickskeller.com. Open Monday through Friday 11:30 A.M. to 2:00 A.M., Saturday 6:00 P.M. to 3:00 A.M., and Sunday 6:00 P.M. to 2:00 A.M. Inexpensive—if
you stop after only one beer.

P.S. If you've ever wanted to live over a major-league beer hall and all the
bar food you could possibly handle, you'll be interested to know that the top
three floors of the Brickskeller's building are taken up by *The Brickskeller
Inn,* a small hotel with over 40 smallish and spartan rooms.

None of Massachusetts Avenue's great mansions reflects power and wealth
more than *Anderson House,* whose massive facade fairly oozes authority.
Now the headquarters of the Society of the Cincinnati, a venerable organization of Revolutionary War descendants, Anderson House was for many years
the home of wealthy career diplomat Larz Anderson. In keeping with the
"Washington's Newport" reputation of this neighborhood, the Andersons used
this colossal house for only a few months every year.

Keep in mind that Anderson House suffers from a touch of schizophrenia.
You'll start off on the ground floor with the Society's impressive collections of
Revolutionary War memorabilia and paintings by John Trumbull, Gilbert Stuart,
and other early American artists. But on the second floor, the Anderson House
suddenly becomes a treasure trove of eclectic antiquities and furnishings that
largely reflect Anderson's years in Europe and Asia as the American ambassador
to Japan and Belgium. Several rooms hold rare Japanese and Chinese carvings
and lacquers acquired during Anderson's years in Asia, while others are strictly

AUTHOR'S FAVORITES IN DUPONT CIRCLE

Phillips Collection	Adams Morgan
Second Story Books	Kalorama Walk
Kramerbooks and Afterwords Cafe and Grill	Embassy Row

European, including the highly traditional English parlor with Hepplewhite chairs and portraits by Reynolds and Hoppner.

What makes the very rich different from you and me becomes obvious in the Anderson's sumptuous dining room. You know you're not back home in your cozy breakfast nook when you see how the Andersons, even *à deux*, dined at a table for twenty-eight in a room graced with Carrara marble floors, seventeenth-century Belgian tapestries, and priceless Japanese screens. After dinner the ambassador and his wife led their guests downstairs to their vast ballroom, which conjures up visions of black-tie evenings in a long-vanished Washington. Outside the ballroom there's the garden and, in the center, a grand seventeenth-century Buddha. Amid this elegance and ostentation you'll find indications that this regal couple also had a nice sense of humor; in the solarium you'll see the amusing cartoon of the Andersons tooting along in their open touring car and a map tracing their favorite drives around Washington. Anderson House, at 2118 Massachusetts Avenue NW (785–2040), is open Tuesday through Saturday 1:00 to 4:00 P.M., but call before coming.

capitalquote

"Massachusetts Avenue runs the whole length of the city, and is inserted on the maps as a full-blown street, about four miles in length. Go there, and you will find yourself not only out of town, away among the fields, but you will find yourself beyond the fields, in an uncultivated, undrained wilderness. Tucking your trowsers up to your knees you will wade through the bogs, you will lose yourself among rude hillocks, you will be out of the reach of humanity."

Anthony Trollope
in *North America* (1862)

In the Phillips Mansion at Massachusetts Avenue and 21st Street, you'll find one of America's finest collections of modern art. Private at first, the **Phillips Collection** went public in 1921, when wealthy collector Duncan Phillips opened a few rooms of the family home to art lovers. The collection has since expanded to occupy the entire mansion and a recent annex.

The collection reflects Phillips's refined and diverse tastes, especially his love for the French Impressionists. Here, in an intimate and charming setting, you'll find Renoir's *Luncheon of the Boating Party* and other treasures such as Degas' *Dancers at the Bar* and masterpieces by Bonnard, Cézanne, Matisse, and Daumier. There are also important works by neoclassicists and realists such as Corot and Courbet along with American modernists Georgia O'Keeffe and Edward Hopper. As you wander through this explosion of great art, you'll also be able to inspect the public rooms of the Phillips mansion, including the grandiose Music Room, with its intricate Italianate ceiling. The Music Room is also the site of the collection's Sunday afternoon concerts, which are held at 5:00 P.M. September through May. The concerts are free with museum admission, but it's a good idea to arrive early. The Phillips Collection, 1600 21st Street NW (387–2151; www.phillipscollection.org), is open Tuesday, through Saturday 10:00 A.M. to 5:00 P.M., Sunday noon to 7:00 P.M.; closed Monday. On Thursday, when there's an "Artful Evenings" program of live jazz, lectures, and a cash bar, the hours are 10:00 A.M. to

diplomatic
niceties

To avoid making a diplomatic gaffe that would embarrass your country, you should know that an embassy is where the ambassador lives. The building where he and his exalted flunkies have their offices is called the chancery.

8:30 P.M. Regular admission is $8.00, but free if you're under eighteen; the charge for Artful Evenings is $8.00.

The Phillips also has an excellent gift shop open Tuesday through Saturday from 10:00 A.M. to 5:00 P.M. and Sunday from noon to 5:00 P.M. Closed Monday. Next to the gift shop, the Phillips Cafe serves coffee, light lunches, and soups Tuesday through Saturday 10:45 A.M. to 4:30 P.M. and on Sunday from noon to 4:30 P.M.

Back on 21st Street, a left turn leads to R Street and a handsome block lined with century-old brownstones. Franklin and Eleanor Roosevelt raised their burgeoning family in the town house at 2131 R from 1916 to 1920, when FDR was the dashing young assistant secretary of the Navy. The house is now the residence of the ambassador of Mali and cannot be visited. The flower-banked marble steps near the corner of 22nd and Decatur Street have been dubbed "The Spanish Steps," even though they bear not the slightest resemblance to the original staircase in Rome. Anyway, they are all that remains of Kalorama (Greek for "beautiful view"), the eighteenth-century manor house that gave this neighborhood its name.

The Beat Goes On

Not far from Dupont Circle, where 20th and O Streets join New Hampshire Avenue, you can wander into tiny **Sonny Bono Park,** a grassy triangle that memorializes the pop star turned politician who died in a 1998 skiing accident. The park, with benches, flowers, and, from an anonymous donor, a TV plaque dedicated to the former congressman, is small but agreeable, which is why on sunny days you're likely to find a few locals reading or dining in this little oasis.

Gallery Scene

It's only natural that the Phillips would become the hub of a thriving gallery community in its neighborhood. Here are a few to start you out:

In Hillyer Court, a tiny mews that cuts through the two wings of the Phillips, you'll discover two distinctive galleries at number 9, a converted carriage house. *The Gary Edwards Gallery* specializes in vintage nineteenth-century photographs from all over the world. The photos, which might include shots of 1880 Madrid or Rome, come from owner Edwards's personal archives. You can see these evocative and historically significant photographs from Tuesday through Saturday between 11:00 A.M. and 5:00 P.M. 232–5926.

Across the hall, at the *Foundry Gallery,* you'll find a cooperative with nonstop shows by thirty artists, including local printmakers, painters, and photographers. Not only that, you'll be able to schmooze with Washington artists like Peter Robinson, then wonder about why, after all those art appreciation classes you still can't paint like that. 387–0203; www.foundry-gallery.org. Open Wednesday through Saturday 11:00 A.M. to 5:00 P.M., Sunday 1:00 to 5:00 P.M.

R Street, between Connecticut and Florida Avenues, is the real heart of this art neighborhood. Galleryland starts at 2114 R Street with the *Burdick Gallery,* dedicated to the carvings, sculptures, and prints of the Inuit people of the Canadian Arctic. 986–5682. Open Tuesday through Friday noon to 6:00 P.M., Saturday from 11:00 A.M. to 5:00 P.M. and Sunday 2:00 to 5:00 P.M.

At the *Fondo del Sol Visual Arts Center* you won't need a passport to tune in on the vibrant art and cultural heritage of the Americas. Exhibitions here run the gamut from pre-Columbian art down to the most contemporary paintings out of Brazil. The center also sponsors a wide-ranging program of lectures, concerts, and other educational events, plus an annual summer festival of Caribbean music. The center, at 2112 R Street NW (483–2777), is open Wednesday through Saturday 1:00 to 6:00 P.M. Contributions appreciated, amigo.

Across from the Irish Embassy, in the 2200 block of S Street, stands Mitchell Park, which looks like your average urban park, with one exception—there's a dog buried in the sandbox. Back in 1918 Morton and Elizabeth Mitchell donated this choice real estate to the city with the proviso that the grave of Bock, their much-loved poodle, be maintained in perpetuity. And that's why you'll find Bock's burial place protected by that chain fence toward the north end.

A left turn on S Street leads past the Irish Embassy, with a harp over the entrance, to the **Textile Museum,** which just might be the best-kept secret in a city notorious for its leaks and indiscretions. The museum is the creation of George Hewitt Myers (as in Bristol-Myers), whose lifelong love of the textile arts began with an Oriental rug in his dorm room at Yale. Seven decades later,

Two galleries occupy the 1872 townhouse at 2106 R Street NW. Upstairs, you'll find the *Alex Gallery*, a well-established commercial gallery that features contemporary European and American artists. Its downstairs sibling, *Gallery A*, features young and emerging artists. 667–2599; www.alexgalleries.com. Both are open Tuesday through Saturday from 11:00 A.M. to 5:00 P.M.

At the *Robert Brown Gallery*, the focus is on international artists, most of them contemporary, but you might also find art by Giacometti and Henry Moore in this eclectic space. Even more eclectic, ask to see Brown's fascinating collection of Chinese advertising posters from the '20s and '30s. Robert Brown Gallery, 2030 R Street NW, 484–4383; www.robertbrowngallery.com. Open Tuesday through Saturday noon to 6:00 P.M.

The *Marsha Mateyka Gallery*, just off Connecticut Avenue at 2012 R Street, presents a broad array of contemporary styles. This top gallery is located in an 1886 townhouse that has been brought back from the brink and made into a wonderful exhibit space. The building may be Victorian, but this gallery is the place to come for contemporary sculpture, paintings, and works on paper by leading American and European artists. 328–0088; www.marshamateykagallery.com. Open Wednesday through Saturday 11:00 A.M. to 5:00 P.M.

Affrica, as the name tells you, specializes in traditional African art. At this exciting gallery at 2010½ R Street, you'll find textiles, museum-quality masks, and carvings from a continent whose art is all too often overlooked. 745–7272. Open Tuesday 2:00 P.M. to 6:00 P.M. and Wednesday through Saturday from noon to 6:00 P.M.

Myers's undergraduate hobby has become a world-class collection of more than 14,000 textiles and 1,400 carpets that are housed in the elegant rooms of his former town home and the mansion next door. The museum's regular holdings include every conceivable example of the textile arts throughout the ages, from fifth-century Coptic and Islamic textiles and pre-Columbian textiles from Peru down to twentieth-century native weavings from Central America and New Mexico, all splendidly displayed under brilliant spotlights that accentuate their dazzling colors and intricate designs. The museum also hosts visiting collections, often with original themes, including the recent pairing of subtly patterned Amish quilts with boldly colored nineteenth-century Caucasian rugs.

And the gift shop is not to be missed. Just like the visual excitement of the museum's exhibits, its shop, located in the Myerses' former library, is one of the most colorful, attractive—and jumbled—you'll find anywhere; aside from reproductions of classic textiles in various forms, it also offers a fine selection of books on the textile arts. The Textile Museum, 2320 S Street NW (667–0441; www.textilemuseum.org), is open Monday through Saturday 10:00 A.M. to 5:00 P.M., Sunday 1:00 to 5:00 P.M. Docent-led tours can be reserved two weeks in advance. Suggested admission contribution of $5.00.

These days, presidents usually hotfoot it out of town the minute their terms end, but in March 1921, when Woodrow Wilson left office, he actually stayed on in Washington, moving from 1600 Pennsylvania across town to an elegant Georgian Revival home that immediately became nationally known as "the house on S Street." Although the world Wilson helped create at Versailles has changed beyond recognition, his Washington town house has remained much as it was when he died there in 1924. Its combination of personal belongings and White House memorabilia makes **Woodrow Wilson House** both a fascinating presidential museum and a wonderfully preserved upper-class home of the 1920s, from the Wilsons' windup Victrola ready to play a 78 of "Oh You Beautiful Doll" to the box of Kellogg's "Pep" on the kitchen table. Wandering in this time warp, visitors find it easy to imagine that the Wilsons stepped out only a moment ago for a drive in nearby Rock Creek Park.

Wilson House docents say that for most visitors the real center of the house is Wilson's library, a comfortable and cluttered retreat filled with the personal and official mementos of his presidency. Wilson's cabinet chair is pushed back from a desk covered with personal papers; nearby stands a vintage microphone used for a 1923 broadcast. There's a "Graphoscope" movie projector (a 1913 gift from Douglas Fairbanks), and on the wall hangs a map of the brave but fleeting new Europe created by Wilson at Versailles. The house contains many personal and poignant touches. In the living room his massive Steinway and its period sheet music await the former president; in the upstairs bedroom, where Wilson died, a suit, walking stick, and boater are laid out for the next day's activities. A few steps away, in the nurse's room, we see

capital quote

"It is sometimes called the City of Magnificent Distances, but it might with greater propriety be termed the City of Magnificent Intentions. . . . Spacious avenues that begin in nothing and lead no where; streets, mile long, that only want houses, roads and inhabitants; public buildings that need but a public to be complete."

—Charles Dickens,
American Notes, 1842

a crude "shock stimulator" used in treating the paralyzed ex-president in his final months. Woodrow Wilson House, 2340 S Street NW (387–4062; www .woodrowwilsonhouse.org), is open Tuesday through Sunday 10:00 A.M. to 4:00 P.M. Admission is $5.00 for adults; under 7 free.

After leaving the Wilson House you'll be *(a)* standing at 24th and S Streets and *(b)* confronted with two choices, both of which represent an embarrassment of riches for a wonderful stroll. Make that decision the Washington way and waffle. Take both and you'll be doing just like the local politicians, who often feel very strongly about something—both ways.

Your first option is to explore **Kalorama,** one of Washington's and the nation's finest residential neighborhoods. To do this, turn right and walk up 24th Street to explore side streets like California Street, Wyoming Avenue, and Tracy Place, which you'll find lined with elegant homes designed for America's superrich by some of the foremost architects of their time.

One of these homes, the former Walsh-McLean mansion at 1825 Phelps Place NW, is now the **Russian Cultural Centre,** which sponsors musical and other programs that showcase Russian culture. The centre also has a permanent exhibit of icons and paintings, which you can see Monday through Friday from 10:00 A.M. to 6:00 P.M. and on Saturday by appointment. Be advised, however, that you'll be just as impressed by the magnificent rooms and parlors of this knockout mansion as by the art itself. To find out what's showing while you're in town, call 265–3840 or visit www.russianculturalcentre.org.

The forest of colorful flags along these streets tells you that most of these homes are now inhabited by foreign ambassadors. One of them is the Tudor mansion at 2221 Kalorama Road, built in 1911 for a mining millionaire, but that

The Islamic Center

Although the Washington skyline bristles with towers and columns, the most distinctive spire of all is the 160-foot minaret of the Islamic Center at 2551 Massachusetts Avenue NW. Dedicated in 1957, the center was funded by contributions and gifts from a number of Islamic governments. The imposing, two-ton bronze chandelier was the gift of Egypt, while the Shah of Iran donated the elegant Persian carpets. The center's interior courtyard gleams with blue and gold mosaics and tiles. Visitors are always welcome but must observe a modest dress code—no bare arms or legs (translation: no shorts) and women must have head coverings. Visiting hours are daily from 10:00 A.M. to 5:00 P.M.; bear in mind, however, that viewing the center's exquisite interior is difficult on Fridays, when mandatory prayers draw thousands of worshippers. 332–8343.

Kalorama Triangle

If you follow Kalorama Road across Connecticut Avenue you'll enter the historic district known as *"Kalorama Triangle,"* which extends as far as Columbia Road, the main street of Adams Morgan. On early maps of the District, this appears as a hilly woodland cut by ravines—once part of the rural estate of poet-diplomat Joel Barlow—but later developed as one of D.C.'s "streetcar suburbs" that sprung up with the construction of the now-vanished Connecticut Avenue trolley line in 1897. If you wander at random along the streets of Kalorama Triangle you'll be repaid with a look at some of the city's finest residential architecture, including the grand apartment houses at 2029 and 2101 Connecticut Avenue and handsome turn-of-the-twentieth century row houses in the 2300 block of 19th Street. Although many of the former palaces of the Gilded Age's golden people have disappeared, just like their owners, the Triangle still boasts one of Washington's grandest homes, the Beaux Arts Lothrop mansion at 2101 Connecticut. It is now the home of the Russian Trade Office and is not open to visitors.

is now, as you can see from the mammoth tricolor floating from the facade, the residence of the French ambassador.

Close by, at 2401 Kalorama Road, stands what I think is Washington's most magnificent house, *The Lindens,* a wonderful frame Georgian home with the look of colonial New England. And well it should—The Lindens was actually built in Danvers, Massachusetts, in 1754, but in 1934 was dismantled and moved to Washington in sections. Check out the house's windows, which are originals, and the lovely little park and garden that surrounds it. Georgetown's Stone House is the oldest house *built* in Washington, but The Lindens is Washington's oldest house.

Your other possibility is to return to Dupont Circle from 24th and S Streets, strolling past the most splendid palaces of Embassy Row. The opulence starts right away with the Embassy of Cameroon's imposing French château at 2349 Massachusetts, which is one of Washington's premiere Beaux Arts palaces. Architects know this romantic pile as the *Hauge House,* named for the wealthy Norwegian diplomat who built it in 1906. Speaking of Beaux Arts, wandering along Embassy Row you'll see a number of town houses similar to the Croatian Embassy—early twentieth-century buildings with French style that would feel right at home in Paris. The Croatian Embassy at 2343 Massachusetts also offers passersby a fine little statue by sculptor Ivan Mestrovic. Before reaching Sheridan Circle you also pass the magnificent Embassy of Haiti at 2311 and (ho-hum) yet another French château at 2315 that is now the Pakistani Embassy.

At Sheridan Circle, where General Phil Sheridan is spending his eternity directing traffic on horseback, look for the Mediterranean-style stucco house at 2306 Massachusetts. This was the home of Alice Pike Barney, who from 1902 to 1924 used the house as her studio and made it Washington's most dazzling artistic and literary salon. Lucky Washingtonians remember that until a few years ago Ms. Barney's flamboyant house and its paintings were open to the public. Not any more. The Smithsonian is now entrusted with the house, and plans call for it to become a music school.

On Sheridan Circle, between 23rd Street and Massachusetts Avenue, a small granite and bronze monument marks one of Washington's few successful acts of political terrorism. On this spot on September 21, 1976, a car bomb explosion killed former Chilean Ambassador Orlando Letelier and his American associate Roni Moffit. Chilean agents working for Gen. Augusto Pinochet were charged and convicted of this heinous crime.

One block away, on the corner where 22nd Street joins Massachusetts Avenue, you'll arrive at **Argyle House,** a massive Victorian pile. As the date high on the imposing façade at 2201 22nd Street tells you, this mansion was built in 1900, and its owner was Captain Frederick Miller, who was both a senior naval officer and a big time cat fancier. You can see his love for felines when you look up high on Argyle House's roof line and find a large stone cat perched, quietly watching the traffic zoom along Massachusetts Avenue. But tabby isn't the only cat prowling Argyle House; take a look at the fierce lions that support the stone bench in Captain Miller's front garden.

Top-Secret Touring

Curious about what actually goes on inside those sumptuous embassies? If your CIA friend told you, he'd have to kill you, but there's an easier way to get that intelligence. In fact there are two tours that will let you crash those formidable gates.

The **Kalorama House and Embassy Tour** takes place on the second Sunday in September from noon to 5:00 P.M. These self-guided walking tours start at the Wilson House, which sponsors this annual event, and visit both distinguished private homes and embassies all over Kalorama. Tickets cost $18 when purchased in advance or $20 at the Wilson House on the day of the tour. For more details or to order tickets, call 387–4062, ext. 18.

The Dupont Circle House Tour. This October event can take you to homes, apartments, artist's studios, and other historic buildings in the Dupont Circle neighborhood. 265–3222. Tickets $25 in advance or $30 on tour day.

St. Francis of Kalorama

Look carefully across the street from the French residence and you'll spy an antique, robin's egg blue police call box that has been turned into a tiny shrine with a ceramic tile of St. Francis of Assisi. Francis, who is surrounded by friendly birds and carries a red flower, is flanked by colored eggs and a bud vase that often sports spring flowers. This delightful little vignette is part of a D.C. Heritage program to renovate and reuse the 1,500 historic but now-abandoned police and fire call boxes in the city and turn them into neighborhood icons. Under this program, artists are decorating the box exteriors, while neighborhood historians provide documents or images for inside the call box doors such as old photographs, quotes from longtime residents, poems that capture the spirit of the place, or notes on historic events or personalities.

Across Florida Avenue stands one of Washington's great Gilded Age mansions. The **Townsend House,** at 2121 Massachusetts Avenue, was built in 1904 as an eighteenth-century French château by Richard Townsend, a railroad magnate, and his wife, heir to another rail fortune. The Townsends spared no expense in creating this grand home. In fact Frederick Law Olmsted, the designer of Central Park, was their landscape architect. Later the house belonged to Sumner Welles, FDR's Undersecretary of State. It is now the home of the **Cosmos Club,** a private club of achievers in the arts, science, and politics, whose lucky members get to read, dine, and dance in vast and sumptuous rooms once frequented by the superrich of early twentieth-century Washington.

capitalquote

"Washington was the one city in the east where any woman with money and talent could set up housekeeping and become an important hostess."

—Alice Hoge, writing in *Cissy Patterson*

Your walk to the Circle will take you past the Anderson House and then Washington's most overwhelming building, the **Walsh-McLean House** at 2020 Massachusetts. The house was built in 1903 by Thomas Walsh, a fabulously wealthy gold miner whose daughter, Evalyn Walsh McLean, went on to own the Hope diamond. Stupendous doesn't begin to describe this house, which boasts a grand stairwell copied from a *Titanic*-era ocean liner that Walsh took a shine to. The building is now the Embassy of Indonesia. Walk-in visits are not possible, but individual and group tours of the mansion's palatial music and ballrooms can be requested by faxing the Embassy's Information Division at 775–5365 or phoning 775–5295 and stating your preferred dates and number of visitors.

One of the pleasures of wandering in this raffish area is poking into the lively shops and cafes that make the Circle a favorite of window shoppers and serious buyers. Dupont Circle is also a center for Washington's specialty book sellers, so bibliophiles, buyers, and browsers have a field day cruising the neighborhood. But don't forget to look up every now and then or you'll miss seeing that most of Connecticut Avenue's shops and cafes are lodged in what were once some of the city's grandest town houses.

Start your shopping at **Second Story Books,** at 20th and P Streets, a few steps from the Circle. Second Story gets its name from its first location as a small used book store over an Asian restaurant in northwest Washington. It is now one of the largest used and rare book stores in the world, with three outlets in the Washington area. The browsing is intense at Second Story, which is floor-to-ceiling, wall-to-wall books—a paradise for bibliophiles looking for rarities or anyone searching for that out-of-print book that was lent out but never seen again. In good weather the store sets up an outside remnants table with a well-earned reputation as a bargain-hunter's delight. Used CDs too. Second Story Books, 2000 P Street NW (659–8884, www.secondstorybooks.com), is open daily 10:00 A.M. to 10:00 P.M.

If you've been thinking that vinyl records are totally extinct, just stick your head into **DJ Hut,** for a look at one of the last outposts of the LP disk. This shop is always crowded with Washington-area DJs looking for new sounds for their clubs. Since we're not talking Vivaldi or Mantovani here, the audition process can be a trifle noisy, as the jocks check out records by the Dungeon Family or Dilated Peoples on professional turntables. Lots of fun, especially if you're into hip-hop. DJ Hut, on the second floor at 2010 P Street NW (659–2010), is open Monday through Friday noon to 10:00 P.M., Saturday noon to 8:00 P.M., and Sunday 1:00 to 6:00 P.M.

Over on Connecticut Avenue you'll find the Circle's most concentrated shopping, beginning with **Kramerbooks,** one of Washington's top booksellers and one of a dwindling number of its independents. Kramerbooks' knowledgeable staff, personalized service, and impeccably selected inventory make

Florida Bound

Florida Avenue, the western boundary of the Dupont Circle area was, in colonial times, the main highway between the port of Georgetown and New York and New England; George Washington traveled it frequently. Known as Boundary Road in the nineteenth century, it was just that—the District's outer limit.

Hidden Treasure

At first blush, O Street between 20th and 21st Streets is merely a leafy and refined block of elegant brownstone town houses dating from the close of the nineteenth century. However, behind the brass plaque and imposing door of 2020 you'll find something totally unexpected—*The Mansion on O Street,* one of America's most eclectic and imaginative hotels—a small inn created by linking four 1892 town houses to form a luxurious complex containing a grand ballroom, seven dining rooms, twelve conference rooms, eighteen guestrooms, and sixteen fireplaces.

From the entryway you spot a typical Victorian parlor, except that this one holds vintage leather barber chairs and an 1800s pool table. Stairs lead past a cat puppet to an upstairs series of wildly and whimsically decorated theme rooms, including the two-story Log Cabin Suite, complete with a simulated rain forest, and the Art Deco Penthouse Suite with its private elevator, full kitchen, and aquarium above the bed. If you've been missing work, ask for the Corporate Suite, decorated like an office where the bed is headboarded with filing cabinets. And there's much more, including great antiques and a collection of art that ranges from Remington bronzes to rare oils and maps; the mansion also hosts periodic traveling art exhibits. The library has over 1,000 volumes. Luxury touches include a chef, stereo systems, scores of TV sets, and enough soaking tubs, Jacuzzis, and spa showers to bathe some countries. Everything you see in the mansion is for sale, including the shower made from an English telephone booth (if you can wrestle it out to your car). You can arrange to tour the mansion by appointment by calling 496–2020; a charitable donation of $5.00 is expected.

If instead you decide to stay at the mansion, you'll be joining a celebrity-laden guest list that includes Sylvester Stallone, Kim Basinger, and Hillary Clinton. Reservations by e-mail (hotel@mansion.com) and fax (659–0547) only. And, yes, it's expensive. The Mansion on O Street, 2020 O Street NW, (496–2000), www.omansion.com.

this the perfect place to track down that special request or find the right book on everything from poetry to appreciating architecture to tips on souping up your sex life. Speaking of which, at the height of the Lewinsky scandal, Kramerbooks did all of us a favor by tearing up the special prosecutor's subpoena for its records of Monica's purchase of a book for President Clinton (since you asked, it was *Vox* by Nicholson Baker; if you read it you'll understand why it was a thoughtful gift). To read more about Kramer's principled (and costly) rejection of the Starr subpoena, check out the store's Web site at www.kramers.com.

Kramerbooks is also important if you're hungering for more than knowledge. Its ***Afterwords Cafe and Grill*** may be in the rear of the store, but it's a real restaurant and a good one, nothing like the little add-on cafes you'll find in many other bookstores. Breakfasts are notable and inexpensive; the rest of the day you can order entree salads and sandwiches, while dinners can run the gamut from jumbo crab cakes to grilled fish and pastas. On Saturday and Sunday the Dupont literati gather here over brunch for profound, cholesterol-laden discussions of big topics. Kramerbooks and Afterwords Cafe, at 1517 Connecticut Avenue NW (387–1400), are both open Sunday through Thursday 7:30 A.M. to 1:00 A.M. and twenty-four hours Friday and Saturday.

In addition to being a social hub and information center for Dupont Circle's gay community, ***Lambda Rising,*** at 1625 Connecticut, is one of the most comprehensive gay/lesbian bookstores in the country. In fact, it was the original shop for what is now a national chain of bookstores for gay men and women. Lambda Rising, 462–6969, is open Friday and Saturday 10:00 A.M. to midnight; the rest of the week it's 10:00 A.M. to 10:00 P.M.

Best Cellars is probably the most dramatic wine store in the country. No jumble of dusty bottles, hastily scrawled price tags, or underlit shelves here; just a starkly attractive and beautifully illuminated display of top wines. Furthermore, Best Cellars arranges their wines unconventionally, by taste categories such as "fruity," "crisp," and "bold," making it easier for you to match wine with food. Best Cellars, 1643 Connecticut Avenue (387–3146; www.best cellars.com), is open Monday through Thursday 10:00 A.M. to 9:00 P.M., Friday and Saturday until 10:00 P.M.

Upon entering ***Secondi,*** it's hard to believe that you're in a consignment clothing store and not a trendy, definitely upscale boutique. There are serious bargains here, from recycled dinner gowns to barely worn designer dresses with labels that even some men will recognize. Alas, there's a touch of sexism here: All of this secondhand chic is only for women; no men's clothing sold. Secondi, upstairs at 1702 Connecticut Avenue NW, is open Monday, Tuesday, and Saturday 11:00 A.M. to 6:00 P.M., Wednesday through Friday 11:00 A.M. to 7:00 P.M., and Sunday 1:00 to 5:00 P.M. Call 667–1122.

Down on the Dupont Farm

It's a bit incongruous, but this highly sophisticated and hip neighborhood, better known for art than asparagus, has its own farmer's market. Every Sunday from 9:00 A.M. to 1:00 P.M. vendors congregate behind the Riggs Bank just off the Circle at the corner of Massachusetts and 20th Street to sell organic vegetables trucked in from neighboring states. You'll also find a good selection of flowers, exotic fruits, and even handwoven sweaters from Ecuador.

Museum Meander

Nine leading museums and arts sites welcome visitors and provide special musical and other programs during the annual **Dupont-Kalorama Museum Walk,** held on the first weekend of June. The Phillips Collection sponsors hands-on art activities for children, the Fondo del Sol Visual Arts Center goes aural with live Latin music, and there's sheepshearing at the Textile Museum. A free shuttle will take you around, stopping at each site on Saturday from 10:00 A.M. to 4:00 P.M., and Sunday 1:00 to 5:00 P.M. Call 387–4062, ext. 12 for full information or visit www.dkmuseums.com.

To dine in an equally chic restaurant, walk across Connecticut Avenue to *La Tomate.* With its stark white walls, splashy paintings, and sunny Mediterranean look, La Tomate might just have floated in from southern Europe. Those impressions are soon confirmed by a menu that is strong on pastas based on shellfish and vegetables, and second courses like spezzatino di pollo and veal Milanese. As a bonus, this "Italian bistro" has large sidewalk windows perfect for the people-watching that comes with the Dupont Circle territory. La Tomate, 1701 Connecticut Avenue NW, is open Monday through Thursday 11:30 A.M. to 10:30 P.M., Friday and Saturday 11:00 A.M. to 11:00 P.M., and Sunday 11:30 A.M. to 10:00 P.M. It's a good idea to reserve by calling 667–5505.

Ginza specializes in things Japanese, so you'll find a nice selection of Asian items there for your home, office, and garden, including samurai dolls, tea sets, lacquered boxes, and many books on Japan and its art. And if you really must have a samurai T-shirt, this is the place to get it. Ginza, 1721 Connecticut Avenue NW (331–7991), is open Monday through Saturday 11:00 A.M. to 7:00 P.M., Sunday noon to 6:00 P.M.

If you're from out of town or another country and can't wait to find out what's going on back home, head for *The Newsroom,* which carries magazines and newspapers from practically everywhere. There's also a large selection of language teaching manuals and materials. The Newsroom, at 1803 Connecticut Avenue (332–1489), is open 7:00 A.M. to 9:00 P.M. every day.

If you've had your fill of shopping, another good walk involves exploring the Dupont Circle neighborhood east of Connecticut Avenue beginning at 18th and Church Streets, where there's a lovely little garden rimmed with daffodils and azaleas that's just perfect for resting or picnicking. This was the site of *St. Thomas Episcopal Church,* a miniature Gothic cathedral where Franklin and Eleanor Roosevelt frequently worshipped. St. Thomas was destroyed by arson in 1970; all that remains of one of Washington's loveliest and most cherished churches is the fire-scorched north altar wall. Although St. Thomas may physically be gone, its sense of tranquillity lingers on in the park, and its parishioners still hold services in the adjoining rectory, which was undamaged by the fire.

Even die-hard Republicans like to take a bipartisan peek at the **Women's National Democratic Club,** which is located in the delightful Whittemore House, an 1892 charmer built in a free-form, slightly undulating shape with protruding dormer windows and a gorgeous caped roof. Beyond the house's wood paneled entrance hall, a series of spacious and handsomely furnished rooms commemorates Democratic First Ladies—especially Eleanor Roosevelt, a frequent visitor—and leaders of the suffrage movement. The Women's National Democratic Club, 1526 New Hampshire Avenue NW (232–7363), is open Monday through Friday 9:00 A.M. to 5:00 P.M.

Further up 18th Street, at the corner of New Hampshire Avenue, you'll see the Beaux Arts prow of one of Washington's most spectacular homes, the fifty-four-room **Belmont Mansion,** which could have floated in from Versailles. The house now belongs to the Order of the Eastern Star, which admits only members of the Eastern Star, Masons, or their guests. If you qualify you can take your chances by turning up at the door during tour times, which are Monday through Friday from 9:00 A.M. to 3:00 P.M., or apply online at www.eastern star.org. Get more information by phoning Tommy Poindexter at 667–4737. If you get in, you'll pass through a regal entrance hall, climb a granite double staircase under amethyst chandeliers, and go upstairs to the Belmonts' former parlors with their gold piano and a grand dining room that sports a ceiling from the Doge's Palace in Venice. If you're not cleared, you'll have to settle for standing outside and admiring the magnificent Louis XIV style of the building and its lovely gardens of unclassified tulips and azaleas.

Exotic Eats

The stretch of 18th Street between R Street and Columbia Road has blossomed into a veritable United Nations of storefront restaurants with exotic cuisines rarely represented on any city's culinary lineup. For a change of pace try one of the following:

Mt. Everest,
1805 18th Street;
462–3980.
The pinnacle of Nepalese, Tibetan, and Indian cooking. Try the Nepalese potato curry or the tasty Tibetan chicken dumplings.

Caravan Grill,
1825 18th Street;
518–0444.
Persian delights such as yogurt soup or a kebab from the restaurant's long list. Also a large buffet at lunch and dinner. Closed Monday.

Adams Morgan

If you're fond of Ethiopian food, you could easily end up spending many evenings in Adams Morgan, which, along with its other multicultural dining possibilities, boasts a disproportionate number of Washington's Ethiopian restaurants. The specialties at each include a wide range of hot or mild chicken, lamb or beef stews, and tasty, subtle vegetable dishes, all accompanied by injera, the spongy pancakes you'll use to mop up your plate. No silverware, grazie. Here are four of the best; all are inexpensive to moderate in price.

Addis Ababa,
2106 18th Street, NW;
232–6092.
Open noon to 12:30 A.M. daily. Live entertainment on the weekend.

Fasika's,
2447 18th Street NW;
797–7673.
Open Sunday through Thursday 5:00 P.M. to midnight, Friday and Saturday 5:00 P.M. to 1:00 A.M. Live jazz Friday and Saturday from 10:30 P.M. to 3:00 A.M.

Meskerem,
2434 18th Street NW;
462–4100.
Open Monday through Thursday noon to midnight, Friday through Sunday, noon to 1:00 A.M. Live Ethiopian music after 11:30 P.M. on Friday and Saturday.

Red Sea,
2463 18th Street NW;
483–5000.
Open daily 11:30 A.M. to 11:00 P.M.

Around the corner on R Street, the ***National Museum of American Jewish Military History,*** which operates under the auspices of the Jewish War Veterans of the U.S.A., documents the contributions that Jewish men and women have made to American military efforts in every war. The museum's exhibits include medals, weapons, and other military memorabilia, along with photos, diaries, and letters from the museum's large photographic and documentary archive. Recent shows have included the story of General Julius Klein's service as a teenage spy in World War I and a major general in World War II, as well as profiles of Jewish women in the military and Jews who fought in the Civil War and the Revolution. The museum, at 1811 R Street NW (265–6280; www.nmajmh.org), is open Monday through Friday 9:00 A.M. to 5:00 P.M. and Sunday 1:00 to 5:00 P.M.; closed Saturdays and Jewish holidays. Contributions appreciated.

That residential block of brownstones on S Street between 17th and 18th Streets is a survivor of what Washingtonians call the ***"Strivers' Section."*** The "Strivers" in question were the cadre of prominent black professionals and intellectuals who, in the 1920s, were fighting for recognition and equality in what was then a thoroughly Southern city. In this block, which is now on the National Register of Historic Places, lived Benjamin Davis, the first African American to become a U.S. general (at 1721 S), poet Langston Hughes (1749 S), and noted jurist Charles Houston (1744 S).

You'll find good eats for your pooch at **Doggie Style Bakery,** where you can buy Fido a personalized birthday cake, cheese balls, and peanut butter rabbits. I (I mean my dog) really liked the personalized bones and doughnuts. Veggie bagels too! Special events include doggie happy hours and a Halloween costume party. Doggie Style Bakery, 1825 18th Street NW; 667–0595. Before visiting give your best friend an advance peek at the menu by visiting www.doggiestylebakery.com. Hours: Monday through Saturday 11:00 A.M. to 8:30 P.M., Sunday 11:00 A.M. to 6:00 P.M.

Now you're nearing the point on 18th Street where Dupont Circle ends and the area known as **Adams Morgan** begins. Adams Morgan (or Madam's Organ, as it is sometimes called) is one of the District's most tumultuous

Cool Rules

Finally, if you're looking for a combination of good food and cool sounds, here are two possibilities:

Felix,
2406 18th Street;
483–3549,
www.thefelix.com
Features "imaginative American" cooking, with heavy emphasis on seafood, including roast sea bass, halibut, arctic char, and mussels. The martinis are divine, but go easy if you're staying around for Felix's nightly program of live music, which varies every evening from Sinatra swing night on Wednesday to groovy jazz and funk on the weekends. Sunday through Wednesday the music starts at 9:00 P.M., but on the weekends it runs from 11:00 P.M. to 2:00 A.M. While you're there check out the intimate Spy Lounge next door, where a DJ spins cool jazz on weekends. Moderate.

The Blue Room,
2321 18th Street NW;
332–0800,
www.blueroomdc.com
The food is mainly tapas-style dishes involving fish and pastas, and it's accompanied by ultra-cool music that plays here every night but Monday. Tuesday the entertainment is live, while DJs rule from Wednesday through Sunday. The crowd is definitely urban chic and the music you'll hear may be acid jazz or down tempo, but it will never be the top 40. Moderate.

neighborhoods and a social center of the city's Latino, Caribbean, and African residents. Perfectly routine and quiet by day, Adams Morgan really comes to life at night, when it becomes Washington's liveliest restaurant scene. If you go, keep in mind that Adams Morgan has no Metro station, that the Dupont Circle stop is at least thirty minutes away, and that the parking situation is catastrophic. Take a cab. Here are a few restaurants to think about:

In spite of the pun, the ***Grill from Ipanema*** is a top Brazilian restaurant, where you can guzzle caipirinhas, made with limes, sugar, and million-proof rum. It's a good idea to have only one before ordering conch chowder, Brazilian grilled meat, or Brazil's national dish, feijoada, a feast of black beans, brined beef, sausage, and cuts of pork. The restaurant is at 1858 Columbia Road NW; 986–0757. Inexpensive.

Cashion's Eat Place, 1819 Columbia Road NW (797–1819), will remind you of a 1937 Parisian bistro—the intimate atmosphere, the bar with habitués sitting under a painting of a nude, and more than a whiff of romance in the air; somewhere cool jazz is playing. The food is even better than the setting, an eclectic menu that swings from roast leg of lamb to duck breast with foie gras, or veal cheeks. Chef-owner Ann Cashion changes the menu daily, but not to worry, you'll be in good hands. Reservations are a must, especially for the yummy Sunday brunch. Moderate.

Places to Stay in Dupont Circle

The Carlyle Suites,
1731 New Hampshire Avenue NW;
234–3200,
fax 387–0085;
www.carlylesuites.com
This converted apartment house on one of Dupont Circle's quieter residential streets announces its Art Deco origins in a lobby covered with louvered sconces and other Chrysler Building touches. The Carlyle, with its 170 comfortable suites with mini-kitchens and dining areas, offers comfort and value, especially for families. The handsome restaurant, open daily 7:00 to 11:00 A.M. and 5:00 to 10:00 P.M., offers mainly light fare such as pastas, soup, and sandwiches, but also grills steaks and fish. Moderate.

The Churchill,
1914 Connecticut Avenue NW; 797–2000,
fax 462–0944;
www.thechurchillhotel.com
The National Trust for Historic Preservation just added the Churchill to its list of historic North American hotels. This grand old Beaux Arts structure began life in 1906 as a luxury apartment house, but was later converted into an elegant and equally comfortable hotel with 144 guest rooms and suites. And you can't beat the location right on Connecticut Avenue, Dupont Circle's main stem, and on the edge of Embassy Row. Moderate.

The Dupont at the Circle,
1604 19th Street NW;
332–5251,
(888) 412–1000;
www.dupontatthecircle.com
Located just off the Circle, this is one of the District's most elegant bed-and-breakfasts, with seven handsome, if not downright swanky, rooms and suites, each with its private bath. If you stay in the period Lincoln Room, you'll get presidential treatment, including a chance to sleep in a replica of the famous Lincoln Bed (no campaign contribution

required). Basically moderately priced, but the larger suites, including the spacious Plum Suite, are expensive.

Hotel Tabard Inn,
1739 N Street NW;
785–1277,
fax 785–6173.
A British writer once described this inn as "the sort of place favored by Englishmen who prefer 'character' to room service and by Americans who want to assert their individuality." That's a pretty good description of this small, laid-back hotel with a distinctly British feel: big rooms with Victorian decor, occasionally quirky furnishings, and moderate prices. Also notable is the hotel's restaurant, a cozy, casual favorite with the locals. Moderate.

The Inn at Dupont Circle,
1312 19th Street NW;
467–6777,
fax 293–8819;
www.theinnatdupontcircle
.com
This new bed-and-breakfast is located in an 1895 Victorian town house right at the Dupont Circle stop of the new shuttle bus service to Georgetown and only steps from the Circle itself. The inn's six Victorian-style rooms boast 12-foot ceilings and most have fireplaces complete with the original tiles. Downstairs in the salon an 1872 rosewood grand piano awaits your delicate touch—anyone choosing to leave the room can flee outside to the inn's charming little patio and garden with a heated solarium. Rates are moderate and include a full buffet breakfast.

Jurys Normandy,
2118 Wyoming Avenue NW;
483–1350;
www.jurysdoyle.com
One of Kalorama's few hotels, Jurys Normandy is a handsome hideaway not far from Dupont Circle and handy to the Connecticut Avenue bus lines. The Normandy is very much like a small European boutique hotel (after all, it's Irish-owned) from the gentlemen's club lobby to the seventy-five well-furnished rooms. Even without its great location, the Normandy is a real find anywhere in the city. Inexpensive to moderate.

Jurys Washington,
1500 New Hampshire Avenue NW;
483–6000.
Because it's right on the Circle and next to the Metro station, you can't get much more centrally located than this D.C. outpost of Ireland's largest hotel group. The hotel's 300 plus attractive rooms are often filled with business travelers and foreign officials visiting on State Department grants, so it pays to reserve in advance. The Irish theme carries over into the hotel's atmospheric pub, where Bushmill's is the national pastime, and its restaurant, where, you'll be happy to hear, the cooking is better than in Dublin. Moderate.

The Kalorama Guest House,
1854 Mintwood Place;
667–6369.
The Kalorama is actually a collection of three turn-of-the-century town houses located in the 1800 block of leafy Mintwood Place, one of the quieter streets in sometimes raucous Adams Morgan. The guest house offers thirty rooms and suites, all nicely furnished; breakfast is included. Moderate.

Swann House,
1808 New Hampshire Avenue NW;
265–4414;
www.swannhouse.com
This is one of the District's few bed-and-breakfasts, and it's a good one. This redbrick Victorian mansion, which was built in 1883 by a noted Washington architect and artist, has more than its share of elegant period touches—the crown moldings, 12-foot ceilings, inlaid floors, and other features you'd expect from a Victorian beauty. But more to the point, many of its twelve spacious rooms come with tasteful antiques, working fireplaces, and whopping bathrooms, plus fax machines and dataport phones that make Swann House a business favorite. And, thankfully, not an antimacassar or sherry bottle anywhere in sight. Swann House also has its own swimming pool, which is small, but just what you want during those sizzling Washington summers. Moderate.

Topaz Hotel,
1733 N Street NW;
393–3000,
fax 785–9581;
www.topazhotel.com
The theme of this new boutique hotel is wellness, but other words that might describe the Topaz are "colorful" and "sophisticated." Colorful starts when you check in with desk clerks wearing iridescent orange

and green silk tunics, then drift into the Topaz Bar with its blue pencil lights and settle into a floor to ceiling settee to start your stay with an energy cocktail. Upstairs, all of the Topaz's ninety-nine rooms are large, comfortable, and handsomely furnished, but several are set aside as special yoga rooms, with meditation space, New Age music, and instructional videos. Following the Topaz's wellness theme, the hotel also offers "energy rooms" with exercise possibilities. The hotel also offers special weekend rates that include aromatherapy sessions and massages. Every night the relentlessly cool Topaz Bar draws crowds of young, with-it professionals, possibly looking for the bar's specialty, the potent "Blue Nirvana" cocktail, emphatically not an herbal potion, but which does deliver a certain feeling of wellness (or is that buzziness?). All of this excitement and a great location between downtown and Dupont Circle. Moderate to expensive.

Windsor Park Hotel,

at 2116 Kalorama Road (corner of Connecticut Avenue); 483–7700; www.windsorparkhotel.com If the idea of living in Kalorama appeals to you, if only for a few nights, then check into the Windsor. This clean and comfortable budget find, with its forty nicely furnished rooms, gets a big play from diplomats in town to consult at their Washington embassies and from Americans lured by its strategic location for bus travel all over the city. Moderate.

Places to Eat in Dupont Circle

Addis Ababa,

2106 18th Street NW; 232–6092.
See page 164 for full description.

Afterwords Cafe and Grill,

1517 Connecticut Avenue NW; 387–1400.
See pages 160–61 for full description.

Bistrot Du Coin,

1738 Connecticut Avenue NW; 234–6969, fax 234–6965.
If you've been pining away for your Paris favorites—the escargots, moules marinières with frites, and all kinds of tartines, leave your passport in the drawer and head for this authentic French bistro that has somehow migrated successfully from the Seine to the Potomac. Lunchtime is pretty restrained, but the noise level and fun build into the evenings, especially on the weekends, where you'll need a reservation to shoehorn in for your onion soup and choucroute garnie. And every Sunday the Bistrot observes the ancient French tradition of *le brunch.* Bonne chance. Open Monday to Wednesday 11:30 A.M. to 11:00 P.M., Thursday through Saturday 11:30 A.M. to 1:00 A.M., and Sunday 11:00 A.M. to 11:00 P.M.

The Blue Room,

2321 18th Street NW; 332–0800.
See page 165 for full description.

Brickskeller,

1523 22nd Street NW; 293–1885, www.thebrickskeller.com See pages 148–49 for full description.

Cashion's Eat Place,

1819 Columbia Road NW; 797–1819.
See page 166 for full description,

Caravan Grill,

1825 18th Street NW; 518–0444.
See page 163 for full description.

City Lights of China,

1731 Connecticut Avenue; 265–6688, www.citylightsofchina.com This citywide favorite invariably makes everyone's list of their favorite restaurants. One reason for that is great food, from specialties like the shark's fin soup and crispy noodles with seafood to the usual Chinese fare of Szechuan beef or Kung Pao shrimp. The other is the combination of reasonable prices and excellent service. Open Monday through Friday 11:30 A.M. to 10:30 P.M., Saturday noon to 11:00 P.M., and Sunday noon to 10:30 P.M. Moderate.

Etrusco Trattoria,

1606 20th Street NW; 667–0047.
It's hard to imagine a better dining experience than Etrusco, where you'll swear you're back in Siena as you enjoy outstanding Tuscan dishes like ribollita, papardelle slathered with a rich duck ragu, and grilled sea bass in a wine and rosemary sauce. Owner/chef Francesco Ricchi also makes great osso buco and splen-

did, homemade sausages and a robust soup of mussels and clams; for dessert try his chocolate Grandfather's Cake. Just as memorable is the atmosphere of a great Italian restaurant with fresh flowers and attractive decor where the sounds you hear are of happy people having a great time enjoying terrific food. Maybe the exceptional wine list has something to do with that, or perhaps it's the friendly, professional service. Reservations a must. Open for dinner only, Monday through Saturday. Moderate.

Fasika's
2447 18th Street;
797–7673.
See page 164 for full description.

Felix,
2406 18th Street;
483–3549.
See page 165 for full description.

Ginza,
1721 Connecticut Avenue NW;
331–7991.
See page 162 for full description.

Grille 88,
1910 18th Street NW;
588–5288,
www.grille88.com
See page 163 for full description.

Grill from Ipanema,
1858 Columbia Road NW;
986–0757.
See page 166 for full description.

The Iron Gate Inn,
1734 N Street NW;
737–1370.
If you're thinking about having an intimate tryst at one of Washington's most romantic dining spots, you can't do better than the Iron Gate's vine-covered patio. In cool weather just move inside to a table in one of the restaurant's firelit rooms. The Iron Gate's menu has an eastern Mediterranean accent, with listings for lamb shank with orzo and roast chicken. Open Monday through Friday 11:30 A.M. to 2:30 P.M., Monday through Saturday 5:30 P.M. to 10:00 P.M. Moderate.

Johnny's Half Shell,
2002 P Street NW;
296–2021.
Johnny's is a great restaurant find for anyone seeking sustenance in the Dupont Circle area. Fish is the specialty at this small, cheery restaurant just off the Circle. Johnny's dense, peppery seafood gumbo is almost a meal in itself, but why stop there when you can move on to the terrific crab cakes, a fritto misto of fried shrimp, calamari, and monkfish, or arguably the best fish and chips in town? A short but well-conceived wine list rounds out the pleasure. No reservations taken, but the wait, which can be considerable, is worth it. Open Monday through Thursday 11:30 A.M. to 10:30 P.M., Friday and Saturday 11:30 A.M. to 11:00 P.M.; closed Sunday. Moderate.

La Tomate,
1701 Connecticut Avenue NW;
667–5505.
See page 162 for full description.

Meskerem,
2434 18th Street NW;
462–4100.
See page 164 for full description.

Mimi's American Bistro,
2120 P Street NW;
464–6464,
www.mimisdc.com

AUTHOR'S FAVORITE PLACES TO EAT IN DUPONT CIRCLE

Sette Trattoria

The Obelisk

Johnny's Half Shell

Etrusco Trattoria

Hotel Tabard Inn

Cashion's Eat Place

Bistrot du Coin

As Woody Allen once said about something else, Mimi's is "the most fun you can have without laughing." Mimi's is the only D.C. restaurant where the waitstaff will serenade you during dinner with show tunes, romantic ballads, and jazz favorites. But don't go to Mimi's for a soulful chat, because the effect of all this excitement and talent is a noisy, happy room. And the food is worth a visit on its own, with a bistro menu that's heavy on grilled fish, aged beef, and rack of lamb; there's also a Mediterranean twist with grilled figs, duck in fruit sauce, and couscous. Reservations strongly advised. Moderate.

Mt. Everest,
1805 18th Street NW;
462–3980.
See page 163 for full description.

The Obelisk,
2029 P Street;
872–1180.
Located in a town house, this might be the city's best Italian restaurant. The Obelisk has a short but exquisite fixed-price menu (at this writing $60), that varies nightly. On our latest visit the antipasti choices included peppers prepared with vegetables and cheese or stuffed pig's foot. The first course involved deciding between halibut raviolini and gnocchi with Gorgonzola

cheese, while the entree possibilities included veal tenderloin with juniper relish, pan-cooked grouper, and roast squab with mushrooms and polenta. Memorable desserts and wines too. Reservations are essential. Open Tuesday through Saturday 6:00 to 10:00 P.M. Expensive.

Pines of Florence,
2100 Connecticut Avenue NW;
332–8233.
Although Kalorama has many delights, an active restaurant scene isn't one of them. However, if hunger strikes on your wanderings, this trattoria is a good choice. But with all those southern Italian favorites and the hearty red sauces, shouldn't it be renamed Pines of Palermo? Open Monday through Thursday 11:00 A.M. to 10:30 P.M., Friday until 10:00 P.M., Saturday noon to 11:00 P.M., and Sunday noon to 10:00 P.M. Inexpensive.

Red Sea,
2463 18th Street NW;
483–5000.
See page 164 for full description.

Rosemary's Thyme,
1801 18th Street NW;
332–3200.
The food at Rosemary's Thyme is as handsome and lively as the surroundings in this "Mediterranean-Creole bistro," which is saying a lot.

You come here for big salads, shellfish pastas, unbelievable lamb shanks, and a long list of kabobs; wraps of freshly baked *pide,* a Turkish flat bread, are another specialty. The long and fairly priced wine list is a plus. Reservations recommended. Open Monday through Thursday 5:00 to 11:00 P.M., Friday and Saturday 11:00 A.M. to midnight, Sunday 11:00 A.M. to 10:00 P.M. Moderate.

Sette Osteria,
1666 Connecticut Avenue NW;
483–3070;
www.setteosteria.com
Walking into this sparkling newcomer is about as close as you'll come to finding Italian summer on a gray day in D.C. Italian wicker chairs with bright fabric cushions, vivid Deruta tiles set in terra-cotta floors, and major ceramics from Orvieto all frame an equally cheery menu. The pizzas and pastas, along with the entrees, are mainly Southern Italian. Aside from some of the southern standards, you'll find seldom-seen dishes such as penne with bacon and pecorino and pizza with escarole, anchovies, and prosciutto. Good salads and antipasti as well. The mainly southern wine list is long, well chosen and fairly priced. The Sette Osteria Web site alone is worth a visit. Moderate.

Shaw and U Street

As soon as you see the stunning mural of Duke Ellington on the wall opposite the Lincoln Theater, you have a pretty good idea of what this neighborhood is all about. Music in general and the Duke in particular are the soul of Shaw, an area that for decades has been Washington's answer to New York's Harlem and Chicago's Bronzeville. Shaw is the traditional center of the city's black cultural, professional, and educational world in what was for many years a strictly segregated national capital. An intellectual hub as well, Shaw is the home of Howard University, founded during Reconstruction in 1867, a magnet for American black leaders and still one of our premier historically black universities.

Unique among Washington's neighborhoods, Shaw has always been black, starting in Civil War days when freed slaves began living modestly in what was then a rural setting within the District. Black professionals erected their own homes in Shaw during Reconstruction, and began to form a cultural and social legacy that made Washington the center of African-American life in the United States. One result has been that this area has some of the city's handsomest Victorian row houses and business buildings, mostly built, financed, and designed by African Americans.

Duke Ellington grew up in Shaw, at 1212 T Street in the years before World War I, when U Street was a musical mecca. During those years the clubs along U Street, Washington's elegant "Black Broadway," made the neighborhood the center of African-American cabaret and social life, especially in the 1920s and 1930s, when ragtime and cakewalk began to morph into "jass." Duke played his first gig ever on the top floor of the True Reformer's Hall at 12th and U, a building now being renovated, after which he advertised in the Washington Yellow Pages that he and his band of "colored syncopaters" were open for business.

Already in decline since the 1950s, U Street was hard hit by the 1968 riots that followed Martin Luther King Jr.'s assassination, after which the area became an urban war zone, where drug markets, crack houses, and vice of every kind flourished. Happily, Shaw is now in the midst of a vigorous recovery. Historic buildings are being restored and the neighborhood is experiencing a minor real estate boom, with new dwellings being built and historic ones being renovated by black upscale professionals, known hereabouts as "buppies." And on 14th Street, once Washington's "automobile row," plays and concerts are drawing theatergoers to a street that is slowly recovering from the trauma of 1968.

Best of all, nightlife is once again flourishing along U Street. The *Washington Post* attributes its recovery to the coming of the Metro in 1991 and a gentrification movement that has affected much of the District. Whatever the reason, U Street is back and, although you'll still want to exercise the usual nighttime caution, it's once again an area where Washingtonians go to enjoy nightlife and have a good time.

Another local community now undergoing revitalization is **Le Droit Park,** an urban enclave with a definite small-town feel and quiet streets with names like Spruce, Elm, and Larch. Its architecture is also small town, mostly 1870 vintage romantic Victorian, with styles like Queen Anne and Gothic cottage. Le Droit Park has traditionally been associated with the intellectual life of its neighbor, Howard University, and has been the home of many black leaders and

TOP ATTRACTIONS IN SHAW AND U STREET

Lincoln Theater	Logan Circle
The Whitelaw	African-American Civil War Memorial
Mary McLeod Bethune Council House	Ben's Chili Bowl

educators, including the Reverend Jesse Jackson and the Duke himself, who lived at 420 Elm Street NW.

Le Droit Park is also the home of the ***Squished Penny Museum.*** If you're one of the thousands of people who have put pennies on the tracks to have them flattened by a train or squashed Lincoln's profile in those arcade machines all over America, you're really going to appreciate this special museum. Run by internationally renowned squishers Pete and Christine, it features a permanent exhibit of pennies they have been personally flattened at tourist attractions all across the country, including the Circus Museum in Sarasota, Florida, and the Osmond Museum in Branson, Missouri. But that's only part of their 56,000–penny collection, which goes back decades to the hobby's earliest roots. While you're there you'll probably run into one of the many Americans and foreigners who gather in this mecca of squishdom to swap stories or trade coins. You can also squish your own pennies at a machine bought from an arcade in Georgia, buy a T-shirt announcing "I'm on a Squishin' Mission," or pick up a copy of the museum's magazine, which is named, you guessed it, The Centinel. Pete and Christine will also make custom pennies with your personal design for use as party favors, weird calling cards, or to commemorate births and weddings. Souvenir pennies with Washington designs are also available.

thehowardtheater

One Shaw musical landmark yet to be restored and saved from decay is the Howard Theater, a sumptuous palace at Seventh and T Streets NW, which opened in 1910. This is where Ellington and other jazz greats like Jelly Roll Morton and Ella Fitzgerald performed regularly. Unfortunately, it is unrestored and falling into decay and is emphatically not open to visitors.

The museum is located at 416 T Street NW, and is open by appointment only. Call 986–5644 or e-mail petey@squished.com. The Web site is www .squished.com.

But we'll start our tour a few blocks away at ***Logan Circle,*** the epicenter of some of Washington's most elegant architecture, a treasure trove of grand Victorian town houses and mansions. Logan Circle's ongoing restoration and historic preservation present a classic example of how a neighborhood can be restored and revived through community cooperation. For more about this comeback, visit www.logancircle.org.

After taking in the grand homes that ring the Circle, head down Vermont Avenue to the ***Mary McLeod Bethune Council House.*** At this handsome Victorian town house just off Logan Circle, you'll find the museum and archives that preserve and interpret the life of one of the great figures in African-American history, the remarkable woman who became a friend and valued adviser on minority matters to Eleanor and Franklin Roosevelt. Before coming to Washington to advise the Roosevelts, Bethune was already a prominent political activist for black causes and an educator who founded the school that is today Florida's Bethune-Cookman College.

The ground-level parlor holds mementos of Ms. Bethune, including her grand piano and photographs of her and her colleagues in the black women's movement. In the rear a video traces the history of the movement and the close relationship Ms. Bethune established with both Roosevelts. On the same level you'll see an excellent bookstore and shop with items dedicated to African-American history. Upstairs, in Bethune's bedroom, more pictures and photographs capture the essence of a remarkable life. The house also holds extensive archives of the National Council of Negro Women, which she founded in 1935, and other documents connected with the struggle of African-American women. The Mary McLeod Bethune Council House, 1318 Vermont Avenue NW (673–2402, www.nps. gov/mamc), is open Monday through Saturday 10:00 A.M. to 4:00 P.M. Access to the archives is by appointment only; to get one, call the archivist at 673–2402. Metro: McPherson Square (orange and blue lines).

The food is better than the pun at *Thaitanic,* where first-rate Thai cooking includes fish cakes and curried duck. The decor is ultrahip, with Formica tables and vinyl chairs straight out of Planet Eisenhower. And not an iceberg in sight. Thaitanic, 1326 14th Street NW; 588–1795. Open 11:00 A.M. to 10:00 P.M. Monday through Thursday, until 11:00 P.M. on Friday and Saturday, Sunday noon to 11:00 P.M. Metro: U Street-Cardozo (green line).

At 1337 14th Street NW, *Hamburger Mary's* is a major local hangout in a large industrial space just off Logan Circle. Big also describes the salads and the burgers, which defy description. Hamburger Mary's, 232–7010, is open

AUTHOR'S FAVORITES IN SHAW AND U STREET

African-American Civil War Memorial	Ben's Chili Bowl
Lincoln Theater	U-topia
Logan Circle	Florida Avenue Grill

Monday through Friday 11:00 A.M. to 10:00 P.M., Friday and Saturday until midnight, Sunday 10:00 A.M. to 11:00 P.M. Metro: U Street-Cardozo (green line).

Stop by **Reincarnations,** at 1401 14th Street to see a massively eclectic mix of furniture and accessories ranging in style from classic to retro and the highly contemporary pieces from leading European and American designers. Reincarnations also offers colorful painted furniture and decorative tiles. And all at surprisingly reasonable prices. Call 319–1606. Open Tuesday through Sunday 11:00 A.M. to 8:00 P.M.; www.reincarnations.com.

Fusebox, in the spare, industrial exhibit space at 1412 14th Street NW, is well worth a visit for its works of cutting edge, highly imaginative artists and photographers. Open Tuesday through Saturday noon to 8:00 P.M.; 299–9220; www.fuseboxdc.com. Metro: U Street-Cardozo (green line).

The **Studio Theater,** at 1333 P Street NW, offers three stages of performances of contemporary theater. In its twenty-three years, the studio has earned a national reputation and praise in the national press for innovative, imaginative theater and, along the way, has garnered dozens of national awards. To find what's playing during your visit, call the box office at 332–3300, or drop in between 10:00 A.M. and 6:00 P.M., Monday through Friday. For a virtual visit, it's www.studiotheatre.org. Metro: U Street–Cardozo (green line).

If you're looking for a map to chart your hike across New Guinea, or some ideas for your next safari along Namibia's Skeleton Coast, **Candida's World of Books** is the place to visit—a bookstore offering one of the city's largest collections of travel guides and literature. Aside from its planet-wide selection of books, the store also has language courses, phrase books, dictionaries, and serious study guides for most languages you've ever heard of, from Tagalog to Serbo-Croat. You'll also find guides to art and architecture, international cookbooks, and guides aimed at young travelers. Candida's World of Books, at 1541 14th Street NW, is open Monday through Saturday from 10:00 A.M. to 10:00 P.M. and Sunday from noon to 6:00 P.M.; 667–4811; www.candidasworldofbooks .com. Metro: U Street-Cardozo (green line).

Rice, a sleek and spare Thai restaurant at 1608 14th Street NW, serves up some of the best and totally authentic Thai dishes in town in Zen-like serenity. Favorites include shrimp dumpling soup, a variety of green and red curries, Panang chicken, and of course, pad Thai. All go great with the Singha beer from Bangkok. Open for lunch daily from 11:00 A.M. to 2:30 P.M. Dinners Monday through Thursday from 5:00 P.M. to 10:30 P.M.; Rice is open Friday and Saturday from 11:30 A.M. to 10:30 P.M.; 11:30 A.M. to 10:30 P.M. on Sunday. Call 234–1400. Moderate.

Jazz aficionados will definitely want to think about visiting **HR57,** where open mike, straight-ahead jazz sessions lure crowds every Wednesday and

Friday night. The sessions here are laid-back and impromptu, and usually feature visiting or local professional musicians. HR57, more formally known as the Center for the Preservation of Jazz and Blues, takes its name from the 1987 House Resolution that designated jazz as an American treasure. And you'll hear the best of it here in this storefront jazz mecca. There's also a set dinner each night, usually fried chicken, red beans and rice, and potato salad, not to mention the ambrosial fresh lemonade. The action at HR57, 1610 14th Street NW (667–3700), starts at 8:00 P.M. on Wednesday and 9:00 P.M. on Friday and Saturday. Admission is $8.00; the fixed-price dinner will run you another $6.00. Metro: U Street–Cardozo (green line).

For a blast from the past, drop into *Sparky's Espresso Cafe,* at 1720 14th Street NW, a neighborhood diner where you can live (or relive) the 1950s in red plastic booths. Order breakfast, specialty coffees, or sandwiches from the blackboard menu, then join the locals in reading or, in the evening, listening to poetry and, sometimes, live bands. Exhibits by local artists, too. Open Monday through Thursday 7:00 A.M. to 11:00 P.M., Friday and Saturday 7:00 A.M. to 1:00 A.M. and Sunday 9:00 A.M. to 8:00 P.M. Call 332–9334; www.sparkyscafe.com.

You might have a Hallmark store in your home town, but no matter what they have in stock, it's a far cry from the assortment at *Pulp,* at 1803 16th Street. I won't do any quoting here—let's just say that Pulp is perfect if you're looking for a greeting to mark any and every, repeat every, possible occasion, romantic problem, or embarrassing social situation. In addition you can buy quirky stuff like Nico, the barista action figure, an Elvis lunchbox, Votivo candles in many scents, and dozens of refrigerator magnets, some of them quite naughty. Upstairs there's a Frida Kahlo shrine with night-lights and finger puppets honoring the great Mexican painter. Open Monday through Saturday 11:00 A.M. to 7:00 P.M., Sunday noon to 5:00 P.M.; 462–7857.

The words "cool" and "hardware store" rarely appear in the same sentence, unless the writer is talking about *Home Rule.* This ultratrendy storefront is packed with nifty tools and gear to take home, including retro Italian toasters that Mussolini might have used, jazzy picture frames, and great glassware. Home Rule, at 1807 14th Street NW, is open Tuesday through Saturday from 11:00 A.M. to 7:00 P.M. and Sunday noon to 5:00 P.M. Closed Mondays. 797–5544; www.homerule.com. Metro: U Street-Cardozo (green line).

Go Mama Go!, at 1809 14th Street NW, features a mega-eclectic selection of gifts, furnishings, and artwork, ranging from Tunisian glassware, Moroccan mirrors, and lots of Asian prints. Says the store's Thai-born owner Noi Chudnoff, "If it's beautiful, it belongs here." That's obvious. Don't forget to check out the Asian wrapping paper with architectural drawings by Leonardo da Vinci. Open Monday noon to 7:00 P.M., Tuesday through Saturday 11:00 A.M. to

7:00 P.M., and Sunday noon to 5:00 P.M. Call 299–0850; www.gomamago.com. Metro: U Street-Cardozo (green line).

For a look at the best in custom furniture from cutting-edge designers from California and Brazil, stop off at *Vastu,* 1829 14th Street. According to the owners, Vastu is the name of an ancient Sanskrit design school using Earth elements, colors, and textures. And that's what you'll find in the showroom—furniture and furnishings made from warm and inviting natural materials, especially gleaming woods like rosewood and teak. But Vastu also has its share of more unusual textures such as aluminum and microsuede, along with hand-crafted ceramic lamps and vases. And on the walls you'll find a choice selection of art by local artists. Call 234–8344. Open 11:00 A.M. to 7:00 P.M. Tuesday through Saturday and noon to 5:00 P.M. Sunday; www.vastudc.com.

Next door, *Muleh,* at 1831 14th Street, you'll find dining tables, benches, and chairs with classic designs, most of them made from reclaimed teak and mahogany from the Philippines and Indonesia. (Muleh means "welcome" in Javanese) Muleh hours are 11:00 A.M. to 7:00 P.M. Tuesday through Saturday and noon to 5:00 P.M. Sunday; 667–3440; www.muleh.com.

For a lot of local residents music and food on 14th Street mean *Cafe Saint-Ex* at number 1847, and it's easy to see why. Upstairs, it's like being back on Paris' Left Bank in a classic, well-visited brasserie of dark wood, mirrors, ceiling fans, and a serious bar. You'll spot the cafe's aviation theme as soon as you see the walls lined with stained glass images of aircraft and vintage posters of old aviation films. Despite the French feel to Cafe Saint-Ex (it's named for French aviator, war hero, and writer Antoine de Saint Exupery), the menu, is the best in American bistro, with a long list of salads, chops, and pastas. Then it's back to the Latin Quarter for the wine list, where French vintages prevail, and at reasonable prices. After dinner, head downstairs to "Gate 54," what the French would call a cave—a basement room with a hangar atmosphere, where a DJ spins everything from bossa nova to classic jazz. Lots of fun and good food at moderate prices. Open 5:00 P.M. to 2:00 A.M. Monday through Friday; 11:00 A.M. to 2:00 A.M. Saturday and Sunday. Call 265–7839; http://saint-ex.com.

At 14th and U Streets, you've reached the epicenter of this historic neighborhood. A right turn on U Street takes you to 1324 U Street, where *Kuna* has been drawing strong reviews from critics who like its combination of good Italian country cooking, a nicely priced wine list, and reasonable prices. Kuna does everything well from opening with "carta di musica" bread and a finale of desserts like chocolate torte. However, the pastas are the main attraction, especially the lusty puttanesca and the meaty Bolognese. To answer your question, the owner named it after his grandmother's village in Croatia. Open Monday through Thursday 6:00 to 10:00 P.M., Friday and Saturday until 11:00 P.M. Reservations suggested; phone 797–7908. Metro: U Street-Cardozo (green line).

A right turn takes you down U Street past **Polly's,** at 1342 U Street NW (265–8385). This neighborhood favorite is cool and laid-back, with great music to listen to by the fire. The excellent bar food is another reason Polly pulls them in, with a menu that offers top-notch burgers, portobello mushroom steaks, and fried calamari. Open Monday through Friday 6:00 P.M. to 2:00 A.M., Saturday and Sunday 10:00 A.M. to 2:00 A.M. Inexpensive to moderate.

The Whitelaw, at 1839 13th Street NW, is now a sparkling 1919 Beaux Arts apartment house offering affordable housing to local residents. But until 1945 it was the only hotel in Washington open to blacks. Duke Ellington stayed there, as did Cab Calloway, Joe Louis, and many other visiting notables. During its depths in the '50s and '60s the Whitelaw was a notorious drug den and bordello that was finally closed because of its dilapidated condition, not to mention its reputation. Thanks to a combination of local funding and community pride, the Whitelaw has been beautifully restored to its former elegance. Especially striking is the graceful dining room, with its original stained glass ceiling. Because people live there, you can't just wander around, but if you ring the bell marked *office* and ask nicely, you just might get in. It's worth it.

No doubt about it, the **Lincoln Theater** is one of Washington's hidden treasures. When it was built in 1922, the Lincoln was where African Americans could watch vaudeville shows and first-run films in a city whose theaters were strictly segregated. Duke Ellington and Count Basie also played there, in a mammoth ballroom that once stood behind the current theater. The Lincoln was for years the heart and soul of black cultural and social life, but during the 1950s it fell on hard times. Restored to its original glory in 1994, today it's one of Washington's great interior spaces, where you walk off a busy street into the gilt, architectural detail, and plush of an elegant theater of the 1920s. Call the box office at 328–6000 for details of the Lincoln's rich cultural programs, which include plays, concerts, and dance

Polly's Cafe

Tell Them "Off the Beaten Path" Sent You

Going to *Signal 66* is like visiting a 1920s speakeasy—walk down an alley to a nondescript door marked "926 N," where a buzzer will admit you to a former livery stable that is now one of the District's most exciting arts and communications spaces. Entering the high-ceilinged exhibit space, you might find a "warehouse party" in progress, along with shows by local and other artists in the gallery's three studios. There's a lot going on at Signal 66, including musical sessions with top local pop bands. Signal 66 is also the home of a recording studio and Web site operated by its artist-owners. Signal 66, at the rear of 926 N Street NW, is open Wednesday, Thursday, and Saturday from 1:00 to 5:00 P.M., Friday from 6:30 to 8:30 P.M. Find out what's going on by phoning 842-3436 or going to www.signal66.com. The issue-oriented Web site operated at the gallery is www.planetvox.com. Metro: Mt. Vernon Square–UDC (yellow line).

and film festivals. The Lincoln Theater, 1215 U Street NW, is across the street from the 13th Street exit of the U Street–Cardozo Metro station on the green line.

If there were a Michelin guide to Washington, you'd find **Ben's Chili Bowl,** at 1213 U, marked with the red symbols that mean "restaurant of habitues," i.e., all the smart locals hang out there because it's so great. Ben's building was once the Minnehaha Theater, in its day one of the best, which advertised "clean vaudeville" acts. But since 1958 Ben's has been a gathering place for everyone in black Washington, from night workers to students at nearby Howard University to Bill Cosby, who's been coming here for years for the chili half smokes. And you might, as I did, spot Michael Jordan folded into one of Ben's booths. Ben's atmosphere probably resembles those places you knew in the '50s—Formica lunch counters with stools, shiny red plastic chairs, and food served right from the grill. Ben's dishes will also take you back to all those pre-cholesterol days, with dishes like half smokes or Kosher hot dogs doused with spicy chili, not to mention breakfasts highlighted by eggs and scrapple or sausages, or hot cakes with grits or home fries. Funky music too. It's wonderful! Be still my heart (note to my cardiologist: just kidding!). Ben's Chili Bowl, 1213 U Street NW (667–0909; www.benschilibowl.com), is open Monday through Thursday 6:00 A.M. to 2:00 A.M., Friday and Saturday 7:00 A.M. to 4:00 A.M., Sunday noon to 8:00 P.M. Reservations—are you kidding? Inexpensive. Metro: Shaw–Howard U (green line).

One of the great finds during the preparation of this guide was **The Islander,** a modest storefront at 1201 U Street specializing in Caribbean cookery, with a friendly atmosphere just as relaxed as the islands themselves. The dishes show the islands' African/East Indian roots. Start off with callaloo (a spinach-okra mix) or plantain, then shift into high gear with the excellent calypso chicken with a mild red sauce, roti, a curried wrap with Indian over-tones, or a curried shrimp or goat accompanied by peleau (fried chickpeas and rice) and a bottle of Trinidadian beer. The Islander is open Tuesday through Thursday noon to 11:00 P.M., until midnight. Friday and Saturday, and Sunday 1:00 to 6:00 P.M. Live jazz most Sundays. Metro: Shaw–Howard U (green line). Call 234–4955.

The second floor auditorium in the recently restored ***True Reformers Hall*** at 1200 U Street is where Duke played some of his earliest gigs. The hall is not open to the public, but on the building's ground floor the ***African-American Civil War Museum*** has interesting exhibits of memorabilia, includ-ing photographs, maps, and uniforms that show vividly the contributions that African-American troops made to the Union cause. The museum's founder/ director, Frank Smith, will be glad to answer your questions and tell you about special walking tours of this historic neighborhood. Call 667–2667; www.afro amcivilwar.org. Open Monday through Friday 10:00 A.M. to 5:00 P.M. and Satur-day 10:00 A.M. to 2:00 P.M. Metro: U Street-Cardozo (green line).

At the intersection of U Street and Vermont Avenue, the ***African-American Civil War Memorial,*** one of Washington's newest national memorials, honors the 210,000 black troops who fought with the "U.S. Colored Troops" during the Civil War. The names of those soldiers are inscribed on this open-air memor-ial's polished metal tablets and are guarded by a statue, *Spirit of Free-dom,* depicting a group of African-Americans who fought in the Union Army. The names of the soldiers are listed by regiment, one of which is the famous 53rd Massachusetts, which fought with distinction at the battles of Forts Pillow and Wagner under a white colonel, Robert Shaw (for whom this area is named); their bravery was dramatized in the film

African-American Civil War Memorial

Glory. The memorial is located at the entrance to the U Street–Cardozo Metro at Tenth and U Streets NW.

The **Black Fashion Museum** is dedicated to the contributions that African Americans have made to fashion and design. This century-old row house highlights Elizabeth Keckley, a former slave who designed Mary Lincoln's dresses and was also her personal confidante; a copy of a Keckley design for Mrs. Lincoln is a major attraction. Another important exhibit honors an already famous Ann Lowe, who in 1953 designed Jackie Kennedy's wedding gown. The Black Fashion Museum, 2007 Vermont Avenue NW, is open only by appointment. To get one, call 667–0744 or e-mail bfmdc@aol.com. Web site: www.bfmdc.org. Metro: U Street–Cardozo (green line).

At 14th and U Streets, a left turn will take you to **Coppi's,** at 1414 U Street NW, just the place for terrific pizza, including some varieties you've probably never seen. Coppi's also features Ligurian specialties such as pesto with scallops and stuffed sardines. Call 319–7773. Open Monday through Thursday from 6:00 to 11:00 P.M., Friday and Saturday 5:00 P.M. to midnight, and Sunday 5:00 to 11:00 P.M. Inexpensive. Metro: U Street-Cardozo (green line).

The utterly funky **U-topia,** at 1418 U Street, is one of the area's most popular and laid-back restaurants, with a good selection of bar food and light fare with a Cajun touch. U-topia's Sunday brunch from noon to 4:00 P.M. is, to say the least, abundant, provided you make it through the potent $1.00 mimosas and Bloody Marys. No reservations. Open Sunday through Thursday 11:00 A.M. to 11:30 P.M., Friday and Saturday 11:30 A.M. to 1:00 A.M., and Sunday 11:00 A.M. to 11:30 P.M. U-topia also offers significant jazz action nightly. Call 483–7669. Metro: U Street-Cardozo (green line).

At 1428 U Street you'll find **Goodwood,** which offers an eclectic collection of nineteenth-century American antiques from local auctions, including stand-up desks, fireplaces, and even a church window or two. Open Thursday 5:00 to 9:00 P.M., Friday and Saturday 11:00 A.M. to 7:00 P.M., and Sunday 11:00 A.M. to 5:00 P.M. Call them at 986–3640. Metro: U Street- Cardozo (green line).

If you're following a no-nonsense, high-carbohydrate diet or ready to indulge your sweet tooth, **Cakelove,** at 1506 U Street NW, is definitely for you. From the sidewalk you can inhale the chocolate, butter, and sugar aromas (only 1,000 calories per breath), then peer in and watch owner/baker (and former lawyer) Warren Brown making cakes, cookies, and his terrifyingly rich chocolate cupcake, all from scratch. Call 588–7100; www.cakelove.com. Open Monday through Friday 8:00 A.M. to 8:00 P.M., Saturday 10:00 A.M. to 6:00 P.M., Sunday 11:00 A.M. to 5:00 P.M. Metro: U Street-Cardozo (green line).

Although 1600 Pennsylvania is the nation's best-known address, the portion of **16th Street** that transits the Shaw-U Street neighborhood is well worth a leisurely stroll. Once a premier residential area, 16th Street fell on hard times and neglect for decades. Now, however, 16th Street is definitely back—once again a good address, as its historic buildings, superb mansions, and stately embassies return to their Victorian Age splendor. If you go, the best Metro stations to use are either Dupont Circle, on the red line for the lower stretch of 16th or, as you approach Meridian Hill, U Street/Cardozo on the green line.

Start your walk at the ***Jewish Community Center,*** at 1529 16th Street NW, one of the District's top, but less well known, cultural assets. The JCC's auditorium is currently the home of the Woolly Mammoth, one of Washington's most original theater companies, and a showcase for young and talented actors and playwrights. JCC also sponsors a Jewish Music Festival, and programs of book talks and discussions by noted Jewish writers along with occasional art exhibits. For a full picture of the JCC's nonstop activities, check out www .dcjcc.org or phone 518–9400.

The center also operates the ***JCC Cafe,*** where you'll find homemade soups and a full roster of tasty salads, sandwiches, and entrees. Their phone number is 387–3246; www.jcccafe.n-i.com/jcccafe. Open Sunday through Thursday 11:00 A.M. to 8:00 P.M. Next to the cafe is the JCC's ***Judaica Gift and Bookstore,*** with jewelry, books, gifts, and toys for the kids. Open Monday through Thursday 1:00 to 5:00 P.M. and 6:00 to 9:00 P.M., Sunday noon to 8:00 P.M. The entrance for both the gift shop and the cafe is around the corner on R Street. Metro: Dupont Circle (red line).

At the end of the nineteenth-century a number of religious groups decided to establish their Washington "embassies" by building prestigious "national" churches in the nation's capital, many of them along 16th Street.

The most obvious, in every way, is the staggering ***National Temple of the Scottish Rite*** at 1733 16th Street NW, which was modeled after the temple of King Mausolos at Halicarnassos, one of the seven wonders of the ancient world. Out in front of this behemoth are two massive sphinxes (one representing "power" and the other "wisdom") that lend an even more pharaonic air to this incredible building. The temple is the headquarters of the Scottish Rite, an ancient order of Freemasonry that stresses education and community service.

You can tour the temple weekdays from 8:00 A.M. to 2:00 P.M. Your tour will take you first through the 200,000 volume library on freemasonry, then to a series of sumptuous meeting rooms and ceremonial chambers, all gleaming with rare woods, intricate mosaics, and marble pillars. You won't forget it. Call 232–3579; www.srmason-sj.org. Metro: Dupont Circle (red line).

Not far from the temple is a much less imposing national church. The ***Church of the Holy City*** at 1611 16th Street NW, is the National Swedenborgian

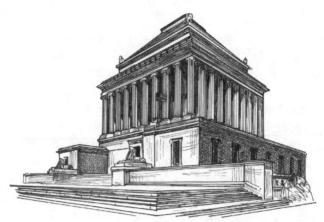

National Temple of the Scottish Rite

church. Peer into this charming English Gothic structure and you'll be rewarded with a wonderful series of stained glass windows illustrating the Bible story. Metro: Dupont Circle (red line).

At the corner of 16th and U Streets, you'll see the grand ***Balfour Apartments,*** built in 1901 as one of the city's first luxury apartment houses. The style is imposing and typical of the period, from its majestic Beaux Arts exterior to the red and gold stone lobby and a grand staircase. Now a condominium, the Balfour is not open to the public. Metro: Dupont Circle (red line).

Further up 16th Street you'll arrive at ***Meridian Hill;*** the name comes from the zero meridian of the United States, which Thomas Jefferson placed along 16th Street: A boundary stone to that effect once stood at the corner of Florida and 16th. In the nineteenth century its high ground and panoramic views made Meridian Hill an enclave of the wealthy and helped turn 16th Street into the city's earlier embassy row: A number of embassies remain there, but many more have left because of security concerns. Meridian Hill's decline, however, seems to have halted and in recent years the area has begun to revive and regentrify.

Two of the neighborhood's great homes remain and attract visitors; both are owned by the Meridian International Center, a nonprofit educational and cultural institution that seeks to promote international understanding through exchanges of people, ideas, and the arts. The center also sponsors a wide-ranging program of briefings, lectures, and other programs on global issues.

The thirty-room ***Meridian House,*** just off 16th Street at 1630 Crescent Place NW, was built in 1920 by steel heir and career diplomat Irwin Laughlin. Shortly after it was completed, the house was called "one of the finest examples of architecture in the French style in America." Sorry to say, Meridian House is open to the public only for weddings, receptions, and other social events. You don't have to get married, however, to wander through the house's lovely terraced garden or peer through the French doors into a vanished world and the public rooms of a classic European chateau.

Meridian House's next door neighbor, the **White-Meyer House,** was built in 1911 for Henry White, a former Ambassador to France, but was occupied from 1929 until 1971 by Eugene Meyer, the publisher of the *Washington Post.* The grand rooms of the White-Meyer House now host a series of internationally oriented art and cultural exhibits on a rotating basis; check the *Post's* Weekend magazine for the latest schedule. The White-Meyer House, at 1630 Crescent Place NW, is usually open Tuesday through Sunday from 2:00 to 5:00 P.M., but since it hosts a number of special events, it's a good idea to call ahead; the number is 667–6800; www.meridian.org.

Meridian Hill Park, at 16th and W Streets, across from the two mansions, is both part of the National Park system and a neighborhood park that may remind you of Rome's Borghese Gardens or Villa Medici. Because of its terraces and dramatic water cascade with thirteen pools, experts call this Renaissance villa park a masterpiece of landscape architecture. A walk around the park will reveal some interesting statuary, including the only known statue of, and monument to, President James Buchanan, called by some "America's worst president." Joan of Arc also rides again on Meridian Hill, while another statue depicts Dante, the Italian Renaissance writer, holding his *Divine Comedy;* just the place for reading poetry, if you brought any along. Aside from its unusual collection of statues, Meridian Hill Park is also an agreeable place where local families take their kids during the day, but avoid after sunset. So should you.

Walking uphill along 16th Street from Meridian Hill Park, you'll find gathered the ghosts of embassies past in Washington's former embassy row, the creation of Mary Foote Henderson, the wealthy and influential widow of Senator John B. Henderson of Missouri. In the early twenteith century Mary, a grande dame of Washington society and certainly no shrinking violet, single-handedly turned this stretch of 16th Street and parts of Meridian Hill into an exclusive neighborhood of mansions, which she built and rented to society figures and foreign governments. The ambitious Mary also wanted a new White House built there, but obviously she failed. She did, however, succeed in getting Congress to designate (briefly) "her" 16th Street as the "Avenue of Presidents." Mary herself lived in Henderson's Castle, a now-demolished red brick pile at the corner of Florida and 16th, a spot now occupied by the Beekman Place condominiums. However, you can still see the castle's walls and turreted gates.

For some years Mary's mansions had fallen on hard times, but now many are being brought back to life. You'll find one of them at 2600 16th Street, at the four-story Venetian Gothic building known locally as the **Pink Palace.** No doge ever lived here and there aren't many gondoliers paddling outside on 16th Street, but this 1906 palazzo has been home to a series of the rich and/or famous, including Mrs. Marshall Field of Chicago and several cabinet members. It is now the headquarters of the **Inter-American Defense Board.**

For more examples of 16th Street's glory days as Embassy Row, check out the former **Cuban Embassy** at 2630 16th (now part of the Swiss Embassy) the French–influenced **Polish Embassy** (2640 16th) and the charming **Lithuanian Embassy** at 2622 16th, with its elaborate stone doorway and windows. The grand rooms of the Polish Embassy are sometimes opened for cultural events; to find out when they're scheduled go to www.poland embassy.org or phone 234–3800. In a class of its own is the former **Italian Embassy** at 2700 16th, now vacant, but a wonderful example of an Italian Renaissance mansion.

One of the best examples is the **Mexican Cultural Institute** at 2829 16th Street, which was built in 1910 for President Taft's treasury secretary as a surprise gift from his wife. Today, the big surprise in this luxurious mansion is one of Washington's most graceful and dramatic staircases, along which unfurls a vibrant, four-story mural of Mexican history by artist Roberto Cueva del Rio. Once upstairs visitors enter a grand, turn of the century mansion with a sunny, blue-tiled conservatory with a fountain and a delightful music room. The institute is open weekdays from 10:00 A.M. to 6:00 P.M. The institute sponsors a comprehensive program of cultural presentations that showcase Mexican art, music, and, dance. For information about their programs, call 728–1628 or check out www.sre.gob.mx/eua/Instituto/Principal.htm.

Places to Stay in Shaw and U Street

Akwaaba,
1708 16th Street NW;
332–4100;
(866) 466–3855
Akwaaba means "welcome" in Ghana, but it also clearly applies to guests of this African-American–themed literary bed and breakfast.

Aside from its rooms named for prominent black writers and poets, a visit to Akwaaba, with its original tiled fireplaces, stained glass windows, and spacious, high-ceilinged rooms, will warp you back to Victorian times, when this grand townhouse was built. All of Akwaaba's eight guest rooms are handsomely appointed and well stocked with volumes of African-American history, literature, and poetry. But if you're

looking for big, sunny front rooms with bay windows and Jacuzzi tubs, ask for the Langston Hughes or Zora Neale Hurston suites. Moderate. Metro: Dupont Circle (red line).

The Embassy Inn,
1627 16th Street NW;
234–7800.
The Embassy is an economical find located near the Dupont Circle and Adams Morgan neighborhoods and an easy walk or bus ride

from downtown. This former apartment house has thirty-eight cheerful rooms and a European feel that includes a continental breakfast to help you start your days out there on the unbeaten path. Metro: Dupont Circle (red line).

Shipman House Bed and Breakfast,
1310 Q Street NW; 328–3510; www.bbonline.com/dc/thereeds/index
This 1887 Victorian home has been nicely converted by innkeepers Charles and Jackie Reed into a bed-and-breakfast that has received national press attention for its restoration and elegant features. The house abounds in period touches like stained glass windows and grand fireplaces, not to mention its luxurious paneled rooms and garden with fountains. The Shipman House has six guest rooms that will take you straight back to those never-to-be-forgotten days of Grover Cleveland and Rutherford B. Hayes. For longer stays the Reeds also offer a self-contained apartment. Inexpensive. Metro: Shaw/Howard University (green line).

The Windsor Inn,
1842 16th Street NW; 667–0300.
The Windsor, built in 1922, is now on the National Register of Historic Places, in part because of its Art Deco lobby with mosaics and tiles from its early days as a luxury apartment house. The Windsor's forty-six rooms are nicely furnished and the rates are reasonable. You'll also like the neighborhood of handsome Victorian town houses and mansions. Metro: Dupont Circle (red line).

Places to Eat in Shaw and U Street

Ben's Chili Bowl,
1213 U Street NW; 667–0909.
See page 180 for full description.

Cafe Saint-Ex,
1847 14th Street NW; 265–7839.
See page 178 for full description.

Coppi's,
1414 U Street NW; 319–7773.
See page 182 for full description.

Florida Avenue Grill,
1100 Florida Avenue NW; 265–1586.
This classic, counter-and-stools (plus a few booths) neighborhood grill is lined with photos of the political and showbiz leaders who have dined in this Washington institution on "Southern-style food." It's easy to see why. Breakfasts are big here, with possibilities that range from hotcakes to omelettes and sides of scrapple, spicy half smokes, grits with red-eye gravy, or all of the above. Lunch or dinner might be tasty barbecue, pork chops, or real southern fried chicken like the Colonel doesn't make. Open Tuesday through Friday 8:00 A.M. to 9:00 P.M., Saturday 6:00 A.M. to 9:00 P.M. Inexpensive. Metro: U Street–Cardozo (green line).

Hamburger Mary's,
1337 14th Street NW; 232–7010.
See page 175 for full description.

JCC Cafe,
1529 16th Street NW;
387-3246.
See page 183 for full
description.

Kuna,
1324 U Street;
797-7908.
See page 178 for full
description.

Logan Tavern,
1423 P Street;
332-3710;
www.logantavern.com
This lively bistro just oozes
energy and panache. The
dining room is open, with a
large wooden community
table in the center, and old
photos of the neighborhood
on the walls. The food at
Logan is mainly of the
"American Comfort" variety—
pastas, meatloaf, large salads, and grilled fish; judging
from the number of locals
that flock there, those chefs
in the back must know what
they're doing. Logan Tavern
is open Monday through
Thursday from 5:00 to 11:00
P.M., Friday noon to midnight,
Saturday 11:00 A.M. to 4:00
P.M. and 5:00 to 11 P.M.,
Sunday 11:00 A.M. to 11:00
P.M. Brunch served Saturday
and Sunday from 11:00 A.M.
to 4:00 P.M.

Mar de Plata,
1410 14th Street NW;
234-2679.
Hot and cold tapas like
seafood salad, grilled
sausage, and fried pork with
cassava are the specialties in
this bright and cheerful
Spanish storefront. You can
make a meal of the tapas or
forge ahead to second
courses like paella, carne
guisada (Spanish for a tasty
beef stew), and grilled
salmon. A good selection of
Spanish wines and sherries
plus service that makes you
feel that estas en tu casa.
Open Monday through
Thursday noon to 3:00 P.M.
and 4:00 P.M. to 11:00 P.M.,
and Friday to Sunday noon
to 3:00 P.M. and 4:00 P.M.
to midnight. Moderate.
Metro: U Street– Cardozo
(green line).

Polly's,
1342 U Street NW;
265-8385.
See page 179 for full
description.

Rice,
1608 14th Street NW;
234-1400.
See page 176 for full
description.

The Saloon,
1205 U Street NW;
462-2640.
Located in a nicely restored
1890s vintage building, the
Saloon's menu is strictly all-
American, with burgers,
sandwiches, and grills, but
the beer list is international
and includes suds from fifteen countries. The Saloon is
open Tuesday through Saturday 5:00 P.M. to 1:00 A.M.;
live jazz every Friday and
Saturday night. Inexpensive.
Metro: U Street–Cardozo
(green line).

Sparky's Espresso Cafe,
1720 14th Street NW;
332-9334.
See page 177 for full
description.

Thaitanic,
1326 14th Street NW;
588-1795.
See page 175 for full
description.

U-topia,
1418 U Street NW;
483-7669.
See page 182 for full
description.

Indexes

Entries for Restaurants, Lodgings, Children's Sites, African-American Sites, Jewish Sites, Lincoln Sites, House Museums, and Sculptures, Statues, and Memorials appear in the special indexes beginning on page 196.

GENERAL INDEX

RESTAURANTS

U-topia, 182
Venetian Room and Cafe Lombardy, The, 93
Vietnam Georgetown, 120

Wok n' Roll, 34
Xando, 161
Zola, 29

LODGINGS

Akwaaba, 186
Bull Moose B&B, 60
Capitol Hill Suites, 60
Carlyle Suites, The, 166
Churchill, The, 166
Courtyard by Marriott, 36
Dupont at the Circle, 167
Embassy Inn, The, 186–87
George Washington University Inn, The, 91
Georgetown Inn, 117
Georgetown Suites, 117
Governor's House, The, 17
Henley Park Hotel, 36–37
Hotel George, 60
Hotel Harrington, 17
Hotel Lombardy, 91
Hotel Mayflower, 17
Hotel Monaco, 28
Hotel Monticello, 118
Hotel Tabard Inn, 167
Hotel Washington, 17
Inn at Dupont Circle, The, 167
J.W. Marriott, 18
Jury's Washington, 167

Jury's Normandy Hotel, 167
Kalorama Guest House, The, 140
Latham Hotel, The, 118
Mansion on O Street, The, 160
Marriott, J. W., 18
Melrose Hotel, 91
Morrison Clark Inn, 33
Omni Shoreham, 140
One Washington Circle Hotel, 92
Phoenix Park Hotel, 52–53
River Inn, 91
Savoy Suites, 140
Shipman House Bed and Breakfast, 187
Sofitel Lafayette Square, 18
State Plaza Hotel, 92
Swann House, 167
Topaz Hotel, 168
Washington National Cathedral College of Preachers, 126
Washington Suites, 92
Windsor Inn, The, 187
Windsor Park Hotel, 168
Woodley Park Guest House, 140

CHILDREN'S SITES

Chesapeake and Ohio Canal, 107
Corcoran Gallery of Art, 79–80
Discovery Creek Museum, 128
Fort Leslie J. McNair, 67–68
Franklin Delano Roosevelt Memorial, 81
Georgetown Flea Market, 112
Heurich House Museum, 148
International Spy Museum, 29

Korean War Veterans Memorial, 81
Lincoln Memorial, 81
Maine Avenue Fish Market, 63
Marine Museum, 69
MCI Center, 31
National Geographic Society, 16
Navy Memorial, 23
Navy Museum, 69
Old Pension Building, 32

AFRICAN-AMERICAN SITES

JEWISH SITES

LINCOLN SITES

About the Author

William B. Whitman is a former diplomat who spent most of his career in Yugoslavia and in Italy, where he started writing about travel and food. He now lives in Washington, D.C. and writes for major magazines, including *National Geographic Traveler, Hemispheres,* and *Forbes-FYI.* Bill is the author of *The Quotable Politician,* a choice collection of quotations by famous politicians about politics, foreign affairs, and political life in general, published by Lyons Press. Bill has also written two other books, *Literary Cities of Italy,* which takes readers to the literary landmarks of Rome, Florence, and Venice, and *Wines of Virginia,* a comprehensive guide to Virginia's wines and wineries.